Vancouver,
Victoria & Whistler
C O L O

Edited by Gail Buente

Formac Publishing Company Limited
Halifax

Contents

For photo credits and acknowledgements, see page 210.

Library and Archives Canada Cataloguing in Publication

Vancouver and Victoria : colourguide / edited by Gail
Buente. — 5th ed.

(Colourguide series)
Includes index.
4th ed. published under title: Vancouver & Victoria
    colourguide, edited by Constance Brissenden.
ISBN 978-0-88780-833-3

    1. Vancouver (B.C.)—Guidebooks. 2. Victoria (B.C.)—Guidebooks.
3. Whistler (B.C.)—Guidebooks. I. Buente, Gail II. Title: Vancouver,
Victoria and Whistler colourguide. III. Series: Colourguide series
FC3847.18.V34 2009   917.11'33045   C2009-902378-4

Formac Publishing Company
5502 Atlantic Street
Halifax, Nova Scotia B3H 1G4
www.formac.ca

Printed and bound in China

Distributed in the
United States by:
Casemate
2114 Darby Road, 2nd Floor
Havertown, PA 19083

Distributed in the
United Kingdom by:
Portfolio Books Limited
2nd Floor, Westminster House
Keir Road, Richmond
Surrey, UK TW9 2ND

Greater Vancouver Map

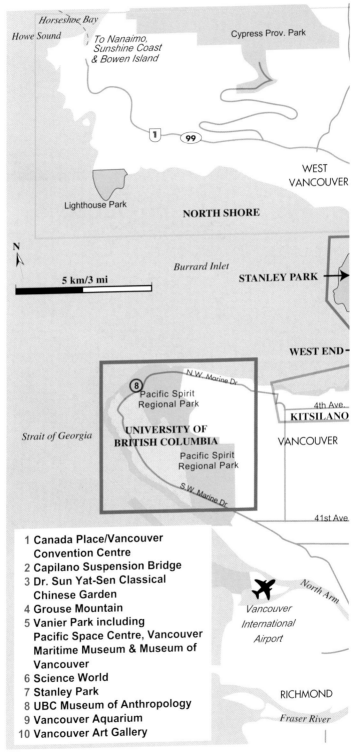

1 Canada Place/Vancouver
   Convention Centre
2 Capilano Suspension Bridge
3 Dr. Sun Yat-Sen Classical
   Chinese Garden
4 Grouse Mountain
5 Vanier Park including
   Pacific Space Centre, Vancouver
   Maritime Museum & Museum of
   Vancouver
6 Science World
7 Stanley Park
8 UBC Museum of Anthropology
9 Vancouver Aquarium
10 Vancouver Art Gallery

▲ Locator Map

N

50 km or 30 mi

British Columbia

Whistler

Garibaldi Provincial Park

Jervis Inlet

Squamish

Golden Ears Provincial Park

Sunshine Coast

(101)

Sechelt

Gibsons

Howe Sound

West Vancouver

Strait of Georgia

Burrard Inlet

Horseshoe Bay

North Vancouver

(1)

Coquitlam

Maple Ridge

(7)

Mission

Chill

(19)

Gabriola Island

(1A)

Vancouver

Burnaby

Departure Bay

Nanaimo

Richmond

(99)

Surrey

(1)

(11)

CAN

U.S.

The Gulf Islands

Tsawwassen

(99)

Abbotsford

Galiano Island

(5)

Washington

Saltspring Island

Mayne Island

Saturna Island

Bellingham

(1)

Duncan

Saanich Inlet

Sidney

British Columbia | Alberta

Vancouver Island

Kamloops

Vancouver Island

• Vancouver

Calgary

Victoria ○

Kelowna

(17A)

(17)

Trail

Port Renfrew

○ Seattle

Olympia

Wash.

Spokane

(1)

Mont.

CANADA

(14)

Victoria

○ Portland

Salem Oregon

Idaho

U.S.A

Burrard Inlet

Prospect Point

Lions Gate Bridge

3

1 The Teahouse
2 Pauline Johnson Memorial
3 Prospect Point Cafe
4 Minature Railway
5 Lumberman's Arch
6 Vancouver Aquarium
7 Petting Farm
8 Malkin Bowl
9 Vancouver Rowing Club
10 Royal Vancouver Yacht Club
11 Totem Park

Stanley Park Dr.

P

Siwash Rock

P

The Hollow Tree

(1A)

(99)

STANLEY PARK

Beaver Lake

Stanley Park Dr.

SS Empress of Japan Figurehead

P

Girl in a Wetsuit

Third Beach

Pipeline Rd.

4

Brockton Point

2

Ferguson Point

5

7

P

P

1

6

11

P

Rose Garden

P

Nine O'Clock Gun

Lions Gate Bridge Rd.

8

Deadman's Island

Seawall Promenade

Lost Lagoon Dr.

9

10

HMCS Discovery Naval Training Station

P

Pitch & Putt Golf Course

Lost Lagoon

Coal Harbour

Second Beach English Bay

Lagoon Dr.

Devonian Hbr. Park

6

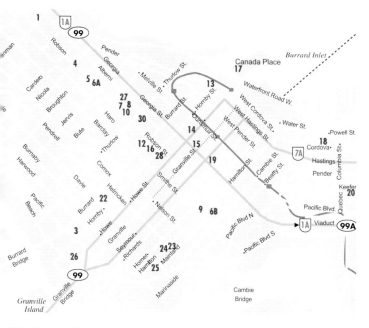

28	Bacchus Ristorante	**4**	Gyoza King
22	Bin 941 Tapas Parlour	**5**	Hon's Wun Tun House
23	Blue Water Café and Bar	**13**	Imperial Chinese Seafood Restaurant
26	C	**3**	Il Giardino di Umberto
1	Café de Paris	**18**	Irish Heather
15	Yew	**27**	Kirin Mandarin Restaurant
10	Cin Cin	**16**	Le Crocodile
24	Cioppino's Mediterranean Grill	**8**	Musashi Japanese Restaurant
14	Diva at the Met	**2**	Raincity Grill
7	Earl's Restaurants	**25**	Rodney's Oyster House
6A	Ezogiku Noodle Café	**30**	Shanghai Chinese Bistro
6B	Ezogiku Noodle Café	**9**	Villa Del Lupo
17	Five Sails Restaurant	**19**	White Spot Triple O
12	Fleuri Restaurant	**21**	Won More Szechuan Cuisine
20	Floata Seafood Restaurant		

▲ Vancouver Accommodation Map

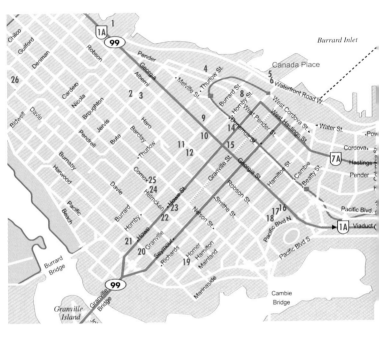

20 Best Western Downtown
Vancouver
23 Bosman's Hotel
25 Century Plaza Hotel and Spa
8 Days Inn Vancouver Downtown
6 Fairmont Waterfront
10 Fairmont Hotel Vancouver
15 Four Seasons Hotel Vancouver
17 Georgian Court Hotel
18 Hampton Inn & Suites
22 Holiday Inn Hotel & Suites
9 Hyatt Regency Vancouver
2 Listel Vancouver
14 Metropolitan Hotel

19 Opus Hotel
3 Pacific Palisades Hotel
5 Pan Pacific Hotel Vancouver
21 Quality Hotel Downtown
4 Renaissance Vancouver Hotel
Harbourside
24 Sheraton Vancouver Wall Centre
Hotel
11 Sutton Place Hotel
26 Sylvia Hotel
12 Wedgewood Hotel
1 Westin Bayshore Resort &
Marina Vancouver
16 YWCA Hotel

About This Guide

Vancouver Skyline

This guide was written to help you get the most out of your stay in Canada's favourite West Coast destinations — Vancouver, Victoria and the surrounding areas, including Whistler and the Gulf Islands. It will enrich your stay by directing you to the top attractions as well as places off the beaten track. The contributors to this book are people who know and love these destinations and want to share their knowledge with you.

The guide is divided by city, with the Vancouver section beginning on page 11 and the Victoria section on page 125. The Vancouver section offers nine chapters focusing on top attractions and activities, and ten chapters dedicated to some of Vancouver's most exciting neighbourhoods.

The Victoria section of the guide includes general information, a brief history of the city, the top things to see and do, and chapters on shopping and dining.

Following the section on Victoria, the guide explores Whistler, the Gulf Islands and the Sunshine Coast. The Listings section at the end of the book provides practical details. City and neighbourhood maps, as well as maps showing the locations of restaurants, hotels and attractions, appear at key points throughout the guide.

Like the other books in the Colourguide series, this is an independent publication. No payments or contributions have been solicited or accepted by the creators or publishers of this guide.

While every effort was made to ensure that the information was up-to-date when it went to press, unforeseen changes do occur. It is always wise to phone ahead to confirm that the information presented here is still current.

Brief biographies of the contributors follow.

MELANEY BLACK (Victoria Shopping) is a Victoria freelance writer.

CONSTANCE BRISSENDEN (Whistler) is a veteran writer and editor, as well as co-author of children's books (www.firstnationswriter.com).

GAIL BUENTE (editor; Vancouver's Top Attractions;Exploring Vancouver; Annual Events) is a writer and editor for magazines and books, with an emphasis on the arts and history.

BRIAN BUSBY (Yaletown) is the author of adult

Stanley Park
Seawall

and children's books and the editor of eight literary anthologies. He lived for many years in Yaletown.

HEATHER CONN (Sunshine Coast; Entertainment) is an author, freelance writer/editor, and photographer who lives in Roberts Creek, B.C.

CHUCK DAVIS (A Brief History of Vancouver) has shared his in-depth knowledge of Vancouver history in countless books and articles.

PATRICIA FRASER (Vancouver Shopping) covers shopping in Vancouver and hosts a contemporary Celtic music program on Fairchild Radio.

GARY HYNES (Victoria Dining) is a Victoria food critic and publisher of *EAT* (Epicure and Travel) magazine.

TRUDE LABOSSIERE HUEBNER (Kitsilano) writes lifestyle pieces about British Columbia and its people for print, radio and television.

LESLEY KENNY (Victoria's Top Attractions) is an administrator at the University of Victoria.

ALMA LEE (Granville Island) is the founder and former producer of the Vancouver International Writers & Readers Festival on Granville Island.

KATHRYN LESUEUR (Gulf Islands) is a writer and award-winning producer who lives in Victoria. Her summers are spent exploring the Gulf Islands.

BOB MACKIN (Activities and Spectator Sports) is a sports reporter for the *North Shore News* and the author of *Baseball Trivia*.

GARY MCFARLANE (Commercial Drive; Visual Art) is a writer and musician who lives near Commercial Drive. He's been active in the Vancouver arts scene for over 25 years.

MARG MEIKLE (Parks and Gardens) is the author of *Garden City: Vancouver*, as well as fact-based books and children's books.

JAMES OAKES (West End) is a veteran journalist who lives in Vancouver's West End.

CHRIS PETTY (UBC), a UBC graduate and historian, edits the *UBC Chronicle* alumni magazine.

D. C. (DENNIS) REID (Exploring Victoria; A Brief History of Victoria) is a Victoria resident, published poet and historical novelist.

LEANORE SALI (Gastown) is the director of the Gastown Business Improvement Society.

ANNEMARIE TEMPELMAN-KLUIT (Kids' Stuff) is a Vancouver native, mother of two, and founder of the website www.yoyomama.ca for Vancouver mums on the go.

BARBARA TOWELL (Downtown Vancouver) has a BA in Art History and an MA in Archival Studies from UBC.

ROCHELLE VAN HALM (North Shore) is a freelance writer who was born and raised and still lives on the North Shore.

KASEY WILSON (Vancouver Dining) is one of Vancouver's leading food writers.

TODD WONG (Chinatown) is a fifth-generation Vancouverite, and creator of Gung Haggis Fat Choy, Robbie Burns Chinese New Year dinner.

Vancouver

Exploring Vancouver

Gail Buente

Vancouver is a city that is constantly reinventing itself. In the early days, it was a rough-and-tumble lumber town and the "Terminal City" of the Canadian Pacific Railway. By the 1940s, it had taken on the trappings of urban sophistication, from neon lights to big-band ballrooms. In the 1970s, it acquired a reputation as Lotus Land, a kind of laid-back Garden of Eden where the population spent its days lying on the beaches and hiking in the mountains. While elements of all these previous personalities still linger, Vancouver today is a vibrant, burgeoning metropolis. For the past two decades, the city has been changing at the speed of light, revved up a notch more since it became the site for the 2010 Winter Olympic Games.

The urban explosion began with Expo 86, the launching pad for the revitalization of areas such as Yaletown, which overlooks the former Expo site on False Creek. Once a rundown enclave of warehouses and railway yards, Yaletown is now a stylish community of high-rises and converted heritage buildings, with chic restaurants deemed some of the best in the West. This change is embraced by those who appreciate the city's range of activities, its lively communities such as the West End, and its expansive transit system. Others satisfy their nostalgia for Vancouver's former relaxed atmosphere by frequenting neighbourhoods such as Kitsilano and Commercial Drive.

Visitors will benefit from improvements that are reshaping an urban centre already known as one of the best in the world both to live in and to visit. For the

Greater Vancouver area, road and transit improvements include a faster link from downtown to the Vancouver International Airport.

An Ideal City

Vancouver is a superbly livable place. The weather is moderate, as befits a coastal rainforest, the grass is ever-green and flowers bloom year-round. The Coast Mountains make a scenic backdrop to the city skyline, especially in winter when they are brushed with a fresh coat of snow. All in all, it's an environment that's hard to beat, which explains why Canadians and immigrants flock here to live. At the last census, in 2006, the city centre was home to more than 578,000 people, while the fast-growing Greater Vancouver area counted 2,116,581 residents.

Lions Gate Bridge

Growth is good news for Vancouver's tourist attractions, services and infrastructure. What was once a small provincial town is now a cosmopolitan Pacific Rim player, with excellent hotels, impressive restaurants and plenty to see and do. The mix of people here is a unique multicultural blend of West meets East, with a large percentage of the population Asian and other visible minorities. Over half of Vancouver's population has a mother tongue other than English or French, Canada's two official languages. Vancouver also has many First Nations people. Their art and design is evident in the city's galleries, museums, and stores.

Traffic here can be hectic, and visitors will discover that the easiest way to get around is by public transit. The TransLink system includes buses, the SkyTrain light rapid-transit, and the SeaBus pedestrian ferry in Vancouver Harbour. With a day pass, you can visit the North Shore cities of West Vancouver and North Vancouver, or head south to explore Richmond and the historic Steveston fishing village. For real efficiency, check with TransLink for routes and schedules at 604-953-3333 (www.translink.bc.ca). You don't even need a car to travel the 120 kilometres (75 miles) to Whistler: transportation is available by bus, rail, and air. If you prefer driving, the roads in and around Vancouver are good, but allow extra time at rush hour.

Below: Stanley Park cyclist
Bottom: Snowboarding at Cypress Mountain

Favourite Spots to Explore

Ask Vancouverites where the best places are to visit, and they'll enthuse about their favourite things to see and do in the city. For some, it's a walk along English Bay to Stanley Park. Keep walking and the path becomes a seawall continuing right around the park. You may decide to explore the interior of the famed park, or simply stop at a park bench and watch the world stroll, skate, or bike by. Granville Island, a spot that gives Stanley Park some competition as most

Harbour Centre

popular, is crowded with shops, studios, and a busy farmers' market, but it also has its quiet spots and quiet moments. The 99 B-Line express bus will take you to the University of British Columbia (UBC) campus, a city within a city, boasting a lovely campus, several theme gardens, and the Museum of Anthropology, which holds one of the world's greatest collections of aboriginal art.

Across the water, on the North Shore, the pace of life slows, with strolls along Ambleside Beach in West Vancouver and picnics in Mt. Seymour Provincial Park in North Vancouver. Grouse Mountain offers expansive views of Vancouver from the top of the peak. Rivers have carved deep canyons through the lush forests. These canyons can be viewed at several spots, the best-known of which is North Vancouver's Capilano Suspension Bridge.

A quick way to get to know the Vancouver area is to contact a local tour company. If you'd like to tour and explore at the same time, the Vancouver Trolley Company's "jump on, jump off" bus is ideal. Many other types of tours are available, from horse-drawn wagons through Stanley Park to harbour cruises.

Unique and informative walking tours are available in several of the city's neighbourhoods. If you're interested in history, Walkabout Historic Vancouver offers walking tours of downtown, Gastown, Chinatown, and Granville Island from mid-March to mid-November. For a 360-degree view of the city and the North Shore, visit The Lookout! atop Harbour Centre Tower. The revolving observation deck is 167 metres (547 feet) up via glass elevators.

This guidebook takes you through many of Vancouver's fascinating neighbourhoods. For more information, the Tourism Vancouver Visitors' Centre is

Seawall at Stanley Park

extremely helpful. Its website, www.tourismvancouver. com, provides lots of great information. If you visit the

centre in person, the staff can make reservations for you at hotels throughout B.C. You can also book your hotels online. For current information on entertainment, attractions and dining in Vancouver, check the daily *Vancouver Sun* or *Province*, and the free Thursday weekly *Georgia Straight*.

This book also explores the highlights of Victoria. For more on Victoria, see the Exploring Victoria section. The Top Attractions sections give in-depth descriptions of the main attractions in each city.

For detailed information on climate, travel arrangements, currency, customs, shopping, dining, accommodation, emergency care, telephone numbers, and other key information, refer to the Listings section at the end of this guide.

A Brief History

Chuck Davis

There are several accounts relating to Vancouver's origins, but a favourite involves the 1792 meeting between a Spanish exploration party and some of the local Salish people. (An earlier expedition, by Don José Marie Narvaez in 1791, marked the first contact between Europeans and Native people in this area.) It happens that 1792 was the same year Captain George Vancouver was exploring these waters. In fact, Vancouver met Dionisio Galiano, the leader of the Spanish expedition, here and the two men hit it off and became friends. Vancouver gave the name Spanish Banks to the area where that meeting occurred, and it still bears that name more than 200 years later. Aside from Indian Arm, part of the Burrard Inlet (today the city's harbour), Vancouver bestowed no Native-inspired names even though he had the Musqueam, the Squamish, the Kwantlen, the Tsawwassen, and many other groups to choose from. Some of these groups were seasonal, coming down from the interior to the mouth of the Fraser River when the salmon were running.

Top left: Captain George Vancouver
Above: Sunset at Siwash Rock, Stanley Park

Simon Fraser made a very brief visit in 1808 before being chased back up the river by angry Musqueam men. Nearly 60 years were to pass before the white people returned ... this time to stay. What attracted them first were the area's magnificent trees. The forest industry then attracted other kinds of enterprise.

Origins

September 30, 1867, marks the arrival in what is now Vancouver of John "Gassy Jack" Deighton. The

15

Statue of Gassy
Jack in Gastown

City officials in front
of a tent serving as
City Hall after the
Great Fire, 1886

Yorkshire-born Deighton, with a complexion, according to a chum, of "muddy purple," rowed into the Burrard Inlet with his Native wife, her mother, her cousin, a yellow dog, two chairs, and a barrel of whiskey. A busy sawmill stood where Gassy landed on the south shore of the inlet. A busier, bigger one existed on the North Shore. A kilometre or so to the west through the trees, three fellows (derisively nicknamed the "Three Greenhorns" for paying the exorbitant price of $1 an acre for their land) were trying to make bricks from a vein of clay.

Gassy, retired from his career as a riverboat captain, jovially greeted the men who worked at the mill. He knew that the nearest drink for these thirsty fellows was a five-kilometre row east along the inlet to the North Road, then a long walk along a rude trail built by the Royal Engineers to New Westminster and through the forest, the elk, and the bears. A saloon near the mill on the South Shore was an ideal business opportunity. Gassy avowed that if the mill workers helped him build a bar, they could have all they could drink. The Globe Saloon was up within 24 hours.

The Globe is gone now, but it stood in the heart of what is now Vancouver's Gastown. The voluble Mr. Deighton, who well deserved his nickname because he never shut up, chose his location more wisely than he knew. The new country of Canada had been formed just two months earlier. British Columbia would soon join this Confederation, lured by the Canadian Pacific Railway's promise that it would link B.C. to Eastern markets. If they had known it would take 15 years to arrive, they might not have agreed so readily. But in 1871, B.C. signed on, and now British Columbians were also Canadians. The population grew and Gassy Jack thrived. So did the Three Greenhorns. Their landholdings became today's apartment-crammed West End.

By the spring of 1886, there were enough people in Vancouver to form a city. The little ramshackle collection of tents and wooden shacks was incorporated on April 6 of that year. A little more than two months later, on June 13, the whole thing was destroyed by fire. A freak wind sprang up while some CPR workmen were burning brush, and in less than 45 minutes, the town disappeared. "Vancouver didn't

16

burn," one of the survivors said, "it exploded." The heat was so intense that the bell at St. James Anglican Church melted into a puddle. You can see it today at the Vancouver Museum. The survivors began to build, more solidly this time, while the ashes were still smoking.

The Railway

The CPR's first train arrived on July 4, 1886, at Port Moody. Contrary to expectations, it didn't stop there: the railway extended the line to Coal Harbour, which is now part of the Vancouver waterfront. That enraged the speculators who had bought land at Port Moody based on the CPR's promise to put a terminal there. It turned out that the water at the end of the inlet wasn't deep enough for the ocean-going ships that were part of the CPR's plans to establish links to China and other Far Eastern points.

Complaints were useless; the CPR was a hard-nosed firm, led by a single-minded, stocky, bearded bull of a man named William Van Horne who ran his railway his way. Van Horne named Vancouver. It was originally named Granville, for the colonial secretary of the time, but Van Horne declared no one would ever know where "Granville" was. But "Vancouver," now that was a different matter. Everyone knew of Captain George Vancouver's famous Pacific Coast explorations. Van Horne had his way. He nearly always did.

Inset: William Van Horne
Bottom: First CPR train arrives in Vancouver

William Van Horne was an American. Americans have played an important part in Vancouver's past: William Shaughnessy, a later CPR president and the man for whom the city's old-money neighbourhood is named, was an American. So was Benjamin Tingley Rogers, who built the huge B.C. Sugar Refinery company. L. D. Taylor, the man elected mayor of Vancouver eight times (more often than anyone else), was from Michigan.

The first thing Vancouver's first city council did in 1886 was petition the federal government to lease it a 400-hectare (998-acre) military reserve at the entrance to the harbour. The heavily forested reserve had been established as a potential defense point just in case the bumptious Americans tried to

Top: The Second
Hotel Vancouver
Above: Fairmont
Hotel Vancouver
today

take over the area. That's how Vancouver got Stanley Park, one of the world's great city parks.

The railway, which had received thousands of acres of free land in return for coming into Vancouver, established the hotel named Hotel Vancouver some distance south of Gastown which, in effect, pulled the city's downtown around it. When Van Horne arrived in the city and saw the hotel, he confronted the architect: "So you're the damned fool who made it look like a hospital!" You see today the third Hotel Vancouver. This imposing, green-turreted landmark (now Fairmont Hotel Vancouver) has hosted royal guests since 1939, beginning with King George VI and Queen Elizabeth, later the Queen Mother.

One very tangible result of the Great Depression of the 1930s is still visible in Vancouver: the Lions Gate Bridge. This big, splendid, and beautiful bridge opened in 1938, paid for and built by the Guinness Brewing Company of Ireland. The brewers had bought, at distress Depression prices of less than $19 an acre, a vast tract of land on the wooded slopes of the North Shore and began to sell the property. They built the bridge to encourage traffic, and buyers, to come on over. It worked. British Pacific Properties is still the most affluent neighborhood in Greater Vancouver. The residents in one of its postal zones have the highest per capita income in the country.

New Growth

After some years of relative quiet, Vancouver began to show signs of growth in the 1950s, and since then has steadily developed into the unique and lively city it is today. The city has given Canada some important architects, including Ron Thom, Bing Thom, Bruno Freschi, C. B. K. Van Norman and, pre-eminently, Arthur Erickson. Erickson's distinctive buildings dot the metropolitan area, and his Robson Square provincial courthouse complex still draws admiring crowds in the city's downtown heart. His MacMillan Bloedel Building at 1075 W. Georgia (no longer occupied by the giant forest company) is a striking and lofty landmark, noted for its immensely deep windows. Erickson's magnificent Museum of Anthropology on the University of British Columbia campus to the west is further evidence of the brilliance of this internationally known architect.

At the other side of town, Erickson's Simon Fraser University, in the suburb of Burnaby, provided a cool

Simon Fraser University

setting for the hotbed of student revolt in the 1960s, when Vancouver was developing a reputation as a laid-back "Lotus Land." In 1986, global attention was heaped on the city during Expo 86, a world exposition that attracted more than 22 million paying visitors. The Expo lands were sold to Hong Kong financier Li Ka-Shing at a bargain-basement price and spawned a high-rise boom. In the past two decades, Lotus Land has been overtaken by the same frenetic energy that has infused cities worldwide. Today, the up-and-coming live in lofty high-rises, bristling with high-tech features. What remains of the old Vancouver are the breathtaking views, the harbour, and the looming Coast Mountains.

Influx of Newcomers

Both urban and suburban areas continue to grow to this day, and so does the number of newcomers. The increasingly multicultural Lower Mainland attracts immigrants from all over the globe, but predominantly from Asia. Today in the Vancouver area, you'll see people with roots in all parts of Asia, Latin America, Europe, Africa, and the Middle East. They've established neighbourhoods: suburban Richmond is one-third Chinese; the fast-growing Surrey has attracted thousands of East Indian residents; and North Vancouver has a large Iranian population. By opening shops and restaurants and participating in the business, social, and community lives of the region, these newcomers have added verve to the Lower Mainland.

Chinese New Year Parade

In the face of recent downturns to the economy, Vancouver and its suburbs are undergoing shifts in trade and commerce. The slow decline of resource-based industries is being counterbalanced by growth in biotechnology, computer-related, and media trades. Tourism is now one of the pillars of B.C.'s economy, and Vancouver is consistently ranked as one of the world's most livable cities.

Top Attractions

Gail Buente

A view of Burrard Inlet from Stanley Park at Prospect Point

Stanley Park

Ask any Vancouverite to recommend one must-see attraction, and the answer will be Stanley Park. Larger than New York's Central Park, it is a welcoming oasis in the heart of the city. Almost entirely surrounded by salt water, the park includes a forest, an inland lake and a lagoon. Adjacent to Vancouver's densely populated West End, its accessibility adds to the pleasure of a visit.

In 1889, Governor General Lord Stanley dedicated Stanley Park "to the use and enjoyment of people of all colours, creeds, and customs for all time." With an estimated 8 million visitors a year, this 400-hectare (1,000-acre) urban wilderness is treasured by all. Any time of year, the trails and footpaths buzz with the sound of dozens of languages, spoken by diverse people of all ages, races and beliefs.

Stanley Park's Miniature Train

The 100-plus years since it became a park are only a brief moment in the eventful life of this ageless patch of earth, and Stanley

Park as it looks now is just one of many incarnations. Fossils indicate that semi-tropical palms and sequoia trees thrived here millions of years ago. Cougars prowled in the not-so-distant past. Remnants of Indian middens (garbage dumps) tell of thousands of years of Native habitation. Lumberman's Arch was once the site of the Squamish village of Whoi Whoi, and Deadman's Island, now a military base, was once a Native funeral ground.

In modern times, the park has undergone two major makeovers at the hands of Mother Nature. In 1962, Hurricane Frieda felled more than 3,000 trees, but after a full year of hauling away debris, park staff put the new clearing to good use as a home for a miniature railway for the enjoyment of visiting families.

Seawall, Vancouver

The second storm hit in December 2006, with strong winds that left 10,000 toppled trees in its wake and seriously damaged the seawall. Following the storm, city crews worked hard for the next two years to restore the park to its previous beauty, and more than 16,000 seedlings were planted to replace the lost trees. Prospect Point underwent an extensive upgrade to make it safer, with more stunning views than ever. The seawall is back to normal. Strollers, joggers and cyclists are again enjoying its 8.8-kilometre (5.5-mile) circular route as it weaves past rowing and yacht clubs,

Stanley Park Totem

the Vancouver Aquarium, cricket and rugby fields, a petting farm and miniature railway, a pitch-and-putt course, lawn bowling, and tennis courts. On weekends artists display their works at an impromptu gallery on the grass, and on summer evenings Malkin Bowl rings with the sounds of Theatre Under the Stars. When you've worked up an appetite, numerous restaurants — the Teahouse, Prospect Point Café, the Fish House, and the Stanley Park Pavilion — offer casual snacks or chic dinners.

A walk along the seawall also takes you past the Girl in a Wetsuit sculpture, the Brockton Point Lighthouse, the huge wooden Lumberman's Arch monument and the legendary Nine-O'Clock Gun. Originally, the gunshot helped mariners set their chronometers, but now continues simply out of affection

21

Lost Lagoon

for tradition. Nearby, sightseers snap pictures of nineteenth-century totem poles by Haida, Kwakwaka'wakw and Nuu-chah-nulth carvers. At Second Beach you'll find a swimming pool, playground, baseball diamonds and picnic areas. The aroma of fish and chips, a Stanley Park tradition, wafts by. Lost Lagoon is perhaps the most representative feature of the outer park. Once a favourite canoeing spot for Mohawk poet Pauline Johnson, it now provides a spot to feed swans in the shade of willow trees.

The interior park, in contrast, is densely forested, with a network of bike and footpaths crisscrossing beneath fir and cedar boughs. Beaver Lake, the inner park's counterpart to Lost Lagoon, is a natural-state pond, edged with cattails and teeming with frogs croaking from atop water lilies. When venturing into the park's wilder interior, don't be misled by the apparently easy-to-follow trailways. It's quite possible to get lost. Taking a trail map along is a good idea.

Vancouver Aquarium Marine Science Centre

Since 1956, when it opened in Stanley Park, more than 30 million visitors have been entertained and amazed by the Vancouver Aquarium Marine Science Centre. The aquarium's displays provide an up-close look at the 70,000 aquatic creatures living here.

In the steamy jungle environment of the Amazon Rainforest Gallery, two caimans, second cousins to the crocodile, set the tone. Every hour, "rainstorms" are created inside this space. Adding to the atmosphere are scarlet ibises, a pair of sloths and giant freshwater Amazon fish that play a vital role in the survival of the rainforest.

Once a day in the Tropical Gallery, a research naturalist dives with the sharks. Twice a week, the diver feeds the sharks, with dramatic results. The waters literally thrash as the sharks gulp down their food. The gallery is designed to mimic a tropical reef at Indonesia's Bunaken National Marine Park, including black-tipped reef sharks, stone fish, and rainbow-coloured tropical species.

Sea otter

Five beluga whales in the Arctic Canada Habitat can be viewed through an underwater gallery on the lower level. Among them are three generations: grandmother Aurora, mother Qila, and baby Tiqa.

Outside, in the Wild Coast exhibit, three sea otters, Milo, Elfin, and Tanu, keep company. The sea otters, like the belugas, are under constant study. Nyac, one of the last sea otter survivors of the Valdez, Alaska, oil spill of 1989, lived at the aquarium until her death of leukemia in 2008, and provided scientists with valuable data on the long-term effects of oil exposure. Public education and scientific observation are important functions of the aquarium. So is entertainment. Beluga training sessions, playful shows starring the Pacific white-sided dolphins, and feeding times for the sea otters are all popular daily outdoor events.

Local waters are the focus of Treasures of the British Columbia Coast. Elusive wolf eels and a giant Pacific octopus dwell here. In Clownfish Cove, children eight years of age and younger will delight in an interactive play zone. Featured are live creatures such as seahorses, horseshoe crabs, toads and of course, clownfish. In a make-believe marine mammal rescue hospital, little ones take care of a sick or injured seal pup.

After viewing the galleries, visitors

Below: Discovering marine life at the Aquarium
Bottom: Beluga Encounter Program

23

can drop by the UpStream Café and the colourful ClamShell Gift Shop, where souvenirs from soapstone carvings to local postcards come in many price ranges.

Acclaimed for its innovative programming, the aquarium was the first in Canada to add professional naturalists on-site. Its Marine Mammal Rescue and Rehabilitation Program is respected worldwide.

Science World

Science World activity

The hugely popular, hands-on family attraction Science World is housed in Telus Science World, a geodesic dome built in 1986 for Vancouver's world exposition.

Originally called the Expo Centre, it was affectionately dubbed "the golf ball" at the time. Three years later, in 1989, the silver ball reopened as Science World, with Queen Elizabeth II on hand for the ceremonies. By day, the exterior reflects the waters of False Creek. At night, the dome sparkles with 391 exterior lights.

Nearly 700,000 people visit Science World each year and enjoy the constantly changing and expanding programs designed to demonstrate just how much fun science can be. It certainly works. Hundreds of creative exhibits guarantee that even science dropouts can find something intriguing and new. One exhibit makes your hair stand on end; another lets you blow square bubbles.

Telus Science World holds six permanent galleries, including Kidspace, an evolving environment for children three to six years of age, and Eureka!, where children of all ages learn about everything from heat sensitivity to making music with their feet. Visitors can also check out the Feature Gallery to see the bright and unusual variety of exhibitions that Science World hosts throughout the year.

Eureka!, Science World

The Omnimax Theatre is found inside the multi-million-dollar geodesic dome. The steeply raked, 400-seat viewing room boasts one of the world's

largest screens, capable of projecting an image nine times larger than a conventional movie. There are no bad seats in the house, but the most comfortable viewing experience is near the top of the amphitheatre. Fifty-minute documentaries vary in subject from dolphins to the mysteries of Egypt. The theatre presents six shows each weekday, with an added show at 5 p.m. on weekends and holidays. An additional fee is charged for these Omnimax shows.

For lunch or a coffee, the White Spot Triple O Café overlooks False Creek. Science World's Kaleidoscope Gift Shop displays some of the most amusing souvenirs in the city, including kid-pleasing choices like a science book featuring "really gross experiments."

The Museum of Anthropology

In the Great Hall of the Museum of Anthropology (MOA), sunlight streams in through 15-metre (50-foot) glass walls. Immense totem poles, graceful cedar canoes and many other First Nations artifacts appear as they might have in remote coastal villages. Displays include sturdy boxes, made by steaming red cedar planks, which were used for everything from cooking to cradles to coffins. Bowls and feast dishes take the form of mythical beings like Tsonoqua, the wild woman of the woods. All these objects conjure images of huge potlatches: traditional ceremonies where social status was publicly affirmed, lavish feasts were served, and gifts exchanged.

Movingly displayed, the University of British Columbia Museum of Anthropology's research collection of approximately 230,000 artifacts includes ethnographic and archeological materials from Europe, Africa, the Americas, Asia, and the South Pacific. Undeniably, the focal point of the museum is its collection of Kwakwaka'wakw, Nisga'a, Gitksan, Haida, and Coast Salish art. Experts agree it is one of the finest collections of Northwest Coast First Nations

Great Hall of the Museum of Anthropology

House Posts circa 1906 at the MOA

art in the world.

While the museum gives careful treatment to these as historic objects, they are also appreciated as works of art. Only the most fragile items are kept in darkness, and even those are accessible through innovative "visible storage" in glass-topped drawers and glass cabinets. While most museums display only 2 to 5 percent of their collections, more than 90 percent of the Museum of Anthropology's permanent collection is viewable. Row upon row of Kwakwaka'wakw dance masks stare out in an eerie display of variations on a theme. Forty-three black raven heads with wild cedar-bark manes raise their red beaks defiantly, and look out through steely, white-rimmed eyes.

Newly renovated Great Hall of the Museum of Anthropology

The museum pioneered both the visible storage system and the use of natural light, a concept that has since been incorporated into the National Gallery in Ottawa. The MOA's innovation continues with its recent renewal project, which increases its size by half and makes the collections even more accessible to the public.

The architecture, suggestive of the plank houses of the Northwest Coast First Nations, is by Vancouver's Arthur Erickson. His unique challenge was to create a building to house an already well-established collection. From its beginning in 1949, with a humble collection of oceanic materials housed in the basement of the university's main library, the holdings had grown over many years. Erickson's design is magnificent, worthy of its subject matter and its majestic location overlooking Howe Sound.

In the Masterpiece Gallery, exquisitely carved jewellery and small sculptures of argillite, silver, gold, and bone are evidence of an age of painstaking craftsmanship.

In the museum's central rotunda, a skylight illuminates master artist Bill Reid's sculpture *Raven and the First Men*. The massive yellow cedar carving portrays the magical trickster Raven as, according to

Haida legend, he discovers the first humans in a clamshell and coaxes them out. The Museum of Anthropology's collection of Bill Reid's art is the largest assemblage anywhere of his influential works, which fuse modern design with traditional Northwest Coastal Native forms.

The Vancouver Art Gallery

The Vancouver Art Gallery houses British Columbia's largest collection of artworks, from classical to avant-garde. Established in 1931, it moved into its present location in 1983. Formerly a provincial courthouse, the neo-classical–style heritage building, designed by renowned architect Francis Rattenbury, was redesigned by the equally renowned Arthur Erickson to accommodate an additional 3,700 square metres (40,000 square feet) of exhibition space. The internationally recognized gallery touches all the bases, with exciting touring exhibits alongside an outstanding permanent collection of close to 9,000 works.

The Vancouver Art Gallery mission statement calls it a place "to inspire and please through visual art," and that describes it well. Visit the four floors of exhibition space and you'll find numerous surprises: shows by established and emerging artists, thematic shows, and blockbuster travelling exhibitions from the world's top museums. You may see an exhibit of familiar paintings by Impressionist masters, or a show of vibrant new works by up-and-coming local artists.

Yet for many guests, the highlight of the gallery is the permanent collection of works by B.C. artist and

Top: Exhibit at the MOA
Above: Painting by Emily Carr at the VAG

Below: Vancouver Art Gallery

George Norris's stainless steel sculpture *The Crab* outside the H.R. MacMillan Pacific Space Centre

writer Emily Carr. Now well-known internationally, Carr's art was ignored for most of her life. Though respected by other painters, including Canada's influential Group of Seven, many saw her as simply an eccentric Victoria boardinghouse keeper with a penchant for pet monkeys. This dowdy, down-to-earth, independent woman carted her paint box and canvases with her wherever she went. Her treks in a dilapidated caravan took her deep into the ancient forests to capture the essence of coastal British Columbia.

When success finally did arrive, the modest artist was unprepared for it. In 1937, when the Vancouver Art Gallery purchased its first Carr painting, *Totem Poles, Kitseulka*, she wrote in her diary that "this sudden desire to obtain 'Emily Carrs'" made her afraid that the attention might "knock me into conceit." The Vancouver Art Gallery's Carr holdings, including 150 paintings and 100 works in other media, constitute the most important single Carr collection. Among them are some of Carr's most famous works, including *Big Raven, Tree Trunk,* and *Scorned as Timber, Beloved of the Sky.*

H.R. MacMillan Pacific Space Centre

Tours and gallery talks add to the enjoyment of the Carr exhibit as well as many of the touring exhibitions. Finish your visit by browsing for quality posters, books, and artist-made gifts in the Gallery Shop before making a relaxed stop at the licensed Gallery Café and patio.

Museum of Vancouver, H. R. MacMillan Space Centre, H. R. MacMillan Planetarium, Vancouver Maritime Museum

Four Vancouver gems are clustered in Vanier Park, on the south shore of English Bay.

Some say the Museum of Vancouver resembles a First Nations woven hat. Outside its front door is the equally distinctive stainless steel sculpture *The Crab*. The museum got its start just a few years after the birth of Vancouver, when a far-sighted group of citizens gathered a few artifacts in a rented space on Granville Street. By 1905, the museum had moved into the Carnegie Library at Main and Hastings streets, now a community centre. The collection moved to its present site in 1968, becoming the largest administered and interpreted permanent collection of any Canadian civic museum. With over 100,000 items, from Salish artifacts to a large collection of neon signs, the museum presents a dynamic range of exhibits.Vancouver is a city poised between a past that is still fresh and a future that is arriving fast. In a place such as this, a museum is more than just a window on history. It can be a part of the dialogue as the city plans for the next stages of growth.

RCMP Schooner *St. Roch* at the Vancouver Maritime Museum

You can access the H. R. MacMillan Space Centre from the same foyer as the Museum of Vancouver. Launched in October 1997, 29 years after the venerable H. R. MacMillan Planetarium opened, the space centre features innovative programs like the Cosmic Courtyard hands-on gallery. Through multimedia shows and live demonstrations, kids and adults get a chance to fly a space shuttle, touch a real moon rock, feel what it's like to morph into an alien, and journey through the universe.

Evening astronomy shows and laser shows with musical accompaniment, staples of the H. R. MacMillan Planetarium, have long been major draws. Donated by lumber baron H. R. MacMillan in 1967 as a Canadian Centennial gift to the City of Vancouver, the planetarium is a city icon. Its famed multimedia shows are presented in the Star Theatre, where the Zeiss star projector beams a 360-degree view of the

Claridge gallery, Vancouver Maritime Museum

Zeiss Star Projector, H. R. MacMillan Planetarium

night sky onto the theatre dome. Sit back — well, lie back really — in the comfortable lounge chairs and view the night sky unfolding overhead.

A short five-minute walk from the museum and planetarium, you'll find the Vancouver Maritime Museum on the waterfront at the foot of Cypress Street. Permanent exhibits as well as temporary feature exhibits bolster the Maritime Museum's most famous display, the RCMP schooner *St. Roch*, the first ship to cross the treacherous Northwest Passage in both directions, as well as the first ship to circumnavigate North America. Kids will enjoy the Children's Maritime Discovery Centre, with plenty of fun things to do like taking the controls in the full-scale replica wheelhouse of the tugboat *Seaspan Queen*, as well as the area known as Pirates' Cove, complete with a

The newly expanded west wing of the Vancouver Convention Centre

Cruise ship passing
under Lions Gate
Bridge

treasure chest, pirate weapons and costumes. Outside
the museum, Heritage Harbour provides a closer look
at heritage vessels of all types, including a small boat-
building and repair workshop.

Vancouver Convention Centre

Built for Expo 86, Canada Place was designed to give
the stylish Sydney Opera House in Australia a run for
its money. With five white, Teflon-coated "sails"
echoing a nautical theme, the Canada Place complex
stands out against the high-rise hotels of Vancouver's
waterfront. Canada Place continues to be a popular
tourist destination, home to a harbour-view promenade,
cruise ship terminal, the IMAX Theatre, Vancouver's
World Trade Centre, and the domed Pan Pacific Hotel.
It is also the original Vancouver Convention Centre.
In 2009, an expansive new building was added to
accommodate larger conventions than the original
facility alone could handle. Not only does the sleek
new structure triple the size of the Convention Centre,
it was built for sustainability, incorporating such
environmental features as extensive use of local wood,
a green roof, and waste-water recycling.

   The complex is a fascinating place to visit, both for
its architecture and for its views of the harbour. The
open-air promenades around both buildings afford the
best views of busy Port Vancouver. The parade of
working vessels, cruise ships, SeaBuses to the North
Shore and seaplanes make this a great place to sit and
have lunch. The IMAX Theatre at Canada Place, open
daily, dazzles viewers with images that are 10 times
the size of conventional 35-mm film. The 440-seat,
steeply pitched amphitheatre features a towering
five-storey screen and six-channel Digital
wraparound sound.

Capilano Suspension Bridge

What an adventure it must have been in the late
nineteenth century when George Mackay's buddies,
calling themselves the Capilano tramps, trudged to the
pioneering Scotsman's secluded cabin on the north
shore of Burrard Inlet. Seventy metres (230 feet) above
the Capilano River canyon, George suspended a

Capilano Suspension Bridge

rickety rope-and-cedar bridge for what certainly must have been a petrifying crossing. Today's bridge, built of sturdy steel cables, still petrifies and captivates 800,000 visitors each year. The 140-metre (450-foot) bridge is certainly safer and more accessible now, but the lush forest property is no less breathtaking than in Mackay's time.

Capilano Suspension Bridge's swaying span is the world's longest and highest suspension footbridge. Since 1899, when the original bridge was built, the attraction has been improved and enhanced by each of its six successive owners. The Story Centre traces the history of the bridge and the development of the city around it. Exhibits include an English country garden planted with rhododendrons and azaleas, the Living Forest interactive ecology display, a tranquil nature park and a gift shop. Totem Park features a display of locally carved Coast Salish poles collected since the 1930s. In nearby Big House, visitors can watch First Nations carvers at work and ask them about their techniques.

The newest enhancement, Treetops Adventure, is the most dramatic ever. After its completion in 2005, the park won a National Tourism Excellence Award as Innovator of the Year for its series of elevated boardwalks crossing from one tall Douglas fir to another. Viewers climb ever higher for a bird's-eye view of a coastal rainforest, without endangering the environment. An ingenious compression system allows the walkways and observation platforms to be supported without harming the tree trunks in any way.

Tours, displays, and special activities are designed to give guests a glimpse into the historic and botanical roots of the area. The full-service Bridge House restaurant and two casual eateries serve hungry visitors with fresh West Coast–style cuisine as well as snacks. The suspension bridge is a 20-minute drive from downtown Vancouver.

Grose Mountain
Skyride

Grouse Mountain

It takes only eight minutes for the Grouse Mountain
Skyride to climb to 1,125 metres (3,700 feet) above sea
level. That's the only disappointing part of the Grouse
Mountain experience, because on a clear day, the
panoramic view of Vancouver, the Strait of Georgia,
and far-off Vancouver Island is unsurpassed. From
here, the Peak Chair continues the ascent to 1,250
metres (4,100 feet), providing a 360-degree view that
includes Vancouver Island across the Strait of Georgia.

Grouse Mountain was named in 1894, after a
hunting party caught some blue grouse there. The
mountain was one of the earliest ski areas developed
near Vancouver. In 1911, a Swede named Rudolph
Verne became the first to ski the slope. Today, hearty
types make their way to the top with a strenuous
2.9-kilometre (1.8-mile) hike up a vertical trail known
as the Grouse Grind. The Grind is a badge of honour
for many, with the fittest of the fit running up the steep
rise. But the majority of visitors prefer the more sedate
Skyride.

Grouse attracts year-round visitors. In winter,
downhill skiing, snowboarding, snowshoeing, sleigh
rides, and a mountaintop ice-skating pond are always
fun. Ski lessons and equipment rentals are available.
For summer visitors, there's the Refuge for

Dr. Sun-Yat Sen Classical Chinese Garden

Endangered Wildlife, an enclosed natural habitat of just under a hectare (two acres). Two orphaned grizzly bears, Grinder and Coola, live here year-round. The larger bear, Coola, is a Coastal grizzly, with salmon as part of its natural diet. Grinder, the smaller one, is an Interior grizzly, eating a diet that is up to 85 percent wild vegetation. In the summertime, rescued peregrine falcons, red-tailed hawks, a golden eagle and a barred owl join the grizzly pair on display. Naturalists are on hand to share insights into these magnificent birds. Loggers' shows, forest hikes, and rides to the top on the Peak Chair add up to hours of activity.

If you're not the outdoorsy type, enjoy the free Theatre in the Sky show. The theatre features a high-definition video presentation, *Born to Fly,* as part of the Skyride pass. Fine dining at the Observatory (advance reservations allow you to ride the Skyride free) makes the most of the views. Open daily are the Bar 98 Bistro, a casual dining area with a large outdoor rooftop patio, and Lupin's Café for fresh, self-serve food.

Dr. Sun Yat-Sen Classical Chinese Garden

In Vancouver's Chinatown, local families in search of the freshest vegetables mingle with out-of-town visitors exploring exotic herb shops. Traffic crawls alongside throngs of pedestrians crowding the sidewalks. In the midst of all this kinetic energy, it would be easy to miss the tranquil Dr. Sun Yat-Sen Classical Chinese Garden tucked away just a few steps off Pender Street. But you won't want to miss this peaceful "Refreshment for the Heart."

Enter the garden near the intersection of Pender and Carrall streets, through a whitewashed wall behind the

Chinese Cultural Centre. As soon as you pass through the doorway marked Yi Yuan, or Garden of Ease, you'll find yourself slowing your steps to the pace of another time and place.

Classical Chinese gardens are an art form 20 centuries old. The most famous are in the city of Suzhou in China's Chiangsu province. These contemplative "scholar's gardens" have influenced garden design worldwide. In 1986, the Dr. Sun Yat-Sen Garden became the first full-scale classical Chinese garden outside China, and the first to be built anywhere in nearly 500 years. Built in Ming dynasty style, the garden reflects nature through the four elements of rock, water, plants, and architecture. Inside, a microcosmic world of less than half an acre is cleverly laid out to maximize its intricacy and complexity. Framed by round moon gates and lacy latticework, glimpses of exquisite vistas emerge, disappear, and reappear to create infinite visual space.

Dr. Sun-Yat Sen Classical Chinese Garden

More than 50 skilled Chinese artisans came to Vancouver to build the garden using centuries-old techniques, ancient tools and authentic building materials. The Yun Wei Ting gazebo, for example, perches atop a miniature mountain built of a unique rock found only on the bottom of Lake Tai in Suzhou. But the garden is also an original, incorporating local plants and materials.

Admission to the Dr. Sun Yat-Sen Classical Chinese Garden includes tea and a tour. The gift shop features a large selection of English-language books about Chinese culture.

Gulf of Georgia Cannery's National Historic Site

Silence reigns inside the Gulf of Georgia Cannery's huge main building, once the busiest of 15 bustling Steveston-based fish canneries. The working canneries are long gone, but the multi-timbered edifice remains as an homage to the West Coast's once-rich salmon harvests. The historic fishing village of Steveston, now a part of Richmond, B.C., reveres the presence of this grand dame overlooking the South Arm of the Fraser River. A visit to the cannery (open May to early

October) can be combined with a tour of the village, with its gift shops and tempting fish and chip restaurants. Or take out your snack and stroll along the adjacent Richmond Dyke to Sturgeon Banks as part of your day.

The cannery's exhibits show the fish-packing industry as it was in 1894. Conveyor belts for transporting empty tins, slime tables for cleaning the fish, the retort oven where the canned salmon was cooked, and the so-called "Iron Chink" canner sit as if ready for the next shift to begin. Processing fish in the busiest fishing port in the world, cannery workers produced two million cans a year or more, most bound for ports in England and Europe.

Within the walls of this old building — now one of Canada's national historic sites — the ghosts of thousands of fishermen and cannery workers linger. Guided tours conjure them up. Knowledgeable guides take visitors through each step of the canning process. The first cannery workers were Chinese men who had come to Canada to build the railway. Soon Japanese and Aboriginal workers joined them on the assembly line. Life in the cannery was demanding, but it was a job that could be done without proficiency in English. The remainder of the crew was made up of their wives and children. While the men hauled and gutted the big fish, the women did the cleaning. Children dropped tin cans into a chute that lined up to a conveyor belt, ready for filling, cooking, and packing. A free film also expands on the history of the early fishing industry, while the cannery's gift shop offers books and fish-themed souvenirs.

Before leaving Steveston, drop down to the public fish sales float, where working boats sell varieties of fresh and frozen fish and seafood off their decks. The fresh catch of the day may include prawns, lobsters, crab, and salmon.

Gulf of Georgia Cannery

Dining

Kasey Wilson

Pacific salmon dinner

Vancouver's culinary reputation is built on fresh food and fresh flavours. The variety of dining experiences continues to grow each year, with some of the country's finest chefs bringing distinction to food that is innovative and, in many cases, unique to the West Coast.

If there is a quintessential West Coast food, it is wild salmon. It comes in five varieties: sockeye, pink, coho, spring, and chum, and can be cooked in a multitude of ways. The original inhabitants, First Nations people on the Pacific and on the inland rivers, barbecued or baked it. Today, specialty restaurants like Salmon House on the Hill feature traditional delicacies such as alderwood-grilled wild British Columbia salmon.

Go Fish, Vancouver

With some 30 percent of Vancouver's population of Asian origin, it's not surprising that Oriental cooking is plentiful throughout the city. No matter where you go within Vancouver or its neighbouring suburbs — Richmond, Burnaby, New Westminster, or the North Shore communities of North and West Vancouver — you'll find the diversity of Asia represented in

B.C. salmon dinner

the kitchens. With a light touch, the chefs offer up a tasty mix of texture and colour, flavour and flair. These days, dining in Vancouver encompasses a great many nationalities: French, Italian, Lebanese, Hungarian, Swiss, Persian, Portuguese, and Spanish are but a few examples. No matter what the style, cooking on the coast is buoyed with top-quality ingredients, brought in from the individualistic farms and ranches of the hinterlands.

The perfect complement to fine dining in Vancouver is the internationally recognized icewine from the Okanagan Valley. Canada is now recognized as the world's leading producer of icewine. Unlike any other dessert wine, icewine is made from grapes hand-harvested at night while they are frozen, during the months of December and January, when the temperature in the Okanagan reaches –8° C (18° F) or colder. Just as wonderful are the ales, beers, and stouts from local micro-breweries. And don't forget the coffee. It's not just a pick-me-up, but a way of life in the multitude of coffee bars that dot the city's streets.

Chinese

Chinatown is, of course, the first place to go in search of Chinese food. Getting a table at the Floata Seafood Restaurant on Keefer Street shouldn't be hard,

Hon's Wun-Tun House

even at the notoriously busy dim sum hour. With 1,000 seats, it is immense. The ease and skill evident in the service and cooking, however, belie its size. A second Floata Seafood serves Richmond. A bit farther along Keefer Street is Hon's Wun-Tun House, an institution revered for fast, inexpensive Cantonese-style rice and noodle dishes and vegetarian dim sum.

Not far from Chinatown, the Pink Pearl Chinese Seafood Restaurant on East Hastings is crowded with discriminating Chinese families, especially between 11 a.m. and 2 p.m. on weekends, when dim sum is a tradition. Lunch-time dining is easy here for visitors: servers urge you to make choices from the dishes displayed on their carts. Coming for dinner instead? You could catch a glimpse — and get an earful — of a

Chinese wedding banquet, usually a boisterous affair.

The Chinese food experience doesn't end at the Vancouver city limits. Across the Oak Street Bridge in Richmond are a number of Asian-style malls, complete with eateries. The Yaohan Centre's food courts offer a wide range of Asian street eats at bargain prices. Next to the Yaohan Centre, the Radisson President Hotel harbours the Richmond Mandarin Chinese Restaurant, distinguished by its creative dim sum menu and masterful repertoire of Cantonese dishes.

Outside the modern Asian centre of Richmond and the pioneering region of Vancouver's Chinatown are literally hundreds more Chinese restaurants. The popularity of humble Hon's, for instance, has translated into additional venues in downtown Vancouver, Richmond, New Westminster, and Coquitlam. Hon's has also spawned a thriving take-out trade in frozen potstickers, buns and dim sum, as well as won-ton noodles and chili oil. Most visiting food writers dine at Sun Sui Wah Seafood Restaurant on Main Street in Vancouver, designed by noted B.C. architect Bing Thom. Owner Simon Chan developed the Cantonese-style menu of dim sum specialties. The Won More Szechuan Restaurant serves reasonably priced hot and sour soup, potstickers and other dishes, mainly spicy, in a crowded, upstairs space in West End Vancouver and bigger, slightly more expensive digs in Kitsilano. At the downtown Shanghai Chinese Bistro, a skein of noodles makes its first appearance as a rope of dough, undergoes a fascinating

Beef and mixed veggies at Hon's

Kirin Mandarin

ritual of twisting and stretching, and ends up on your plate as Tan Tan noodles with peanut sauce. Szechuan cuisine reappears in a slightly costlier incarnation at the Szechuan Chongqing Seafood Restaurant, with locations in both Vancouver and Burnaby. Both restaurants showcase cooking from the Chongqing region and specialize in seafood.

The Imperial Chinese Seafood Restaurant brings Chinese fine dining with a view to the downtown business district. Its serene atmosphere frequently breaks down in the face of giggles from its younger patrons. It's equally likely to be shattered by the adults, whose unsuppressed admiration for a perfect, glistening rock cod, whole and steamed with ginger and scallions, is often hearty and spontaneous. Look to the elegant Kirin Mandarin, also downtown, for specialties such as Shanghai smoked eel, Beijing duck, and Szechuan hot and spicy scallops.

Japanese

The popularity of teriyaki, teppan and especially sushi has taken Japanese food far from the small stretch of Powell Street known as Japantown. At Tojo's, on busy

Tojo's Restaurant

West Broadway, the privileged and prudent few who reserved a place at the 10-seat sushi bar are treated to a show of Hidekazu Tojo's consummate skill with sushi. Tojo's edible masterpieces are the main draw for the knowing Japanese business people, filmmakers, and celebrities who crowd the establishment, but a wide range of non-sushi dishes round out the somewhat pricey menu. In contrast to tiny Tojo's, the large and lush Kamei Royale, in its second-floor downtown location overlooking Burrard Street, is home to a steady stream of barbecue grill dishes, free-style special rolls and, of course, a wide range of sushi.

The West End's Musashi Japanese Restaurant offers more sensibly priced sushi and sashimi. Its menu includes the usual soups, salads, tempura, teriyaki chicken and beef, as well as rice and noodles, many assembled nicely into combination dinners. Yuji's Japanese Tapas offers a unique menu of Japanese

Vij's Restaurant

appetizer dishes perfect for snacking and socializing at reasonable prices.

Gyoza King has a much narrower focus. While noodle dishes and inexpensive specials do appear on the menu, there's no sushi to be seen in this West End eatery. The place is crammed with locals and tourists alike, who consume one plateful of plump meat, seafood or vegetable gyozas after another. And for ramen in all its forms — regular (pork), miso, and soy — try Ezogiku Noodle Café, a short walk away, where little else (only a fried rice dish, a fried noodle dish, a curry, and gyozas) is offered. There's a second Ezogiku near the Vancouver Public Library.

South Asian

In many parts of Greater Vancouver, South Asian restaurants in all price ranges are easy to find. Vij's Restaurant showcases B.C.-influenced Indian curries and other specials. The west side's Maurya has an incredible wine list and the tandoori quail served over spinach and chickpea cakes is a must. There's a moderately priced lunch buffet Monday to Sunday. Both places are modern, high-profile eateries.

Thai and Other Asian

Thai restaurants represent yet another sector of the city's multi-faceted Asian community. Montri's Thai in Kitsilano is hot, in every sense of the word (but you can ask for milder). Often cited as the city's best Thai, Montri's presents authentically spiced dishes that make the scaled heat ratings — from one chili (mildest) to five chilies (hottest) — required reading. The Phnom Penh is family-run, with a focus on Vietnamese and Cambodian food. While the surroundings may be rather plain, the hot and sour soup, tender flash-fried squid tubes, and fresh-oyster omelettes are anything but. For a fast, inexpensive meal, try one of the abundance of little Korean restaurants along Robson Street.

French, Italian, Mediterranean

For French dining, look to Le Crocodile. Located downtown, it offers roomy, luxurious surroundings with a patio, and French wines and Alsace regional dishes that are well worth the expense. Owner and chef Michel Jacob's Alsatian onion tart has been hailed as the best in Vancouver. For a bistro experience, try Café de Paris in the West End. The warm dark wood, wine racks

Le Crocodile

Quattro on Fourth

and lace curtains instantly bring to mind a Paris bistro. The menu includes moderately priced classics: duck confit, steak tartare, and cassoulet, all served with the pommes frites that have become legendary in the city. A table d'hôte, as well as original contemporary French creations, is available. Saveur, on Thurlow, sources local organic produce to create fine French dining at a prix-fixe of under $40 dollars. Bistro Pastis also produces solid country fare. Look for an outstanding cheese plate and, in cooler weather, satisfying braises, cassoulets and roasts. The Smoking Dog Grill will sate a hunger for uncomplicated food such as coq au vin, steak au poivre, duck à l'orange and salade niçoise. On a sunny afternoon, watch the Kitsilano crowd from the patio.

Il Giardino di Umberto

In West Vancouver, the unpretentious La Régalade is winning awards for no-nonsense country cooking inspired by the neighbourhood bistros in France. Don't miss the escargots or the homemade pâtés. Italian, French, and Spanish flavours meld at Cioppino's Mediterranean Grill, where chef and owner Pino Posteraro infuses his philosophy of "cucina naturale" into light, fresh dishes. In the same Yaletown area, Villa Del Lupo delivers a generous and contemporary menu of excellent pastas and favourites such as lamb shank osso buco.

Another bit of Italy resides in Il Giardino di Umberto, a seaside villa recreated on Hornby Street. The Tuscan menu emphasizes pasta and game. And at Quattro on Fourth and Gusto di Quattro, the rooms are mosaic-tiled and mahogany-trimmed. Quattro prepares some unusual Italian pastas; the combination plate provides a good overview. Voted the city's best for Italian cuisine and best ambience, CinCin Ristorante and Bar is an elegant spot for wood-fired cucina in a warmly embracing setting.

Raincity Grill

Pacific Coast
Plentiful, readily available seafood is a characteristic of Pacific Coast cuisine. The

Yaletown area is an urbane enclave of streetside cafés and stylish diners. At Rodney's Oyster House, oysters are the main attraction: a dozen or so varieties lie on ice, in long stainless steel beds, while customers line the oyster bar. Other fresh seafood, chowders, and slapjacks are also popular. Exceptional seafood is served at Blue Water Café and Raw Bar in a century-old heritage warehouse. Provence Marinaside's husband-and-wife team have matched a rustic décor with Mediterranean fare, in a perfect location overlooking False Creek. The trendy Global Grill & Satay Bar is yet another Yaletown winner. Try the regional dishes such as grilled veal chops and tuna tartar.

Stilton Cheesecake
at Diva

An established favourite, and still worth searching out, The Cannery Seafood Restaurant serves up fresh seafood dinners and brunches in its isolated location among the Burrard Inlet wharves. The Beach House, on the other side of the Burrard Inlet, is also especially strong on seafood; it offers a marvellous view of the West Vancouver waterfront.

At the Raincity Grill, near English Bay, the menu changes according to whatever fresh, local ingredients are on hand. Wine is available by the glass from an extensive, award-winning wine list. The West Coast theme is upheld by a duo of hotel restaurants as well. The Five Sails at Canada Place presents an imaginative West Coast menu that's good enough to compete with the spectacular harbour view. Diva at the Met optimizes an airy, natural space with multi-tiered seating, and out of its Waldorf-style open kitchen come stylish,

Above: Smoked
Black Alaska Cod
from Seasons
Restaurant in Queen
Elizabeth Park

Bottom: The Fish
House in Stanley
Park

C Restaurant

contemporary meals under the direction of executive chef Dino Renaerts.

The Fish House at Stanley Park has an enviable location, surrounded by trees, tennis courts, and lawn bowling greens in one of the world's best urban parks. Flaming prawns are one of the most popular dishes, and Chef Karen Barnaby's ahi tuna steak Diane with mashed potatoes has become a classic. Bishop's location streetside in Kitsilano, away from the harbour and the beach, lets you fully appreciate master host John Bishop's superlative standards of service and cuisine. Should your attention stray to the modern Canadian art gracing the walls, the whole roasted quail in mission fig glaze or the grilled rare albacore tuna with Dungeness crab and stinging nettle strudel will easily recapture your interest. The Pear Tree in Burnaby lures Vancouver visitors and residents out to the suburbs with the promise of Scott Jaeger's reasonably priced and inventive menu, which might, for example, offer a braised lamb shank with seared scallops and roasted pear risotto.

In the midst of all the West Coast innovation, a bit of tradition stands firm. Patrons at the famed Teahouse Restaurant at Ferguson Point in Stanley Park won't

Grilled prawns

allow traditional favourites such as the Teahouse's crab, shrimp and mascarpone stuffed mushroom caps off the menu. Seasons in the Park, in Queen Elizabeth Park, also has a menu that focuses mostly on fish and poultry. The restaurant overlooks the beautiful quarry garden and the Vancouver cityscape against the mountains.

Fine Dining and Hotel Dining

As the founding restaurant in the Vancouver Aquarium's Ocean Wise Program, C specializes in sustainable seafood dishes, cooked with a light touch. Executive chef Robert Clark and chef de cuisine Quang Dang create distinctive dishes that taste as intriguing as they sound: twice-cooked sablefish, smoked trout salad, and Bamfield pinto abalone. West regularly wins awards regionally, and is known internationally as the best of the best in contemporary West Coast cuisine. From Queen Charlotte halibut to Okanagan lamb, executive chef Warren Geraghty utilizes the best in regional ingredients to create his original interpretations of the classics.

At Lumière, executive chef Dale MacKay, working in consultation with international star chef Daniel

Boulud, uses mainly West Coast ingredients to make imaginative and consistently top-quality creations. Next door is their casual dining bistro, DB Bistro Moderne.

Some of the city's best restaurants are ensconced within downtown hotels, including the Five Sails and Diva at the Met (see Pacific Coast, page 43). Fleuri may be tucked away at Sutton Place, yet it is widely known for its Chocoholic Bar, afternoon teas, Sunday brunch, seafood buffet and ever-changing, always excellent, menu. The staggering new Shangri-La Hotel (to find it, you just need to look up) is home to Market by Jean-Georges, a restaurant, bistro, and raw bar combination overseen by celebrity chef Jean-Georges Vongerichten, working with on-site chef David Foot. The menu is reliable and surprisingly affordably priced.

The Bacchus Restaurant in the small, exclusive Wedgewood Hotel is a beautifully and discreetly lit room that unfailingly delivers fine food.

Specialty

The Hart House in Burnaby is remembered as much for its Tudor-style, heritage-home setting on Deer Lake as it is for its service and food. Menu items are unpretentious and range from seared halibut to smoked Fraser Valley duck breast.

Vegetarians seek out Planet Veg. Close to Kitsilano Beach and Vanier Park, the popular spot cooks up East Indian, Mexican, and Mediterranean vegetarian fast foods. Lineups are fairly frequent but takeout is an option. Order ahead or at the door (no delivery available). You won't find vegetarian fare at Memphis Blues Barbeque House, with locations on West Broadway, Commercial Drive, and Lonsdale Avenue in North Vancouver. All the favourites — pulled pork, ribs, beef brisket, and their signature cornish game hens — are served in hearty portions, with sides of baked beans, coleslaw, and cornbread.

Tapas are served at Bin 941 downtown, a warm, close room where the tasting bowls are generously filled and reasonably priced. A similar concept operates at Bin 942, near Granville and Broadway. The room is larger, but has much the same atmosphere and offers repeats of many of the menu items.

Casual

For many families, Earl's, which has several Vancouver locations, is the restaurant of choice. The service is fast and the food is fresh and healthy. It has an enviable wine list, and many of the locations have patios. Another long-time Vancouver family favourite is White Spot, which has lately expanded its traditional menu of burgers and fries with original dishes created by local celebrity chefs. Tomato Fresh Food Café in Kitsilano distinguishes itself from other diners with healthy, colourful comfort food such as BLTs, tomato and pesto sandwiches, and vegetarian chili. On Commercial Drive, or "The Drive" as it's universally known, Waazubee Café is casual and upbeat. The very hip Subeez with its 30-speaker sound system fits in well with its Yaletown neighbours. Don't miss the killer fries with garlic mayo, chicken and brie burger, or any of the vegetarian dishes.

The Dockside on Granville Island fuses a casual restaurant with a micro-brewery and pub. In summer, the smashing outdoor patio is open for business. The large open kitchen is versatile, alternating between pub grub and up-market fare. The lounge offers a full bar of spirits and a range of lagers and ales from their highly regarded brewery. However, some say the best beer in town flows from the custom-designed taps at Steamworks, an extraordinary Gastown brew pub with a wide-ranging brunch, lunch and dinner menu.

Patisserie Lebeau (near Granville Island) has fine Belgian waffles, delicious pastries and a selection of French breads and croissants for pâtisserie purists. A few doors down, Les Amis du Fromage supplies you and many top chefs with more than 350 cheeses at affordable prices. A new, unlikely location on E. Hastings sports an attached wine bar, Au Petit Chavignol. Solly's Bagelry's three locations are worth seeking out for their kosher comfort food and the best cinnamon buns in town.

In Gastown, The Irish Heather is the delight of owners Sean and Erin Heather's eye, and many others. A multitude of brews, as well as single malt and Irish whiskies, tickle the taste buds, washing down homemade bangers n' mash and beer-battered cod in a fish n' chips combo. And for some of the freshest fish in town, Go Fish is a takeaway on the waterfront near Granville Island. The fish is truly fresh, coming directly from the fishing boats docked nearby.

Steamworks brew pub

Shopping

Patricia Fraser

Stand at the corner of Granville and Georgia streets and you'll find yourself at the centre of Vancouver life, with skyscrapers above and the SkyTrain below them. This is the heart of cosmopolitan Vancouver. It's also the starting point for some serious shopping. No matter which direction you take, you'll find something to tempt you: malls (Pacific Centre and Sinclair Centre), shopping promenades (such as Robson Street), boutiques specializing in locally designed fashion in Gastown, and home décor and designer baubles in Yaletown.

Robson Street at night

Georgia and Granville

On the northeast corner of Georgia and Granville streets is the Hudson's Bay Company, known as "the Bay." Established in 1824 as a network of fur-trading posts, the Bay is a Canadian tradition, and a handy stop for quality goods from scarves to soup plates. The other corners of Georgia and Granville streets also hold the downtown Sears and Vancouver's own London Drugs, an institution in its own right.

Head downstairs through the Bay to the underground Pacific Centre Mall. Running north from Georgia Street, this attractive mall holds chains such as the glamorous redefined Holt Renfrew offering international fashions, personal shopping, and trunk

47

shows. Also on site are Harry Rosen, MaxMara, Hugo Boss, the Gap, Club Monaco, Banana Republic, H&M, and Jacob.

Back above ground, walk west along Georgia and you'll pass the Vancouver Art Gallery, with The Gallery Store bursting with unique gifts, cards, and jewellery. Keep going west until you come to Burrard Street. You could go underground again to the Royal Centre and Bentall Centre malls, or turn south for a block and head up to Robson Street.

Designer shops on Robson Street

Robson Street

Once a quiet street known as Robsonstrasse for its European-style delis and schnitzel cafés, Robson is now an urban carnival of chains such as the Gap, Roots and Rootskids, Banana Republic, and Mexx, interspersed with a bounty of coffee shops and little Asian fast-food cafés. Designer shopping bags swing off youthful arms amidst an up-tempo mix of well-heeled international travellers. Walk further west along Robson to Denman Street and you're deep into the West End. The shopping area here is more residential than Robson Street, with flower stores and framers, fish-and-chip shops and beachwear (just steps from English Bay).

Gastown and Lonsdale Quay

Holt Renfrew, downtown Vancouver

The Gastown area is chock-a-block with tourist shops and restaurants in refurbished heritage buildings along the waterfront. The curios and keepsakes at Salmagundi West raise souvenirs to a higher level. The former Canadian Pacific Railway station is now the terminus for the SkyTrain and the connecting station for the SeaBus to the North Shore. Take the SeaBus for a 12-minute waterborne jaunt across Vancouver Harbour to the dock at Lonsdale Quay Market. Treat yourself to lunch, purchase a hand-crafted souvenir, then head back on the handy, frequent SeaBus.

Granville Island

Granville Island, on the south side of False Creek, is a former industrial peninsula reclaimed by the city and reborn as a shopping and arts centre. The huge Granville Island Market is a collection of vendors of gourmet food items and fresh produce. In the Net Loft, another large building packed to the gunwales with boutiques, find Edie Hats (a Vancouver fashion landmark), Paper-YA's decorative handmade papers, Beadworks' collection of 30,000 beads, and a multiplicity of artists' studios and galleries. Elsewhere on the island, browse for handcrafted pottery, jewellery and gifts, or visit Osake, Canada's first artisan sake maker. The Kids Only Market, a renovated former warehouse at the entrance to the island, is home to over 25 imaginative shops for children.

Antiques and Collectibles
Lovers of antiques and collectibles will want to visit the three areas where shops and galleries are concentrated: West 10th Avenue by the University of British Columbia (Folkart Interiors and others), Granville Street between West 6th and West 14th avenues (Uno Langmann, Farmhouse Collections), and Main Street between 12th and 29th avenues (Second Time Around and Baker's Dozen).

Bookstores
Vancouverites love to read, and whether you're browsing the latest bestsellers or searching for something more esoteric, you're likely to find a treasure in one of the city's many bookstores. Browse for hours in Chapters bookstores (downtown, on South Granville, and at Metrotown mall), each with its own Starbucks coffee shop and a huge stock of books and gift items, or shop Vancouver's own Book Warehouse chain for bargains. For a more intimate and individual book experience, try Duthie Books and new-age Banyen Books on West 4th Avenue, gay lit Little Sister's in the West End, Oscar's Art Books and Kidsbooks on West Broadway or Barbara-Jo's Books to Cooks in Yaletown.

Kids Only Market on Granville Island

Kidsbooks on West Broadway

Canadian Clothing Designers
Western style starts here: First Nations fashion maven Dorothy Grant uses her Haida background as inspiration for clothing based on "button blanket" designs, meeting customers by

appointment only. Zonda Nellis on South Granville has developed a worldwide following for her subtly coloured, elegant hand-loomed designer wear. Canadian RozeMerie Cuevas designs for Jacqueline Conoir, available at JC Studio on West 6th Avenue. In swank Kerrisdale, Margareta Design offers clothing that is conservative and classic.

Children's Stores

Clothing for the well-dressed tot can be found at Bobbit's for Kids! on West 4th, Isola Bella in Kerrisdale, and Please Mum on West Broadway. As for toys and games, check out Kaboodles on

The Toybox on West Broadway

Granville Island and West 10th, and the Toybox and Toys R Us on West Broadway. As well, the Kids Only Market on Granville Island offers a number of shops under one roof, including one devoted to kites.

Activewear

Vancouver's active lifestyle, along with its mild, wet weather, has generated a style of dress that's so comfortable, it's now as popular with couch potatoes as it is with sporty types. Fleece, stretchable materials, waterproof breathables, and the new eco-fabrics are the basis of the West Coast look. Lululemon Athletica, a local company that started out specializing in yoga wear, today dresses active fashionistas all over the globe. It has outlets on Robson Street, in Kitsilano, and in several malls. For outdoors people, Mountain Equipment Co-op is a Vancouver institution that

Colourful beads at Granville Island Market

opened in a hole in the wall back in 1971, and now has a dozen massive stores across Canada. The main store on West Broadway is the centrepiece of a cluster of outdoor retailers that includes another Vancouver mainstay, Taiga, plus A.J. Brooks, Eco Outdoor Sports, and a number of other outdoor apparel shops.

China and Crystal

Apart from the Bay, which has everything, you can find what your heart desires at Atkinson's at West 6th and Granville. The whole store sparkles. Chintz and Company in Yaletown boasts "entertaining tablewares." W. H. Puddifoot & Co. is a favourite in Kerrisdale.

Designer Boutiques

You'll find favourite labels at Vancouver's many designer boutiques. Petites in particular will be

pleasantly surprised at the selection. Nearly one-third of Vancouver's population is of Asian heritage and sizes are appropriately geared to the market. Most shops are temptingly close to major downtown hotels. On West Hastings, there's Chanel, Leone, and Escada; the Gianni Versace Boutique at the Sinclair Centre; Enda B Fashions, Edward Chapman's Ladies Shop, Bacci's, and Boboli are all on South Granville; and Dyanna's Fine Clothing for Women is on Howe Street.

First Nations Arts and Jewellery
Vancouver offers a fine selection of authentic First Nations art and jewellery. In Gastown, Hill's Native Art on Water Street (formerly Hill's Indian Crafts) stocks carved jewellery and chunky, virtually indestructible Cowichan sweaters. The Inuit Gallery, around the corner on Cambie Street, is a respected gallery for collectors of quality Inuit and First Nations carvings and prints. Marion Scott Gallery, a recent newcomer to Water Street, has renowned Inuit artworks. The Lattimer Gallery on West 2nd Avenue near Granville Island offers masks, jewellery, prints, and drums. The Museum of Anthropology at the University of British Columbia has a good selection of jewellery, books, prints and sculpture, including soapstone, a traditional local material.

Japanese lantern, Circle Craft

Gift Shops
You will find well-designed objects from pottery to jewellery at Bookmark in the Vancouver Public Library's downtown branch, at Circle Craft Co-op on Granville Island and in The Gallery Store at the Vancouver Art Gallery on Robson. West Coast–themed gifts can be found at the Clamshell Shop at the Vancouver Aquarium and at the Museum of Anthropology's gift shop. And for birthday, wedding, or anniversary gifts for every budget and occasion, try Chachkas on South Granville, and Moulé on West 4th and Park Royal Mall in West Vancouver.

Spring dress, Yaletown

Home Furnishings
Cosmopolitan Vancouverites enjoy their interiors as well as their city's great natural settings. Near the corner of Broadway and Granville streets, decorators will find classic Jordan's on Broadway, rustic Country Furniture, and urbane Industrial Revolution. Upholstery Arts on Burrard Street near West 8th Avenue offers a huge selection of soft furnishings made to order. Yaletown's Bernstein & Gold sells fine Egyptian cotton linens, Italian bedding and tapestries, and Fortuny lighting in an elegant setting. Like most other stores, shipping is available.

John Fluevog
Boots and Shoes

Boboli on South
Granville

Men's Clothing

High-end establishments well worth a visit include
Boboli on South Granville, Harry Rosen, and Holt
Renfrew in the Pacific Centre, Boys' Co. on Robson,
Leone in the Sinclair Centre, Mark James on West
Broadway, Enda B Men and Women on West 10th
Avenue, and S. Lampman in Kerrisdale. For a sportier
look, try Eddie Bauer at Oakridge Centre and Park
Royal Centre, Roots on Robson Street and Tilley
Endurables on Granville.

Shoe Stores

With shops on Granville Street and in Gastown,
the unique style of internationally renowned
shoemaker John Fluevog tempts those willing to
put an unconventional foot forward. The classic
Ingledew's, downtown on Granville, and Freedman
Shoes on South Granville both offer quality classic
dress and casual footwear.

If your tootsies are feeling tender, the Broadway Shoe Salon
and Walk with Ronsons both have a good selection of comfortable
walking shoes.

Entertainment

Heather Conn

Vancouver offers remarkable entertainment from little-known talented amateurs to marquee-splashed stars. Whether you're a film buff, a music fancier, or someone who revels in live theatre or dance, you'll find events happening every night of the year. Stroll through the downtown entertainment district where many clubs, for all persuasions, provide a lively after-hours scene. Most performing arts productions sell tickets in advance. Ticketmaster has a monopoly in this area, with a telephone line dedicated to arts events. A welcome addition is Tickets Tonight, open daily, which sells day-of-event half-price tickets at the Tourism Vancouver Visitor Centre.

Chan Centre for the Performing Arts, UBC

The Drowsy Chaperone, Vancouver Playhouse

Film

Known for its thriving, close-knit independent film community, Vancouver is a filmgoer's mecca. Its outstanding Vancouver International Film Festival draws devoted attendees from

Stanley Theatre

across North America, screening more than 350 dramas and documentaries representing dozens of countries, at 10 venues. You'll also find innovative and provocative movies at many themed film festivals such as the Latin American Film Festival (www.vlaff.org), the Jewish Film Festival (www.vjff.org), and the Mountain Film Festival (www.vimff.org). In May, DOXA (www.doxafestivals.ca) shows exclusively documentaries, and in August, the Vancouver Queer Film Festival (www.queerfilmfestival.ca) features films with gay themes. For year-round fare, Pacific Cinematheque on Howe Street offers offbeat new releases and delightful rare films and classics. Catch special film events and the best of world cinema at Vancity Theatre at Seymour and Davie.

Live Theatre

Middle: Firehall Arts Centre
Bottom: Vancouver Playhouse's
The Wars

The Vancouver Playhouse (part of the Queen Elizabeth Theatre complex) is one of the best regional theatres in Canada. Plays presented here employ the top actors, directors, designers, and craftspeople from across the country. Since it opened in 1963, the Vancouver Playhouse Theatre Company has often premiered award-winning Canadian plays.

In the 1930s, the Stanley Theatre on Granville Street near Broadway was *the* place for vaudeville. It later became an excellent movie theatre but eventually closed in the heyday of the multiplexes. In the late 1990s, the Arts Club Theatre completed lengthy and difficult renovations to transform the dilapidated but distinguished cinema into a first-class professional theatre. Now called the

Stanley Industrial Alliance Stage, the heritage theatre is a charming 630-seat venue, home to many of Vancouver's most entertaining productions, including many smaller musicals. The plays are equally good at the Arts Club's 450-seat Granville Island Stage. A string of hits, including homegrown and international plays, contribute to the Arts Club's longevity. Having run the Arts Club since it opened in 1972, artistic director Bill Millerd is the most respected, and probably most decorated, theatre practitioner in the country.

54

Bramwell Tovey conducting the VSO

If you thought that Granville Island was just for great market shopping, you'll be surprised at how many live theatres coexist here. Across the walkway from the Granville Island Stage is the intimate New Revue Stage. This cabaret-style venue hosts Vancouver TheatreSports League, offering comic improvisation honed to a science. If you haven't seen a live improv show, catch one of the regular early-evening performances. Vancouver TheatreSports is suitable for the entire family. The 224-seat Waterfront Theatre is another Granville Island venue, noted for performances of new Canadian plays. For independent theatre with an off-the-wall edge, hit Granville Island in the fall for the Vancouver International Fringe Festival. Built in a former fire hall, the Firehall Arts Centre on East Cordova is devoted to new plays, performance art, and dance, and has a reputation for presenting ground-breaking multicultural productions. In addition to its professional theatres, Vancouver has several good community theatres. Presentation House in North Vancouver has excellent offerings. Metro Theatre in South Vancouver's Marpole area presents melodrama, mystery, and British comedy. At the Jewish Community Centre's Norman Rothstein Theatre, live performers fill a luxurious, 318-seat auditorium.

Vancouver Opera's *Ariadne auf Naxos*

The Queen Elizabeth Theatre is the place to go to see New York–style musical productions, touring theatre and dance companies, family presentations, and multicultural shows. The theatre is perfect for all these and the productions of its resident troupes, the Vancouver Opera and Ballet British Columbia. Built in 1959, the theatre is a large venue featuring elegant decor, plush seats, and a 21-metre (70-foot) wide stage with proscenium arch.

Music

From strings to swing to the thrum of indie rock, Vancouver's music scene offers vibrant choices and a diverse history. The Vancouver Symphony Orchestra (VSO), which began in 1919, now performs more than 150 concerts annually, welcoming many outstanding artists. You'll usually find the symphony at the historic Orpheum Theatre, a former vaudeville house built in 1927. At the time, this venue was one of the largest and most impressive theatres on the West Coast. After five years of extravagant renovations in the late 1970s, it still enthralls with its classic ambience of old-time elegance.

Vancouver Opera's *Carmen*

Like the symphony, the opera has long historic roots in Vancouver. The city's first opera performances date to the late 1880s. The Vancouver Opera Company launched in 1960, with a performance of Bizet's *Carmen*. Today, Vancouver Opera is fiercely committed to developing Canadian talent, as well as hiring principal singers of international fame. The company employs its own orchestra and chorus made up of local musicians and singers. Traditional opera fans can relish shows from *Salome* to *Rigoletto*. All performances are at the Queen Elizabeth Theatre.

For jaw-dropping acoustics, try a classical concert at the 1,400-seat Chan Centre for the Performing Arts at the University of British Columbia. The UBC Opera Ensemble appears here a few times a year, as does the Vancouver Symphony Orchestra. For choral splendour, look for the Vancouver Cantata Singers performing at the Chan Centre. This award-winning chamber choir, one of Canada's foremost, is guaranteed to captivate.

For eclectic tastes that lean to rock 'n' roots, try the Railway Club on Dunsmuir downtown or an informal concert at the Commodore Ballroom on Granville Street. Built as a ballroom dance club, its main attraction was its bouncy, horsehair-spring floor. Although the Great Depression hit just after it opened, it managed to survive and go on to greater glory during the big band era. Over the years, it's adapted to host rock, jazz, punk, and many other kinds of musical acts. It's still one of Vancouver's most-loved clubs — and there's still some spring left in that floor. Check in advance to see who's playing. Artists include local, national, and international musicians of every genre.

Folkies and world beat aficionados will want to watch for concerts sponsored by the Rogue Folk Club, and visitors in July can take in the venerable Vancouver Folk Music Festival. For jazz, try The Cellar Jazz Club on West Broadway and O'Doul's in the Listel Hotel. The superb Vancouver International Jazz Festival in June offers both ticketed and free events. A casual spot for upbeat and world beat local bands is the long-running Backstage Lounge on

Simone Orlando in Ballet B.C.'s *Elemental Brubeak*

Granville Island. For rollicking rhythm and blues, put on your boogie boots and head to the Yale Hotel, near the Granville Bridge on the downtown side. Built in 1889, the Yale is one of the oldest buildings in Western Canada. Dress casually and enjoy some beer at this classic blues bar.

Dance

For modern dance, you'll find B.C.'s most diverse performance spaces at Scotiabank Dance Centre on Davie and the Vancouver East Cultural Centre on Venables. "The Cultch" opened on October 15, 1973, with a two-week run of the locally based Anna Wyman Dance Theatre. Today's Cultch, with a renovated historic theatre and new addition, offers a marvellous array of distinctive dance performances and performing arts.

Fei Guo and Shannon Smith in Ballet B.C.'s *Peter Pan*

You might want to keep an eye out for Kokoro Dance, an innovative troupe that performs outdoors and at various venues throughout the city. The long-running Judith Marcuse Dance Projects creates multi-disciplinary dance and theatre productions at various city-wide locations.

For classical and modern dance, Ballet British Columbia has built an international reputation for artistic excellence. The company first performed on April 11, 1986, and was quickly recognized for its combination of talent and creativity. You can see the ballet at the Queen Elizabeth Theatre.

Bar at Opus Hotel

Clubs

For star watchers, the bar of choice is the Gérard Lounge on the first floor of the Sutton Place Hotel. One of Vancouver's trendiest lounges, the luxurious Gérard is exquisitely furnished and the bar prices

Vancouver's Jazz Festival featuring Five Alarm Funk

reflect the surroundings. If you spot some of Hollywood's most memorable faces here, be discreet; Vancouver is known for its politeness. If you're more intent on meeting someone attractive and of the opposite sex, visit Richard's on Richards. The crowds at this big dance club tend to be in their late twenties and early thirties. Music ranges from rock and extreme metal to hip-hop and house.

A few blocks from Richard's, you'll find AuBAR, the place to be seen. The club has a line outside most every night from Thursday through Saturday. Another place to dress up for and be seen is the lounge at the Opus Hotel in Yaletown. Gastown's Fabric Nightclub attracts a casual, youthful crowd to dance in its brick-walled warehouse space. Leading DJs spin hip-hop, Top 40, funk, and alternative and electronic music.

Lineups are the biggest problem with Vancouver clubs. Any place worth going to usually has a lineup after 9 p.m. Smoking is not permitted inside public buildings, so be prepared to smoke outside, away from doorways.

Gay and Lesbian

In Vancouver, gay clubs have the least amount of attitude of any downtown night spots. Celebrities is a longtime favourite of gay, straight, and bi dancers and party lovers. Theme nights such as Latin night, amateur drag nights, and even gay bingo add to the fun atmosphere. If you're looking to make it a long night of dancing, move on to Pulse Nightclub, where another mixed crowd dances the night away. Numbers, a more exclusively gay male dance club, is another option.

For something a little more low-key, Oasis is a lounge and restaurant combo with a patio and tapas menu. Sports fans might want to head over to Score, a gay-friendly sports bar. And for the times when a cocktail and conversation suits the mood better than dancing or partying, 1181 is the place to go. All three clubs are frequented by a gay-positive, mixed crowd.

The Honey Lounge is a cool bar with a good percentage of lesbian patrons. Next door to Honey is a women-only nightclub called Lick, an "All-Girl-Operated Underground Queer Night Club." Patrons here enjoy hip-hop to indie and pop on the club's super sound system. Venues from Celebrities to The Railway Club and the Howard Johnson's on Kingsway host women's DJ dance nights.

Shops along Davie Street in Gastown

58

Visual Art

Gary McFarlane

Vancouver's art scene began to come into its own in the 1930s when Emily Carr and other artists developed a style that reflected the West Coast landscape and images. In the post-war years, artists such as Jack Shadbolt incorporated surrealism, abstractionism, and the other "isms" of the day. During the 1960s and '70s the city became a centre for experimentation. One of the most memorable images of the era was a monocled Mr. Peanut, represented by the artist Vincent Trasov, running for mayor. Over the last two decades, the Vancouver School of photographers has put the city on the international art map. Local art stars include Rodney Graham, Stan Douglas, and Jeff Wall. The Vancouver Art Gallery regularly showcases this city's historic work. Today Vancouver has a thriving art scene. Vancouver's art ranges from lush landscapes to photography to animé-inspired drawings to the unique artist-run centres where anything goes.

Marchessault-Arcetritlires at Bau-Xi Gallery

Inside the Vancouver Art Gallery

Commercial Galleries

South Granville is home to many of the city's most prestigious galleries, running for a few blocks north and south of the Granville Street and Broadway intersection. Equinox Gallery features up-and-coming and senior Canadian sculptors and painters, including Gathie Falk, Liz Magor, and Gordon Smith. They also carry twentieth-century classics such as Warhol and Lichtenstein. Bau-Xi and Winsor galleries specialize in landscape paintings and other figurative works. Douglas Udell Gallery carries work by artists from the

Device to root out evil, Public art, Vancouver

West Coast to the Prairies. Monte Clarke Gallery exhibits younger artists, including writer-artist Douglas Coupland and photographer Karen Bubas. Lawrence Eng Gallery also has a stable of young talent. Heffel Gallery auctions classic Canadian art including the Group of Seven. Historic paintings and antiquities can be found at Uno Langmann and other antique shops that dot Granville Street. All galleries distribute free copies of *Preview — The Gallery Guide* with maps and up-to-date show listings.

Nearby Granville Island has many small galleries and shops featuring printmakers and other artisans: Malaspina Print Makers, Dundarave Print Workshop, Crafthouse, Gallery of BC Ceramics, Circle Craft Gallery, and New-Small & Sterling Studio Glass.

On the east side of town, Catriona Jeffries Gallery features some of Vancouver's most internationally recognized conceptual art, including works by Brian Jungen and Ian Wallace. Located downtown, Buschlen Mowatt Galleries has long been a fixture of the gallery scene and has also organized the eagerly anticipated Vancouver Sculpture Biennale. Also downtown is the Dorian Rae Collection, which deals in museum-quality African and Southeast Asian sculpture and textiles. In the fall, hundreds of local artists open their studios to the public for the Eastside Culture Crawl.

Buschlen Mowatt Gallery

First Nations Art

Canada's vibrant Native art traditions are featured at several galleries. Although the Northwest Coast Haida and Tlingit arts have become synonymous with Native art in British Columbia, Vancouver is a base to discover other cultures — like the Coast Salish, Kwakwaka'wakw, and Tsimshian, to name only three. Douglas Reynolds Gallery on South Granville specializes in historic and contemporary Northwest Coast Native art, including acclaimed artists such as Robert Davidson. Near Granville Island is Lattimer Gallery, which sells masks and other ceremonial art, including limited-edition prints by Bill Reid, Susan Point, and Norval Morriseau. Gastown has many gift shops specializing in Native crafts, and respected galleries including Coastal Peoples Fine Arts Gallery, Spirit Wrestler Gallery, Marion Scott Gallery, and the Inuit Gallery of Vancouver. The world-renowned Museum of Anthropology at the University of British Columbia provides an in-depth look at West Coast Native art.

Exhibit at the Museum of Anthropology

Public and Artist-run Galleries

Vancouver has a wealth of public galleries that belie its relatively small size — and probably has more artist-run galleries than any other city in the world. It's a tradition of do-it-yourself non-conformity, which began in the 1970s with artist-run centres such as VIVO Media Arts Centre and the Western Front. Recent Governor General's Award–winner Eric Metcalfe and influential video artist Kate Craig came out of this environment.

Inside the Inuit Gallery, Gastown

Gastown has become a hub for innovative galleries: Centre A showcases contemporary Asian art; Access and Helen Pitt galleries introduce artists still wet behind the ears; Artspeak specializes in conceptual art; and Gallery Gachet provides a forum for artists informed by mental health issues. Some galleries are barely holes in the wall. Blanket Gallery, which has a growing international reputation for cutting-edge work, is literally tucked away in an alley under a viaduct. Pick up the free local newspaper *Georgia Strait* to see what's hot, what's not, and what's no longer.

Outside of Gastown, the Contemporary Art Gallery and the Or Gallery frequently exhibit the trendiest Canadian artists. On Granville Island at the Emily Carr University of Art and Design, the Charles H. Scott Gallery has thematic shows of international contemporary art. The Morris and Helen Belkin Art Gallery at the University of British Columbia has an impressive exhibition space featuring an important archive on the most influential local artists. If you ask at the desk, they'll let you into Rodney Graham's Millennial Time Machine, a horse-drawn carriage converted into a camera obscura.

Public Art

Vancouver is gaining a reputation for fun, and sometimes controversial, public art; here is a small sample of what you might see throughout city neighbourhoods.

Sculpture at Buschlen Mowatt Gallery

Looking like a weathered Sputnik, Jerry Pethick's *Time Top* is installed on the north shore of False Creek just west of the Cambie Bridge (after being submerged in the Pacific Ocean for two years). Downtown, a life-sized bronze bull by Joe Fafard stands at the corner of West Georgia and Richards. Other more controversial bronze animals can be found at 4078 Knight Street: Tom Dean's *Peaceable Kingdom* includes over a dozen swine and vermin cavorting in a public square while sloths hang overhead, all overseen by a menacing vulture. A classic slab of 1960s modernism by Henry Moore adorns Queen Elizabeth Park. There are also spectacular examples of Native art throughout the city, including Bill Reid's massive *Jade Canoe* packed with mythological figures at Vancouver International Airport. A complete registry of Vancouver's public art is available at http://vancouver.ca/PublicArt_Net.

Parks and
Gardens

Marg Meikle

**VanDusen Garden
(top and bottom)**

It will come as no surprise to visitors that gardening has always been one of the top outdoor leisure activities in Vancouver — it really shows. The combination of a mild climate, plenty of precipitation, and very diverse immigration to this area makes for a wide variety of gardening styles. From the abundant crops of the Chinese vegetable gardens around Chinatown to the amazing tomatoes and grapes of the Italian community around Commercial Drive, from the seemingly out-of-place palm trees on Beach Drive in the West End to the colourful perennial borders in many other neighbourhoods, there is much to enjoy around here. Vancouver is also one of the few cities in the world blessed with two botanical gardens; VanDusen Botanical Garden and the University of British Columbia (UBC) Botanical Garden are both superb living research libraries.

VanDusen Botanical Garden

Lush VanDusen is a 22-hectare (55-acre) garden conveniently located on the edge of Shaughnessy, a well-heeled historic section of Vancouver. Remarkably, the bountiful, mature VanDusen Botanical Garden was only built in the early 1970s on a former golf course. At any time of the year, many of its 255,000 plants, trees, and shrubs will be in bloom. The garden is laid out in themed areas, including the Children's Garden, Mediterranean Garden, Meditation Garden, Rose Garden, and Sino-Himalayan Garden. There's also the Rhododendron Walk, Canadian Heritage Garden, a

maze, a heather garden, and a fern dell.

Many popular special events are held here throughout the year, including Vancouver's most magnificent display of Christmas lights, a big plant sale in April, and an abundance of flower-club shows, concerts, and family programs in the spring and summer. There is a lovely themed gift shop, and the gardenside Shaughnessy Restaurant, serving fresh West Coast cuisine.

Rhododendron in full bloom at VanDusen Garden

UBC Botanical Garden and Other UBC Gardens

The UBC Botanical Garden sits on the ocean edge of the campus, overlooking the Strait of Georgia. Open to the public for wandering, and breathing in that fresh sea air and those gorgeous scents, this 28-hectare (70-acre) themed garden is also used for teaching and research. The various gardens include the Alpine Garden, Asian Garden, Carolinian Forest, Winter Garden, B.C. Native Garden, Physic Garden (herbs), Food Garden, and the Contemporary Garden featuring new plant varieties. The 25-hectare (61-acre) David C. Lam Asian Garden has a huge variety of woody Asian plants, maples, clematis, roses, rhododendrons, azaleas, magnolias, and rare Oriental plants. The best view is from the Greenheart Canopy Walkway, an aerial trail system that weaves through the garden trees. The Shop-in-the-Garden offers a good selection of gardening books and a great nursery, including plants developed through the UBC plant introduction program.

Of special interest at UBC is the classical Japanese Nitobe Memorial

Below: Maze at VanDusen
Bottom: Pond at VanDusen

Garden designed with a very West Coast view by Japanese landscape architect Kannosouke Mori. He used many native trees and shrubs, training and pruning them in traditional Japanese fashion. Within this 1-hectare (2.5-acre) garden are many more: the Tea Garden with a Tea House, the Nightingale Fence, the Tenth Bridge, several water crossings, and a stroll garden.

Queen Elizabeth Park and Bloedel Floral Conservatory

Second only to Stanley Park in popularity, Queen Elizabeth Park is located on Little

Queen Elizabeth Park

Mountain, the highest point in Vancouver. It offers a terrific view of the city and the North Shore's Coast Mountains. June is a particularly showy month for the 52-hectare (130-acre) Queen E. Park, as the locals call

Parrot at Bloedel Floral Conservatory

Inside the Dome at QE Park

it, because the roses are in full bloom. But any time is worth a wander through the Quarry Garden at the peak of the mountain. It was created in the 1960s, and is similar to Butchart Gardens near Victoria, which was built 60 years earlier, also in a quarry.

There is public art of note throughout Queen Elizabeth Park. A Henry Moore sculpture, *Knife Edge-Two Piece*, is close to the Bloedel Floral Conservatory. The conservatory is a huge Plexiglas dome that holds a large variety of tropical, desert, and exotic plants as well as more than 100 tropical birds. It is a particularly great destination on a rainy day, for inside this warm, climate-controlled dome is a jungle of palms, banana trees, and orchids, among other species.

Dr. Sun Yat-Sen Classical Chinese Garden

The Dr. Sun Yat-Sen Classical Chinese Garden, opened in 1986, is the first authentic full-sized classical

Dr. Sun Yat-Sen Classical Chinese Garden

Chinese garden built outside China. In a serene environment behind a wall in the middle of Chinatown, you will find tranquil ponds, natural rock sculptures, courtyards, and an interesting variety of plants. The garden reflects the Taoist philosophy of accentuating harmony in contrasts. Every stone, pine tree, and magnolia flower in the garden has been placed purposefully and carries a symbolic meaning. The garden offers guided tours, which provide perspectives on Chinese culture, life during the Ming dynasty, architecture, and plants. In August, the garden offers the popular Enchanted Evening series. Visitors sip a cup of complimentary tea and enjoy an hour-long music program. The concerts are varied, often featuring Asian classical or popular music. This is an especially nice place to go on a rainy day as the walkways are covered and the tips of the eave tiles are designed to let the drops fall from them in a particularly gentle way.

Stanley Park's Garden Delights

The 400-hectare (1,000-acre) Stanley Park has many attractions, including a variety of gardens. Of special interest in June and July is the Rose Garden, which features hundreds of roses divided in beds by colour. Also noteworthy, particularly in April and May, is the Ted and Mary Greig Rhododendron Garden containing not only rhododendrons, but also camellias, magnolias, maples, and azaleas. The park boasts

Stanley Park

65

Cycling in Stanley Park

many trails throughout the forested area. (See Stanley Park map, page 6.)

Century Gardens at Deer Lake Park
If you like rhododendrons, Burnaby's official flower, this is the place to see a lot of them. Located on the grounds of the Burnaby Art Gallery, this garden was created in 1967 for Canada's centennial. The garden, which overlooks Deer Lake, also has a good collection of roses and azaleas.

Park & Tilford Gardens
Created in 1968 by a privately owned distillery, these North Vancouver gardens have been preserved despite rezoning and other changes in the area. The owners and merchants of the nearby Park & Tilford Shopping Centre now fund the gardens. There are separate themed gardens or outdoor rooms devoted to roses, herbs, rhododendrons, and West Coast native plants, as well as the White Garden, Oriental Garden, Native Garden, Rock Pool, and Display Garden, with features such as hanging baskets, fountains, a Victorian greenhouse, and a Florentine pergola.

Below: Stanley Park

The gardens display plants suitable for the West Coast climate and are developed using organic methods and integrated pest management.

Trees Galore
Vancouver has more flowering trees than any other city in Canada. Trees have been the lifeblood of the economy and define this place. Vancouverites are truly passionate about their trees. Tens of thousands of flowering cherry, plum, magnolia, and dogwood trees make spring a delight throughout the city. As well as the tree collections in the public gardens listed here, consider a free tour of the Riverview Lands Davidson Arboretum. This collection of about 1,800 trees on the 99 hectares (244 acres) of the Riverview Hospital grounds contains more than 150 varieties. Created around 1905, it was one of the first arboreta in Canada.

In the Shaughnessy area is a round park in the middle of The Crescent, one of the most prestigious streets in town. This park has a collection of unusual trees, some of which are more than 100 years old. See if you can spot the Japanese Snowbell, Winged Euonymus, Pyramidal Blue Lawson Cypress, or Eddie's White Wonder Dogwood, the latter developed right here in Vancouver.

66

Activities and Spectator Sports

Bob Mackin

Vancouver is North America's four-season recreation destination. Where else can you start the day on a golf course, race through gnarly trails on a mountain bike at midday, hit the ski slopes or marina before sunset, and then unwind at a professional hockey, soccer, or football game? Both weekend warriors and armchair admirals will find plenty to see and do. One of the best parts is that so many of the outdoor activities come without a hefty price tag.

Dragon boat race

Outdoor Activities

Summer

Beaches

Vancouver's beaches are ideal for relaxing or getting sweaty in the summertime. Kitsilano and English Bay are the most popular, which means space is at a premium on the best days. Downtown beaches include Second or Third Beach at Stanley Park, or venture westward toward the University of British Columbia to Jericho or Spanish Banks. If you can do without clothes, Wreck Beach, steps below the university, is always an alternative. Another good bet is Ambleside, across the Lions Gate Bridge in West Vancouver. All are good for swimming, but the best pool for laps and laughs is the 137-metre (450-foot) Kitsilano Pool, open mid-May to September.

▲ Vancouver

Indoors, you'll be pleased with the Vancouver Aquatic Centre or one of the many other pools operated by City Parks, including one ozonated pool in the Killarney neighbourhood. Suburban Richmond and Coquitlam built modern pool facilities in the 1990s. The city's newest pool is a part of a complex that includes the Vancouver Olympic and Paralympic Centre — the curling venue for the 2010 Games — near Nat Bailey Stadium.

BC Lions

Water Sports

Water, water everywhere. Though you may not want to sip the saltchuck, it is ideal for canoeing, kayaking, or windsurfing. Deep Cove and Howe Sound are good spots for these activities, but False Creek, Kitsilano, Jericho Beach, and Ambleside are also viable options. Watch out for commercial vessels. Vancouver is paradise for ocean kayakers and has many rivers for those looking for that downstream rush. The Capilano River is the easiest to reach.

Windsurfing's best local venue is English Bay, where rental equipment and lessons are available. Experts head to the blustery north end of Howe Sound in Squamish (an hour's drive north of Vancouver) for some of North America's finest conditions.

Cycling

The City of Vancouver and its suburbs have slowly made streets and bridges more bike-friendly. In Vancouver, an extensive network of routes is dedicated to cycling. The Lions Gate Bridge was overhauled to include wider, smoother sidewalks with cyclists in mind. The ride may be windy, but the view from the top of the bridge is magnificent.

Kayaks at Whitecliff Park

A favourite bicycle route is the Richmond dyke system on Lulu Island, which passes through the fishing village of Steveston and goes right by the Richmond Olympic Oval. Built as a speedskating

68

**Tour de Gastown
cycling race**

arena, it is a massive sports and recreation centre where one can play hockey, basketball, table tennis, and indoor soccer. Another popular route is the False Creek to Point Grey waterfront path. The Pacific Spirit Regional Park near the University of British Columbia has a wealth of trails for all abilities. Whistler is also a mountain biking magnet, with accessible, free cross-country trails and a paid course for downhill and free-ride experts on Whistler Mountain. Cypress Mountain in West Vancouver followed suit with a course designed by North Shore mountain-biking legend Todd "Digger" Fiander. The undisputed champ for popularity and accessibility is the Stanley Park seawall; there are bikes for rent near the park entrance. Don't forget a helmet: it's the law to wear one while cycling.

In-Line Skating

If you'd rather have wheels on your two feet than two wheels and a seat, try in-line skating. Helmets, knee and elbow pads, and gloves are highly recommended. The Stanley Park seawall isn't just for bikes. In fact, in-line skaters outnumber cyclists on some summer days. Skate rentals are located near the entrance to the park.

For a more serene skate, try the wooded wonders of North Vancouver's Lower Seymour Conservation Reserve.

**Richmond Olympic
Speed Skating Oval**

Furry Creek Golf Course

Golf

Some people wouldn't take a walk in the park without a club, balls, and a tee. Luckily, there are many places to do that in Vancouver. The area boasts a variety of public, private, and semi-private golf courses. For the novice, there are pitch-and-putt courses at Stanley Park and Queen Elizabeth Park. The University Golf Club and Langara and Fraserview courses are among the closest to downtown. Richmond's Mayfair Lakes offers plenty of water hazards on what was once a farm. En route to Whistler, the Furry Creek course spills down a mountainside, providing unique challenges and an unbeatable view of Howe Sound. Whistler's smorgasbord of four courses includes designs by the likes of Jack Nicklaus, Arnold Palmer, and Robert Trent Jones Jr.

Hiking

Hiking is another popular activity on the West Coast. You don't have to go far to get away from the hustle of city life. In Vancouver, visit Pacific Spirit Regional Park at the University of British Columbia and Stanley

Beach volleyball

Park downtown. In nearby Richmond, the dyke system is flat and close to the Gulf of Georgia and the Fraser River. On the North Shore, Seymour and Cypress provincial parks offer a multitude of trails, as do the Lower Seymour Conservation Reserve and Lynn Canyon Park. Lighthouse Park in West Vancouver is another option. The most challenging of all is the Grouse Grind, a 2.9-kilometre (1.8-mile) hike up Grouse Mountain in North Vancouver. Depending on the avalanche/landslide risk, it's open from April through October. Summer hiking at Whistler offers spectacular views. When climbing or hiking in any of B.C.'s mountains, always be prepared with the proper footwear, equipment, and clothing. Even on the sunniest days, the weather can be unpredictable. And of course, it's best to hike with a buddy.

Winter

Skiing and Snowboarding

Vancouver is known for its abundance of rain. Luckily, on the Coast Mountains, that equals tempting winter snowfalls. On the North Shore, where it's higher and colder, winter sports enthusiasts will find a variety of recreation options. Grouse Mountain, Cypress Mountain, and Mount Seymour all offer top-quality downhill and cross-country skiing, snowboarding, and snowshoeing. Grouse adds sleigh rides and outdoor ice skating. Cypress and Seymour are similarly popular with those who ski, snowboard, and use toboggans and inner tubes. Grouse is the most accessible, with direct public transit service and the SkyRide, a breathtaking eight-minute aerial tram ride, from its parking lot. Cypress is host to the 2010 Olympic Winter Games' snowboarding and freestyle skiing events. Whistler Mountain got the marquee downhill events, while Blackcomb Mountain has the world's fastest bobsleigh, luge, and skeleton track.

Cycling at Whistler

Snowmobiling

For those who like motorized action, there's snowmobiling in Whistler, less than a three-hour drive from Vancouver on Highway 99, also known as the Sea-to-Sky highway, which has been recently upgraded for the 2010 games. Canadian Snowmobile Adventures provides tours on Blackcomb Mountain. An alternative way to tour the trails is on the company's snowcat, a large enclosed vehicle that seats 19 people. In the summer, the company offers all-terrain vehicle tours.

Skiing at Whistler

Family-oriented Winter Sports

Grouse Mountain has turned part of its ski area into a winter wonderland with an ice skating and hockey rink and sleigh rides. It's also one of a number of mountains that offer snowshoeing, the fastest-growing winter sport in North America. It's fun for the whole family and you don't need lessons. Just strap on the shoes and go. Rent them at Grouse, Seymour, and Cypress.

Tubing at Cypress Mountain

Extreme Sports

Highway 99 leads the way to challenging outdoor activities. The town of Squamish is called the outdoor recreation capital of Canada, and the name is well-deserved.

Vancouver Sun Run

Whistler also offers a multitude of choices, from glacier skiing to zip-trekking, and death-defying downhill mountain biking.

Climbing

If it's cold enough and the water freezes (which doesn't happen every year), there's ice climbing at the 335-metre (1,100-foot) Shannon Falls. A few minutes north of the falls is the legendary Stawamus (Squamish) Chief. The big granite rock that looms above the Squamish townsite at the end of Howe Sound was first conquered by climbers in 1961. It's been a provincial park since 1997 and is a popular hiking spot, but it's not recommended for rookies.

Rock climbers and newbies can practice their technique at a variety of indoor rock climbing centres in the suburbs. At 700 metres (2,300 feet), the Chief is the second-largest granite monolith in the world. It's also a popular nesting habitat for the peregrine falcon, which sometimes forces closure of climbing routes.

Soaring and Skydiving

The Vancouver Soaring Association operates from spring to early autumn on the longest turf airfield in Canada, at Hope Airport in the Fraser Valley. The sensation of motorless flight is amazing. Club members are only too glad to take interested newcomers for a ride. If you'd like to free-fall with a parachute strapped to your back, then Pitt Meadows Airport is the place to go.

Coming in for a landing

Whitewater Rafting

The water is cold and fast-flowing, but that's part of the rush of whitewater rafting. There is prime rafting on the Chilliwack River in the Fraser Valley and the Cheakamus River off Highway 99, the Sea-to-Sky Highway.

Zip-trekking and Bungee Jumping

Ever wanted to fly through a forest like a bird or jump from tree to tree like a squirrel? The next best thing is zip-trekking in Whistler. And for those who like the rush of jumping off high objects with nothing attached to them but a giant elastic band, the sport of bungee jumping is still going strong above the Cheakamus River near Whistler.

Spectator Sports

Baseball

Built in 1951 and restored to its former glory in 2008, Nat Bailey Stadium is one of the oldest ballparks in North America. It is also home to the University of British Columbia Thunderbirds during late winter and spring. The Vancouver Canadians of the Single A Northwest League return to action every June through September with a 38-game home schedule. It's the first chance to see tomorrow's Oakland Athletics' stars.

Football and Soccer

There's been one constant since BC Place Stadium opened in 1983: the BC Lions of the Canadian Football League have played there. The season runs from early July to October (or November if they make the Grey Cup playoffs). The stadium will be the site of the opening and closing ceremonies of the 2010 Winter Olympic Games. Summer tours of the interior are available.

The Vancouver Whitecaps soccer team plays outdoors at Burnaby's Swangard Stadium. There's nowhere better to be on a summer night than among the tall trees at Swangard, just a corner kick from Vancouver on Boundary Road and Kingsway. The men play April to September, while the women's team has an abbreviated May to August season. Unlike the rest of Vancouver's sports franchises, many players are homegrown, though quite a few have played internationally. The Whitecaps men's team will join Major League Soccer and move downtown to BC Place in 2011, when the stadium will have a new, retractable roof.

Vancouver
Canucks
in action

Hockey

Vancouver has three hockey teams. The National Hockey League's Canucks play at GM Place downtown (known as Canada Hockey Place during the Olympics). The Giants of the Western Hockey League play in the Canucks' old home, the Pacific Coliseum, where they won the 2007 Memorial Cup national major junior championship. The Chilliwack Bruins debuted at Prospera Centre in the Fraser Valley in 2006. The UBC Thunderbirds play on campus in Thunderbird Arena, the other Olympic hockey rink for 2010.

Horseracing

Hastings Racecourse on the Pacific National Exhibition grounds is more than 120 years old. Its scenic view is the best of any Canadian track, with Burrard Inlet and the North Shore's Coast Mountains in the distance. Thoroughbred racing runs April to November. Hastings' valley cousin is Fraser Downs Racecourse in the Cloverdale area of Surrey, 45 kilometres (28 miles) from Vancouver. Harness racing runs September to June. Both tracks include casinos.

Annual Events

The TELUS World Ski & Snowboard Festival in Whistler is winter's last blast in April. The all-out sports-and-music bash features ongoing parties, films, concerts, and adventure zones. The top professional skiers and snowboarders and some of the latest buzz bands come to play.

The Vancouver Sun Run in mid-April is the second-largest 10-kilometre (6-mile) footrace in North America and the biggest in Canada. In 2009, more than 55,000 people walked or ran from Burrard and Georgia streets to BC Place Stadium to celebrate health and fitness. The first Sunday of May is traditionally BMO Vancouver International Marathon day in the City of Vancouver.

The False Creek waters near Science World host competing dragon boat teams in the latter half of June. The Dragon Boat Festival is a weekend-long celebration of the city's ethnic diversity, with teams representing a number of nationalities and causes.

The red stone streets of Gastown were a stop on bicyclist Lance Armstrong's long voyage to winning seven Tour de France titles. He won the criterium race in Gastown in 1991. Look for the Tour de Gastown in late July. It's part of the B.C. Superweek, which includes races in White Rock, Delta, and Burnaby.

TELUS World Ski & Snowboard Festival

Kids' Stuff

Annemarie Tempelman-Kluit

Vancouver is full of fun for kids big and small. With beaches, mountains and parks as well as lots of indoor attractions, no matter what the weather, there's something to keep the kids entertained.

Below: Treetops Adventure at Capilano Suspension Bridge

Indoor Attractions

When the weather's inclement there's plenty to hold the family's attention. In addition to Science World, the H. R. MacMillan Space Centre, and the Vancouver Aquarium, smaller museums with a kid-friendly focus include the Vancouver Maritime Museum, the Vancouver Police Museum, the Museum of Anthropology, and the B.C. Sports Hall of Fame. In Burnaby, the Burnaby Village Museum and Carousel includes more than 30 authentically restored buildings, and the costumed staff helped to recreate the feel of a 1920s village. The highlight is the beautifully restored C. W. Parker Carousel, circa 1912. All these venues offer special family programs on weekends and holidays throughout the year.

Outdoor Attractions

Part of Vancouver's appeal is the wealth of outdoor fun to be enjoyed. VanDusen

Lynn Canyon Park

Botanical Garden is home to an Elizabethan hedge maze that kids love getting lost in. The hedge is about 1.5 metres (5 feet) high. There are wooden steps throughout, so shorter folk can climb up to see that they are not really lost. In Stanley Park, kids will be drawn to the miniature train that travels about 1.4 kilometres (almost a mile) through a rainforest, and twice a year it's transformed into the spooky Halloween Ghost Train and the Bright Nights Christmas Train. The Children's Farmyard next to the train houses over 200 animals, birds, and reptiles. It's best to check times of operation before going.

Stanley Park's famous seawall offers lots of chances to walk, bike, and push a stroller, but the False Creek Seawall is just as much fun. The newest section, by Vancouver's Olympic Village, is particularly kid-friendly, with climbing stones, sculptural seats, and a bridge. You can walk this seawall all the way from Science World to Granville Island and beyond.

North Vancouver's Capilano Suspension Bridge spans the Capilano River gorge and hangs 70 metres (230 feet) over the raging river's waters. The walk across the swaying 140-metre (450-foot) wood-and-cable footbridge will thrill the whole family. Treetops Adventure — a walk through the treetops on swaying wooden walkways — offers a squirrel's-eye view of the forest below. Other North Shore attractions include Lynn Canyon Park's Ecology Centre, with its own suspension bridge high above Lynn Creek. Maplewood Farm, a two-hectare (five-acre) petting farm focused on barnyard animals, is home to rabbits, goats, cows, horses, donkeys, sheep, ducks, geese, and chickens.

Playland, open from April to the end of September, offers outdoor rides ranging from the traditional wooden roller coaster and Ferris wheel to the Ring of Fire and the Rainbow. The rides at their Kids Playce

Playland at the Pacific National Exhibition Grounds

are for younger children. There are also games, attractions and, of course, cotton candy and foot-long hot dogs. Playland is located on the Pacific National Exhibition grounds on East Hastings Street.

Water Play

Depending on the time of year, Vancouver's 11 sandy ocean beaches offer fine swimming. Lying in tidal pools, digging holes, or building sandcastles and driftwood structures can be a lot of fun. Lifeguards are on duty from Victoria Day to Labour Day at Second Beach and Third Beach in Stanley Park, and at English Bay, Sunset Beach, Kitsilano Beach, Jericho Beach, Locarno Beach, and Spanish Banks.

Vancouver Marine Animal Science Centre

Kitsilano Pool is Canada's longest pool and one of only a few saltwater pools. It is heated, and its graduated slope makes it excellent for small children. It's open from Victoria Day to mid-September. Second Beach Pool, in the heart of Stanley Park, is another favourite outdoor destination. After exhausting the pleasures of the pool's three small waterslides, check out the children's playground, which boasts a real fire engine.

Maplewood Farm

The Granville Island Water Park and Adventure Playground offers water cannons (ground-level spouts that gush water), a safe waterslide and shallow wading areas. The park is supervised in season, and parents can sit on the grass and enjoy the excitement. The Stanley Park Water Park, just north of Lumberman's Arch, offers much of the same action but also has equipment suitable for children with physical disabilities.

Water Park at Granville Island

Festivals and Culture

Vancouver's premiere event for kids is the Vancouver International Children's Festival in Vanier Park each May. It features outstanding international and top-notch local performers. The purchase of show tickets includes admission to the festival site. Check out the box office at the festival gates for often-available rush tickets. Otherwise, a small fee allows you on-site to enjoy the roving entertainers, face painters, a huge sandbox, and the multicultural community stage.

The Pacific National Exhibition (PNE) takes place at the end of each summer. With a focus on agriculture including a 4-H festival, horse shows, and live entertainment, the exhibition runs the gamut from nighttime concerts to daytime family entertainment.

Below: At Second Beach playground
Bottom: Science World exterior

Word on the Street, Vancouver's celebration of reading, happens each fall and includes events just for kids, such as shows and readings. All year round, mini-bibliophiles can hit Vancouver Kidsbooks which has locations in Kitsilano and Surrey, and Main Street's Once Upon a Huckleberry Bush. And the main branch of the Vancouver Public Library has a large children's section on their lower level.

Food

When it's time to eat many restaurants in Vancouver have both good food for the whole family and fun for the kids.

Dunbar Streets Kokopelli Café offers kid-sized portions of their meals, a door wide enough to fit strollers, and a fun kids' play area. You can even buy baby food there. In Kitsilano, the Rocky Mountain Flatbread Company has a menu focused on sustainable and local fare — mostly pizza — and a play kitchen for kids. On Commercial Drive, Little Nest serves delicious food with lots of options for tots and a well-stocked kids' play area. Babyeats in North Vancouver has the largest play area of them all, as well as healthy food and good lattes.

Gail Buente

Vancouver is a city shared equally by hale-and-hearty outdoor types who spend their leisure time communing with nature, and urbane cosmopolites who mainline designer coffees. Both types are fiercely loyal to the city's wide variety of annual festivals and cultural events.

Polar Bear swimmers at English Bay

Winter
On New Year's Day, the notorious Polar Bear Swim attracts upwards of 2,000 shivering participants into the icy waters of English Bay. Another outdoor tradition, the Brackendale Winter Eagle Festival and Count takes place in January along the Squamish River midway between Vancouver and Whistler.

Spring
Spring starts in March and April, when the Vancouver Cherry Blossom Festival stages a variety of events to celebrate the city's 36,000-plus ornamental flowering cherry trees. April also brings the Vancouver International Wine Festival, a fundraiser for the Vancouver Playhouse.

By May, the festivals are in full bloom. Thousands of runners arrive early in the month for the BMO Vancouver International Marathon, Canada's largest marathon.

Later in May, kids have a festival all their own. Featuring dance, theatre, music, puppets, and clowns, the Vancouver International Children's Festival fills Vanier Park with youthful laughter.

Snowshoeing at Whistler Resort

Dragon boat race

In June, False Creek is animated by the annual Rio Tinto Alcan Dragon Boat Festival. Each brightly painted 12-metre (40-foot) boat is powered by a team of 20, paddling in unison.

Summer

Summer in Vancouver is a non-stop festival. Leading off the season is the TD Canada Trust Vancouver International Jazz Festival, embracing samba, free jazz, and blues, to name a few musical styles.

Throughout the summer, Bard on the Beach takes over Vanier Park in Kitsilano. Productions are staged in a backless tent, so the audience can enjoy the play with a backdrop of mountains.

In July, the Vancouver International Folk Music Festival takes centre stage. July also brings the HSBC Celebration of Light fireworks competition to downtown Vancouver.

For two weeks in August, MusicFest Vancouver's remarkable array of classical, jazz, and world music concerts feature top-notch local and touring artists.

The final summer fling, at the end of August, is the Pacific National Exhibition (PNE), the granddaddy of Vancouver festivals. Visitors enjoy old-fashioned fun on the wooden roller coaster, view farm animal exhibits, and chow down on corn dogs and mini-donuts.

Fall

Summer officially ends with Labour Day, but the festivals keep happening, and September visitors can come inside for the Vancouver International Fringe Festival, a theatre event for those who enjoy the new and sometimes outrageous. The beginning of October brings with it the Vancouver International Film Festival, with an emphasis on films from Canada and Pacific Rim countries.

Taking place on Granville Island in October, the Vancouver International Writers & Readers Festival presents a week of readings and chats with the most exciting writers from around the world and around the corner.

Jazz Festival in David Lam Park

Vancouver Neighbourhoods

Downtown

Barbara Towell

Downtown winter night lights

Vancouver is a relatively new city. In 1884, William Van Horne, the influential general manager of the Canadian Pacific Railway, visited what was then the logging village of Granville. He made two recommendations: that the tiny village of approximately 100 buildings become the terminus of the first cross-Canada railway, and that it be renamed Vancouver. In spite of the Great Fire of June 13, 1886, which totally destroyed the new city, a boom was on. By 1889, more than 10,000 people lived here. The Greater Vancouver area today numbers more than 2 million people.

Throughout its brief history, Vancouverites have fought hard to preserve the city's heritage buildings. Downtown Vancouver is proof of some success. A walk in the area reveals a satisfying mix of old and new. "Old" here means buildings from the late nineteenth century and early twentieth century. "New" means whatever grand edifice was completed last week.

Bird of Spring sculpture in Robson Square

Vancouver's history can be traced through the architecture of its downtown core, which encompasses West Georgia Street to the south, Burrard Street to the west, Cordova Street on the waterfront to the north (look for the mountains) and Cambie Street to the east. It's fair to say that politics, business, and faith shaped the city. The result is an eclectic mix of buildings, starting from the château-like Fairmont Hotel Vancouver at Georgia and Burrard and ending with a Roman

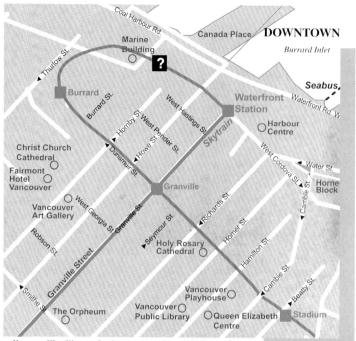

coliseum–like library farther east on Georgia Street. Although the number of permanent residents in the area is minuscule compared to the West End, Gastown, or Yaletown on False Creek, downtown Vancouver does not empty out at night. Because of the many hotels, restaurants, and entertainment venues in the area, the streets of the inner core remain fairly busy until midnight.

Hotel Vancouver

Fairmont Hotel Vancouver

First came the Canadian Pacific Railway (CPR), then came progress. Our walk begins at the corner of Georgia and Burrard where, in 1928, construction began on the Hotel Vancouver. This grand hotel, designed by the CPR in the impressive style of its Château Lake Louise and Banff Springs Hotel, would convince travellers that Vancouver was not a damp parochial backwater but a glistening modern metropolis. The next year, the stock market crashed and construction came to a standstill. For nearly a decade, the hotel's unfinished steel skeleton stood as a reminder of grim economic times. Only the impending royal visit of King George VI in 1939 brought about its hasty completion.

In the intervening period between start and completion, tastes changed. Ideas of tradition gave way to faith in

83

Christ Church Cathedral

the modern. As a result, the lower arcade, lobby, and VIP suites were finished in an Art Deco style rather than the original classical approach. When Hilton took over management in the 1960s, much of the interior was redecorated yet again in a more classical form. Today's updated interior is a glamorous journey into a more luxurious past. Memorable exterior features of the Fairmont Hotel Vancouver include its steep, green copper roof and its sly, slightly impish gargoyles.

Christ Church Cathedral

Across the street from the Fairmont Hotel Vancouver is the lovely and vibrant Christ Church Cathedral (690 Burrard), seat of the New Westminster Anglican Diocese. Designed by C. O. Wickenden, Christ Church reflected the Gothic Revival style that thrived in Canada in the nineteenth century. Each denomination mounted its own modifications to the style (compare Christ Church to the Catholic Holy Rosary Cathedral, noted later). The austere lines and interior atmosphere of Christ Church speak of its ties to Britain. Christ Church was built to serve the growing population of the city's West End, but initial funds were sparse. The inaugural service on October 6, 1889, was held in the granite basement, the only finished part of the building. In the aptly named Root House, 52 parishioners were warmed by a coal-fired boiler. To raise money, parishioners purchased stock in the church's construction company. Within six years, the sandstone structure was complete, with additions in 1909 and 1940. The interior boasts an impressive ceiling with beams of Douglas fir. Of the church's 29 stained-glass windows, three are by William Morris. They were acquired in 1984 on permanent loan from the Vancouver Museum and can be seen on the north-facing wall on the west side. The first organ was installed in 1895, employing an organ blower at the rate of five dollars a month. The pipes of the second organ can be seen in the church, though they are no longer functional. Be sure to check out the regular musical events taking place here. Information is available at the church or on their website at www.cathedral.vancouver.bc.ca.

Harbour Centre

As with many of Vancouver's older buildings, the cathedral was threatened with demolition in modern times. In 1976, after five years of lobbying, the building was named a "Class A" heritage site by the municipality.

Marine Building

A five-minute walk north along Burrard Street
toward the mountains brings you to the spectacular
Marine Building (355 Burrard). Erected in the Art
Deco style, its construction cost its Toronto-based
developers $2.5 million in 1929. By 1930, the
developers were broke and offered the building to
the city for $1 million. When legislators refused to
pay, Britain's Guinness family spotted a bargain and
stepped in, purchasing it for much less. The same
fiscally astute family built the Lions Gate Bridge in
1938 and ran it as a toll bridge until it was sold to
the B.C. government in 1963.

The Marine Building's architects, McCarter and
Nairne, suggested a design reminiscent of a "great
crag rising from the sea, clinging with sea flora and
fauna, tinted in sea-green, touched with gold."
Indeed, no other Vancouver building is more finely
finished. No visit to the Marine Building would be
complete without a venture inside, through its
extraordinary front door decorated with bronze grills
and Art Deco zigzags. The lobby's walls include
terra cotta friezes depicting the history of
transportation and the colonial discovery of the Pacific
Coast. The building was restored in 1989.

Marine Building

Below: Marine
Building exterior
detailing and
interior

Waterfront Station

Crossing over to West Cordova, proceed to Canada Place
with its five white "sails" built for Expo 86. A stroll on the
promenade is in order before moving on to Waterfront
Station (601 West Cordova), built by the Canadian
Pacific Railway in 1914. Two earlier stations stood on
the spot, a timber structure in 1887 (where the first
passenger train arrived on May 23, of that year) and a
château-style station in 1898–99. Waterfront Station is
the only building in Vancouver designed by the firm
of Barott, Blackader and Webster. In the words of
architectural historian Harold Kalman, their creation
is the most "self-consciously pompous building type
[made] in the early part of the century." It is indeed a
grand terminus with an expansive column facade and
pilastered waiting room. It now serves as an entrance
to both SkyTrain and SeaBus public transit systems.

Shops fill the former waiting room, but the public
aspect of the site has eroded, as there are no
longer public washrooms and seating is
scant. Paintings on the upper walls depict
Canadian landscapes set in the West. The
building was restored in 1976–77.

Sinclair Centre

Crossing Cordova, you can enter the
Sinclair Centre from its rear entrance or
head a block up the hill to its main entrance
at 757 West Hastings Street. The building
was completed by the department of public
works in 1910 to house the post office and
other federal offices. In 1939, an extension

Sinclair Centre

was added at 325 Granville Street. The two "faces" of the Sinclair Centre reflect very distinct economic periods. The original building was executed in an Edwardian Baroque style that married architectural influences from both the French and English. Built for $600,000, its rusticated granite basement continues up to smooth columns reaching past the second and third floors. The fourth floor includes dormer windows. The entire structure is finished off with an impressive clock tower. The granite exterior hides an early example of a fireproof steel frame.

King George VI was kept busy on his royal visit to Vancouver in 1939. He not only opened the Hotel Vancouver but also the Sinclair Centre's extension to the post office. The addition could not be more contrary to the design and intent of the original building. The first building was erected during Vancouver's construction and land speculation boom. As a result, it is highly ornate, expressing optimism in the future wealth of the country. The extension, on the other hand, was finished at the tail end of the Depression. Its exterior walls are bereft of decoration except a minimal application of pilasters used to harmonize with its predecessor. Interestingly, it was the original building, not the extension, that was occupied in 1935 by 750 unemployed men, as it more aptly captured the spirit of federal power. Their demands for relief led to a violent backlash from police, and a number of the protesters were hospitalized.

The Sinclair Centre is now an elegant shopping mall, retaining many of its original architectural and decorative highlights.

Harbour Centre Area

Harbour Centre Tower

Exit the Sinclair Centre on Hastings Street and walk east to Simon Fraser University's Harbour Centre at 515 West Hastings Street. There is usually a small but interesting art show in its impressive modern lobby. The view of the harbour from the adjoining ceiling-high window is impressive. Downstairs is a good bookstore and a food fair. The Harbour Centre Tower is home to the Lookout!, a visitor attraction. Though not notable architecturally, the tower does offer one of the finest views in the city.

A block away, at 342 Richards Street, the Century House is worth a peek. Designed by J. S. D. Taylor and completed in 1912, it is noteworthy not because of its classical style (there are other finer examples to be found), but for a particular detail that is best described as magic realism: the building is crowned with a pair of winged beavers. One can only wonder how contemporaries viewed these particularly whimsical little creatures, which are part beaver and part bird. The best view is from across the street.

Holy Rosary Cathedral

Back on Richards Street, you can't miss the Holy Rosary Cathedral (646 Richards). In 1900, when most of Vancouver's buildings were no higher than three storeys, the cathedral's 21-storey peak must have cast an impressive

Winged beavers on
Century House

shadow. As it was built during a period of considerable
church debt, some parishioners questioned the sense of the
monumental Gothic revival structure. The building was
dubbed McGuckin's Folly after the priest whose efforts
made construction possible.

Built from Gabriola Island sandstone with granite
foundations, the church's asymmetrical towers are its most
prominent visual feature. The cathedral bells are of
particular auditory interest. In the east tower, eight bells are
tuned to a full octave, producing up to 5,000 different
sequences. Inside the cathedral, granite-encased marble
columns support an arched ceiling. Among the many
stained-glass windows are eight depicting biblical scenes.
Visitors are welcome.

Holy Rosary
Cathedral

Library Square Area

Continue south a few more blocks to Georgia Street, then
head east to Library Square, the home of the Vancouver
Public Library's central branch (350 West Georgia).
Described as a rectangle within an ellipse, the design —
controversial when first proposed — by Moshe Safdie &
Associates with Downs/Archambault and Partners
resembles a Roman coliseum. Opened in 1995, the nine-
storey-high structure houses the library, an adjoining office
tower, and retail shops on the lower level concourse.
Library Square includes two outdoor plazas, which often
host special events. The concourse, with its six-storey-high
view of the internal workings of the library, is a great place
to catch your breath over an excellent cup of coffee, a slice
of pizza or an ice cream cone then sit, sip, and do some
serious people-watching.

Library Square and the attached federal office tower sit
on the southwest corner of an intersection where you'll
also find Vancouver's Main Post Office, the recently

Vancouver Public
Library

redeveloped studios of
CBC radio and television,
and the civic theatre
complex of the Queen
Elizabeth Theatre and the
Vancouver Playhouse.

When the theatres
were built in 1959, the
hope was that this eastern
edge of downtown would
develop into a cultural
hub. It took much longer
than expected, but when
the city's main library
moved to the district, the
last piece was in place to
enliven the
neighbourhood.

West End

James Oakes

Robson Street

The West End is Vancouver's original residential neighbourhood, occupying the western half of the city's downtown peninsula. Once home to bluebloods in stately mansions surrounded by gardens and quiet streets, the area has evolved into a remarkably diverse community — home to single parents, upwardly mobile singles, gays and lesbians, foreign students, recent immigrants, low-income transients, condo owners, and retirees. The West End, in short, is a success story of urban livability that is the envy of cities across North America.

Boundaries

The West End is the most densely populated square kilometre in Canada. Zoning maps show Georgia and Burrard streets as the northern and eastern boundaries, while Stanley Park and English Bay create the western and southern extremes. Laid out on a simple grid pattern, the main streets of the West End running east/west are Beach,

Manhattan Building

Davie, Robson, and Georgia. The main north/south streets are Denman, Thurlow, and Burrard. Included within the West End's boundaries are three distinct commercial zones, running along Robson, Davie, and Denman streets. Public transit includes the city's brand-new replacement electric trolley buses, running in a loop along these same streets. SkyTrain's Burrard Station is close to the northeast corner of the area, with easy access to Robson Street's glitzy fashion scene.

Map labels

Lost Lagoon

Lost Lagoon Viewpoint

Stanley Park

Lagoon Dr.

West Georgia St.

Park Lane

The Presidio

Chilco St.

Gilford St.

Robson St.

Haro St.

Bidwell St.

The Sylvia Hotel

Ocean Towers

Beach Ave.

Denman St.

Bidwell St.

Roedde House Museum

English Bay Beach

Alexandra Park

Cardero St.

Nicola St.

Cardero St.

Broughton St.

Robson St.

Barclay St.

Bute St.

Alberni St.

Inukshuk Inuit sculpture

Roger's House

Comox St.

Jervis St.

Haro St.

Thurlow St.

Manhattan Bldg.

The Beaconsfield

Bute St.

Pendrell

Thurlow St.

Broughton St.

Davie

Burnaby St.

Davie Village

Burrard St.

Harwood St.

Sunset Beach

Beach Ave.

Pacific St.

Vancouver Aquatic Centre

Granville Island Ferries

Burrard Bridge

Above: Inukshuk sculpture at English Bay

Burger at Moxie's

A West End Walkabout

Probably the best place to start a West End tour is right in the thick of things, by heading west on Robson Street from Burrard or Thurlow. Contemporary, hip, and self-consciously cosmopolitan, Robson has become the city's premiere shopping street, the mecca of Vancouver's young and fashionable — not to mention a party zone when the Vancouver Canucks are winning in the Stanley Cup playoffs. Just step into the stream and join the throng of shoppers, tourists, international students, and local West Enders as they jostle for space on the crowded sidewalks. The corner of Robson and Thurlow is renowned for its two (count 'em) Starbucks coffee shops located kitty-corner from each other. One is in the elegant old Manhattan Building, the West End's earliest apartment block, completed in 1908.

Fashion boutiques dominate the scene at street level along the next block of Robson, overlooked by an excellent selection of upstairs restaurants, including Tsunami Sushi, Moxie's, and CinCin. You can continue along the high-energy Robson stroll for several more blocks, or try venturing into the heart of the residential West End by taking a left at Bute Street. You'll soon come to a leafy little park complete with benches, fountain, and flowerbeds. Overlooking it is the Beaconsfield, a stately, if somewhat run-down, stone and brick structure. This is one of the West End's original Edwardian apartment buildings.

Three blocks farther on — take a right at Barclay Street and proceed down the hill to Broughton Street — you'll come to the Roedde House Museum (1415 Barclay), another architectural treasure of the West End. Roedde House stands among a collection of late nineteenth-century

Roedde House Museum

wood-frame houses in Barclay Heritage Square. Carefully restored with period furnishings, the museum is a journey back in time to the height of Victorian and Edwardian elegance.

After soaking in the atmosphere, head back out to Robson Street and continue west down the hill toward Stanley Park. Although the lower end of Robson is being gentrified with upscale shops and condominiums, it has the friendly atmosphere of an urban village with green grocers, pizza shops, and video rental outlets.

On the far side of Denman Street, in the exclusive area known to locals and realtors as "West of Denman," Robson becomes strictly residential for its final two blocks until it merges with Lagoon Drive. Here, on a slope overlooking Lost Lagoon, visitors are greeted with one of the best city views, a 180-degree panorama of Stanley Park, Coal Harbour, and the North Shore mountains.

Admire the view while walking south along Lagoon Drive, but when you reach Nelson Street, take a moment and look upwards at the row of high-rises bordering the park. Standing among the conventional 1960s and 70s towers is the post-modernist Presidio, designed by Vancouver architect Richard Henriques, who in turn was inspired by Austrian architect Adolf Loos' Villa Karma near Montreaux, Switzerland. Offshore buyers, who reportedly enjoy their residences for only a few weeks every year, purchased many of the Presidio's multi-million-dollar suites in the early 1990s. Once you've come back to Earth, follow the pedestrian path running along the edge of the park until you come to Beach Avenue and the shores of English Bay.

The Seaside

Swimmers began flocking to English Bay when the West End was first developed in the 1890s. By the turn of the twentieth century, summertime crowds travelled to the popular bathing beach on the newly opened Robson and Denman streetcar line.

Today, the Brighton-style pier has long since disappeared, but the holiday-resort atmosphere along the beach is as strong as ever. At the first sign of a sunny day, sunbathers, beach lovers, dog walkers, and windsurfers invade the area.

English Bay Beach

The ivy-clad Sylvia Hotel on Beach Avenue, overlooking English Bay, still offers visitors perhaps the best accommodation location-wise for the money. It was built in 1911 as the Sylvia Court Apartments before the Depression forced the owner to rent it out as a seamen's hostel. After the war, it moved upscale and branched out into the liquor business, opening the city's first cocktail bar in July 1954. A recent renovation has transformed the bar into a smartly sleek spot to admire the view of the bay over a cocktail.

The Sylvia Hotel

Next door to the Sylvia, at 1835 Morton Avenue, stands the Ocean Towers, a jazzily shaped apartment building dating from 1957. Across the street, at the intersection of Denman and Davie, a cluster of imported palm trees completes the exotic "British California" ambiance. A brief side trip along Denman Street reveals funky boutiques, bicycle rentals, cappuccinos, a fresh juice bar, and an amazing variety of international cuisine. Pedestrians like to think they rule the street and traffic moves by at a crawl. For a special treat, order some fresh halibut and chips from the window at the famous Raincity Grill and head to the beach.

English Bay is also an evening destination. Locals and visitors come out to walk along the seawall promenade, listen to musicians, and watch the sun set beyond the anchored freighters and the mountains of Vancouver Island. During the annual HSBC Celebration of Light fireworks festival in July and August, upwards of 300,000 people gather around the bay to watch the spectacular international displays.

At the easternmost end of the English Bay beach, you'll find an Inuit inukshuk sculpture by Alvin Kanak. Commissioned by the Northwest Territories for Expo 86, the large granite blocks represent a human figure with welcoming, outstretched arms. More recently, the symbol inspired the logo for Vancouver's 2010 Winter Olympics.

Alexandra Park bandstand

From here, cross Beach Avenue to Alexandra Park, named after the consort of King Edward VII. It boasts a pretty wooden bandstand constructed in 1914 for outdoor concerts, as well as a marble fountain adorned with a brass plaque honouring the city's beloved Seraphim "Joe" Fortes. Generations of children were taught to swim by this affable Barbadian immigrant, who acted as lifeguard and special constable at English Bay until his death in 1922.

From the northeast corner of the park, walk north on Bidwell to Davie Street, turn right, and head up the hill to the impressive Rogers House at 1531 Davie. One of the last survivors of the West End's age of opulence, this elegant mansion-turned-restaurant was designed by Samuel Maclure, one of Vancouver's most prolific early architects, for local sugar magnate Benjamin Tingley Rogers.

Granville Island
ferries

Roger's House

Window display at
a Davie St. DIY
wine shop

To continue exploring the West End's southern flank, return to the seashore via Nicola Street and then stroll toward the Burrard Street Bridge until you arrive at Sunset Beach. This marks the end of the English Bay Seawall and the entrance to False Creek. At the foot of Thurlow Street stands the Vancouver Aquatic Centre, which houses a 50-metre pool, a children's pool, and other indoor recreation facilities. Behind the aquatic centre you'll find the West End landing of the Granville Island ferries. The little passenger ferries run regularly from dawn until dusk, serving English Bay, Vanier Park in Kitsilano Point, and Granville Island.

The 24-Hour Village

Our final destination, the Davie Village, is about a 10-minute hike back up to the West End's central plateau. Just follow the pedestrian path across from the entrance to the aquatic centre, and head up the stairway leading to the north end of the Burrard Street Bridge. From there, walk north along Burrard for three blocks, then hang a left when you come to the Esso station at the corner of Davie Street.

Here, along the three-block strip of bookstores, cafés, dollar stores, florists, 24-hour supermarket, and drugstore — and a great selection of reasonably priced restaurants — you'll find the sidewalks busy with a colourful mix of West Enders, tourists, and international students. And as the rainbow street banners and fuchsia-coloured bus shelters proudly proclaim, the Davie Village is also the traditional core of Vancouver's gay community. The Gay and Lesbian Centre on Bute Street houses a drop-in centre, lounge, and library. By night, Davie supports a lively social scene. Numbers Cabaret, Fountainhead Pub, and Pumpjack Pub are gay-oriented and usually packed. For midnight snacks, try Hamburger Mary's. On weekends, Oasis Pub is open late with live entertainment and a DJ from 10 p.m. to 2 a.m. When you're ready to take a break from the busy pace of Davie Street, stroll over to Mole Hill, a full city-block of charmingly restored Victorian homes in a bucolically peaceful setting. Once slated for demolition by the Park Board to make way for playing fields, these houses were saved thanks to the persistent efforts of heritage and community activists, and today provide rental housing to a mix of tenants through the Mole Hill Community Housing Society. If you are visiting between June and October, the West End Farmers Market on Saturday mornings in the 1100-block of Comox has an outstanding selection of organic produce from local and up-country growers. Wending your way leisurely along the row of stalls, you'll almost forget that you are within a few blocks of Vancouver's downtown core.

Gastown

Leanore Sali

Gastown, Vancouver's oldest neighbourhood, is not one to rest on its laurels. The handsome facades of the brick buildings reveal a mix of antique stores, boutiques, and street-level galleries that contain a broad selection of Canadian First Nations art. In busy restaurants housed in former warehouses, diners are offered a variety of cuisine and price ranges. The nightlife is lively, with a selection of pubs and clubs that cater to every age group. Gastown is as alive today as when it was the bustling centre of industry in the mid-1800s. Today's annual Tour de Gastown bicycle race, held in July, is a case in point. Nearly 40,000 spectators crowd Gastown's red brick streets to watch nearly 200 riders during B.C. Superweek, the province's prestigious week of racing.

Stand in Maple Tree Square looking west along Water Street and people-watch: local residents stop to chat with

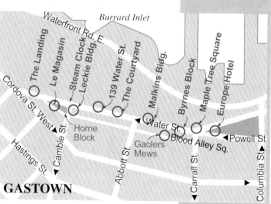

93

Steam clock

neighbours, international students rush to classes, business people dodge the throngs to lunch appointments, and visitors from around the world stop en route to pose for photographs by Gastown's world-famous steam clock. In Gastown, residents and tourists have learned to enjoy the street scene in much the same way Europeans do.

Gastown's Historic Past

Granville, the original settlement around which Vancouver grew, was unofficially known as Gastown after its first settler, Captain John "Gassy Jack" Deighton. The Yorkshire man, who'd been a sailor, prospector, steamboat pilot, and saloon keeper, arrived at Burrard Inlet in the fall of 1867, opened his Globe saloon, and soon prospered. Almost immediately, others came to join him.

By the 1870s, Gastown was a multicultural community of saloons, hotels, and grocery stores catering to mill workers, lumbermen, ships' crews, and whalers. During the next decade, the community underwent a growth spurt following the announcement that it would be the site of the Canadian Pacific Railway terminus. By 1886, it had 1,000 buildings and 3,000 residents. On April 6 of that year, it was officially incorporated under the name Vancouver.

Shortly after, on June 13, 1886, a brush-clearing fire blazed out of control and burned the town to the ground. By destroying the old town, the Great Fire spurred the biggest building boom in West Coast history. The area prospered until Vancouver's economic boom collapsed in 1914. From the 1930s to the 50s, Gastown, once the heart of Vancouver, became a virtual backwater.

Gastown remained in decline until the early 1960s when a few enterprising merchants and property owners recognized the architectural heritage underneath the grime of the old buildings and began to restore them. City Hall joined in the cause. New street lamps were installed, streets and sidewalks were bricked, and the meandering courtyards and mews were left intact. In 1971, the Province of British Columbia designated Gastown a historic district.

Europe Hotel

Gastown Tour

Start your tour at Gassy Jack's statue in Maple Tree Square. Facing east, you'll see the Europe Hotel, built in 1908 by Angelo Calori. A flatiron-shaped building built to fit the triangular lot, the Europe was the earliest reinforced concrete structure in Canada and the first fireproof hotel in Western Canada.

The building directly behind Gassy Jack's statue is the Byrnes Block (2–8 Water Street). Built in 1886 by George

Byrnes, a former sheriff of the Cariboo during the gold rush days, this was one of the first brick buildings in Vancouver. It once housed the Alhambra Hotel, one of the city's fancier establishments at the time.

Take the entrance off Carrall Street to the central courtyard known as Gaolers Mews. This is where the town's first jail and the home of Gastown's first constable were located. Vancouver's first city council meeting was held here. The site later housed the city's first post office and later the city's first fire hall. The building was renovated in 1974 to create the interior courtyard and the office and retail complex.

Gastown; Gassy Jack's statue at Maple Square

Exit onto Water Street. As you stroll west along Water, take the time to browse through the galleries and shops along the way. Many galleries specialize in West Coast and Inuit art, offering the largest selection in Western Canada and representing internationally renowned First Nations artists.

On the north side of the street, you'll see a large building housing the Old Spaghetti Factory Restaurant (55 Water). It was built in 1907 as the warehouse and headquarters for Malkins, one of B.C.'s main food wholesalers. The upper floors were renovated in 2002 to accommodate live-work studios.

Continue along Water Street, crossing to the north side at the corner of Water and Abbott streets. As you continue your stroll west along Water, notice the courtyard, built in 1974 and designed to blend in with its older neighbours. Just west of the courtyard is 139 Water Street, built in 1898 as the first warehouse for Malkins wholesale grocery business. Renovated in 1996 into

Gastown shoppers

apartments, this building is an excellent example of Gastown-living today.

At the corner of Water and Cambie streets is Gastown's famous steam clock. Although built in 1977, the movements of the steam clock are based on an 1875 design. Its creator, horologist Raymond Saunders, designed it to run on a continuous supply of steam that feeds the clockworks from the steam vent beneath the street. For souvenir photo-takers, this is a must-visit site, with bursts of steam every 15 minutes.

Cross over to the south side of the street. The red brick

Goaler's Mews

building on the southeast corner of Water and Cambie is known as the Leckie Building. It was built in 1910 by the Leckie family as a shoe and boot factory. Renovated in 1990 for office and retail use, the Leckie Building is an excellent example of the timber construction used in early Gastown buildings.

Stroll south on Cambie to Cordova Street. Turn right at the corner and meander west along Cordova. The buildings along this strip of Cordova Street once housed merchants outfitting gold seekers headed for the Klondike. Today, this area is an emerging fashion district offering designs by Vancouver's up-and-coming fashion designers.

The building on the northwest corner of Cambie and Cordova was built in 1888. It was known as the Masonic Temple, as it housed the Masonic Grand Lodge. Next door is the Horne Block, built by land investor and city politician J. W. Horne. Designed by Nathaniel Stonestreet Hoffar, the city's first important architect, the Horne Block was the mid-1880s' most exquisite venture into the Victorian Italianate style of architecture.

At the entrance to the alley off Cordova is the Le Magasin building. Check out the face ornaments on the fibreglass frieze. These face ornaments are life masks of notable entrepreneurs from Gastown's 1960s revitalization. Take the back entrance and walk through the building to exit onto Water Street. On both sides of the street you will see the best examples of 1890s architecture still standing in the city.

Cross over and continue west along Water Street until

Horne Block

you get to the Landing (375 Water). This converted warehouse, built by the Kelly Douglas grocery company in 1905 from profits made from outfitting Klondike gold seekers, reflects the general history of wholesaling in Gastown. The building was renovated in 1988 as a retail and office complex.

Just around the corner is Steamworks, a casual brew pub that makes an ideal lunch stop. Directly across, in Waterfront Station — originally the CPR terminus and now a transportation hub for SkyTrain, SeaBus, and the West Coast Express — is the Transcontinental, Steamworks' more upscale sibling. Both establishments retain a touch of Gastown's past in their decor.

Chinatown

Todd Wong

Vancouver's Chinatown is the second-oldest in Canada (after Victoria), and the second-largest in North America (after San Francisco). Vancouver's Chinatown is a symbol both of the city's historic past and its future, spanning centuries as the "Gateway to the Pacific" for both gold-seeking pioneers and modern jet-setting entrepreneurs. East meets West and old meets new, as Vancouver's Chinatown struggles to balance the conflicting forces of change: urban decay vs. revitalization, historical preservation vs. condominium development. Competing "mini-Chinatowns" in suburban centres and other neighbourhoods now challenge Chinatown businesses for customers.

But everything exciting still happens in Chinatown: Chinese New Year parades, summer festivals, moon festival, night markets, community dinners, and even the occasional political protest.

Herbal store in Vancouver's Chinatown

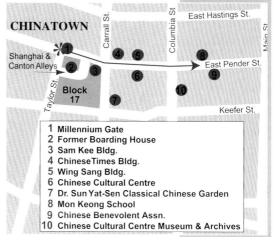

CHINATOWN

Shanghai & Canton Alleys

Block 17

East Hastings St.
Carrall St.
Columbia St.
Main St.
East Pender St.
Keefer St.
Taylor St.

1 Millennium Gate
2 Former Boarding House
3 Sam Kee Bldg.
4 ChineseTimes Bldg.
5 Wing Sang Bldg.
6 Chinese Cultural Centre
7 Dr. Sun Yat-Sen Classical Chinese Garden
8 Mon Keong School
9 Chinese Benevolent Assn.
10 Chinese Cultural Centre Museum & Archives

Vancouver's Chinatown is a photographic feast with hanging BBQ duck, live fish and crab tanks in food stores, and deer antlers and dried sea horses at the herbalist stores. Chinatown is an enticing place to shop and eat, and to visit the Chinese medicinal stores for remedies and treatments. It is home to a famous Ming dynasty–style garden, the world's skinniest building, and the largest Chinese restaurant in North America, and it boasts not one, but two, Chinese gates.

Food and Shopping

No trip to Chinatown is complete without eating. Vancouver has some of the best Chinese restaurants in North America. Dim Sum means "pieces that touch the heart," and you will find exquisite shrimp dumplings, sticky rice, spare ribs, and duck feet that are indeed mouth-watering. Floata Seafood Restaurant (400–180 Keefer) has seating for 1,000, so it's no wonder it is the favoured location for many banquets and events. If you prefer somewhere more intimate, check out Park Lock Seafood Restaurant (544 Main).

Up the street is Hon's Wun-Tun House (268 Keefer), famous for its good, inexpensive meals, and regularly topping polls for best noodle house. Poke your head into Kent's Kitchen (232 Keefer) to see the busiest, biggest, and cheapest buffet for $5 a plate. Stop in at New Town Bakery (158 E. Pender) for delicious apple tarts, moon cakes, and other Chinese pastries. For a blast from Chinatown's past, check out Foo's Ho Ho Restaurant (102 E. Pender), the only restaurant serving "old-style" Cantonese cuisine, and one of the few surviving restaurants from the Chinatown of the 1960s, which was alive with neon and night-clubs.

Lots of stores are filled with imported wicker, clothing, and porcelains. Check out antiques in Peking Lounge (83 E. Pender), or folk craft and mementos of Mao-era China at Bamboo Village (135 E. Pender). Chinese toys can be found at many stores such as Cathay Importers (104 E. Pender), but also check out the paintings and Chinese chop stamps at Art de Chine (101 E. Pender). Dragons Martial Arts Supplies (28 E. Pender) has everything you could possibly need, including colourful lion and dragon costumes for parades. Kiu Shun Trading (261 Keefer) is one of the largest herbal stores in Western Canada. If you see something intriguing but unfamiliar, don't be afraid to ask about it.

Top: Chinatown Market
Above: Silk Road banners

Sam Kee building

Summer visitors may want to arrive at dusk for the Chinatown night market, held Fridays through Sundays. Several streets are closed to traffic, attracting throngs browsing for bargains on clothing, accessories, electronics, toys, and gift items — and snacks, of course.

History Tour

Chinese people first arrived in 1858 from the gold fields of California in search of "Gum San" or "Gold Mountain" as word spread of gold in B.C. Others arrived by sailing vessels to work on building the Canadian Pacific Railway. Some became merchants or worked in the canneries and lumber mills.

Many Chinese immigrants settled along Shanghai Alley and Canton Alley, just a few steps west of Carrall and Pender streets. The Millennium Gate, spanning Pender Street at Taylor, marks the site of early Chinatown. It is in the heart of what was known as Block 17. By 1890, Block 17 was home to more than 1,000 Chinese residents. These tiny streets once teemed with shops, restaurants, barbershops, and even Chinese opera theatres. Walk down Shanghai Alley to see the West Han Dynasty Bell, a gift from the city of Guangzhou to its "twin city" of Vancouver. Story panels depict details about important figures, such as Won Cum Yow, the first Chinese born in Canada, and Yip Sang, a successful merchant who became the Chinese agent for the Canadian Pacific Railway Company. This was the vibrant hub of Chinatown when Dr. Sun Yat-Sen visited Vancouver and, according to legend, attracted a crowd of 1,000 people to see him at the 500-seat Sam Kew Theatre.

Many of the residents were the "married bachelors" who had to leave wives and children behind in China because they couldn't afford the exorbitant head tax imposed in 1885 to deter Chinese people from coming to Canada. Newspapers ran stories and cartoons about the "heathen" Chinese who lived in "overcrowded rabbit warrens" and took work away from White people. In 1907, when the Asiatic Exclusion League met at Vancouver City Hall two blocks away at Main and Hastings, tempers flared and an anti-Asian crowd walked to the alleys of chinatown, destroying shop windows and doors.

Many of the buildings have long been torn down, but some important buildings still stand. Sam Kee Building (8 W. Pender) is the narrowest building in

Top: Chinese Cultural Centre Museum and Archives
Middle: Chinatown neighbourhood
Above: Bust of Dr. Sun Yat-Sen

Millennium Gate

Historic building on Pender Street

the world, according to the Guinness World Records. Originally, a standard nine-metre (30-foot) lot was owned by Chang Toy, but most of it was expropriated by the City of Vancouver in 1912 in order to widen Pender Street. Local legend says that Chang Toy's neighbour wanted to ad the remaining two metres (six feet) to his property, at a bargain price. But to spite him, Chang Toy had a building constructed to fit the narrow property. Look down through the glass tiles in the sidewalk, and you will see where once stood an underground bathhouse.

Look north across the street at the former Chinese Freemasons Building (5 W. Pender) and you will see where the last Chinese tailor shop, Modernize Tailors, still stands. It opened in 1913 and was passed down to Bill and Jack Wong by their father. Their brother Milton Wong, a prominent community leader, has bought and restored the building. The business made most of the "zoot suits" in Vancouver during the swing era, and in 2007 was the subject of a documentary, Tailor Made: *Chinatown's Last Tailors*.

Up the street is the Wing Sang building (51 E. Pender) where Yip Sang built his dynasty and his home for several wives and families. Today, developer Bob Rennie has restored the building with plans to create an art gallery and modern condo units where Yip Sang's families used to live. The Chinese Benevolent Association (CBA) building (108 E. Pender) housed the association which gave resources to the community and helped it resist anti-Asian laws. These buildings display the classic blend of eastern and western architecture typical of Chinatowns in North America. The recessed balconies are similar to Mediterranean buildings that were constructed in colonial Hong Kong, Macau, and Southern China.

Mon Keong School

In front of the Chinese Cultural Centre is the white marble China Gate. Walk under the archway to discover a bronze picture of Chinese railway builders. Opposite is a list of the names of Chinese-Canadian veterans, who fought for Canada in World War II. Walk into the nearby courtyard to discover mosaics of each animal of the Chinese zodiac. Straight ahead is a bust of Dr. Sun Yat-Sen, the father of modern China, who came to Vancouver three times in the early 1900s to raise funds to overthrow the Qing dynasty and help found the Republic of China. From here, go west to the entrance of the exquisite Dr. Sun Yat-Sen Garden, south into the slightly less elaborate Dr. Sun Yat-Sen Park (free admittance) or east to the Canadian Chinese Monument to pioneers and war veterans, built at Keefer Triangle. At the east end of the park is the Chinese Cultural Centre Museum and Archives (555 Columbia). Both the Cultural Centre and the Sun Yat-Sen Garden offer tours.

Commercial Drive

Gary McFarlane

Everyone calls it "the Drive," but the best way to experience Commercial Drive is a leisurely walk past its diverse array of shops, cafés, parks and community and cultural centres. Local residents know this, and stage car-free Sunday street festivals each summer.

Like much of Vancouver, the area was densely wooded late into the nineteenth century. The Salish Indians once hunted elk here. Long-gone forests fed the historic Hastings lumber mill. The first homes were built in the working-class suburb of Grandview in the early years of the twentieth century. The streets east of the Drive are still lined with grand and eccentric turn-of-the-century buildings, some decaying rustically, others lovingly restored.

Italian Neighbourhood

Following the First and Second world wars, waves of Italian immigrants settled in the area. Commercial Drive is still an excellent place to shop for prosciutto, sausages, great rounds of cheese and biscotti at the numerous delis and produce markets. During soccer season, sitting in Abruzzo Cappuccino Bar (1321 Commercial) is a sensation not unlike being in downtown Naples at rush hour. Sip an espresso under a reproduction of the Sistine Chapel at Calabria Bar (1745 Commercial), rub elbows with Roman sculptures and peruse portraits of Italian stars. Check out the First Ravioli Store (1900 Commercial) for the best

fresh pasta in the city. Then stand in line for fresh gelato at Gelateria Dolce Amore (1590 Commercial).

While it has retained its Italian flavour, the Drive in recent years has been a landing place for successive waves of immigrants from Asia, Latin America, and Africa, each bringing a legacy of culture and food. The Drive has great restaurants, most very gentle on the wallet.

Restored home along Commercial Drive

Coffee and Culture

Social life on the Drive begins in its cafés. Coffee is taken seriously here, and not only by Italians. Local Ethiopian eateries feature a ritual that includes coffee beans roasted at the table. Addis Café is particularly intimate and friendly. Vegetarians throng to Bandidas Taqueria (2781 Commerical) and Juicy Lucy's Sports Café. Little Nest is a gourmet brunch spot which is — surprise — child-friendly. Dutch Girl Chocolates (1002 Commercial) makes their own imaginative homemade treats — have you ever tried a champagne and black pepper truffle? Havana Restaurant features an art gallery and a theatre, and their outdoor seating is one of Vancouver's best places for people-watching. Whether you're in the mood for sushi, tapas, pupusas, or pho, you'll find them on the Drive. Or satisfy a craving for Belgian beer and mussels at Stella's Tap and Tapas Bar (1191 Commercial).

Lamb chops at Dallas Souvlaki on the Drive

Quirky specialty shops abound. Worth browsing are Ten Thousand Villages for fair trade handicrafts, Highlife Records (1317 Commercial) for world music, and Beckwoman's (1314 Commercial), a curiosity shop crammed to the ceiling with clothing, beads, and political posters.

Local cultural meccas include the Vancouver East Cultural Centre, also known as "the Cultch," a theatre situated in a former Methodist church, recently expanded to include a second small theatre. Several restaurants feature live music in the evenings: Libra Room Café serves up local jazz; Lime (1130 Commercial) mixes sushi with alternative sounds; Falconetti's East Side Grill is a watering hole with pounding rock music. The funky Waazubee Café has turntabling DJs on many evenings, and Café Deux Soleils has alternative music and poetry slams, as well as on-tap beers from an acclaimed local micro-brewery, Storm Brewing.

Havana Restaurant

Yaletown

Brian Busby

Urban Fare

Yaletown is at once one of Vancouver's oldest and newest neighbourhoods. The original residents were railway workers from the Fraser Canyon town of Yale who, quite literally, picked up their houses and moved to the area after the completion of the transcontinental railway. During the early years of the last century, most homes were replaced by dozens of timber, brick, and concrete warehouses. The rail yards remained until the 1980s, when the land was cleared for Expo 86, the world exposition. During the past decade, Yaletown has experienced dramatic upward growth: dozens of tall residential towers, built in the aftermath of Expo 86, now overlook False Creek. The new buildings, in combination with an extended seawall and a series of new parks, attract a varied population, making Yaletown a neighbourhood much admired by urban planners.

A Walk Through Yaletown

An appropriate place to begin exploring Yaletown is at Emery Barnes Park, located on the northwest corner of Davie and Richards streets. A U.S. Olympic athlete and professional football player, Barnes arrived in Vancouver in 1957 to play for the BC Lions football team. He later became a dedicated social worker and for 24 years served as the local member of the provincial legislature. Barnes was one of the first two Black Canadians elected to the legislature and was the first to take on the role of Speaker. A narrow, mosaic-bottomed stream running between a small artificial waterfall and a large fountain bisects the park, which is one of the newest in the city.

Crossing to the southeast corner of the intersection,

Emery Barnes Park

The old Canadian Linen Company building

you'll find the old Canadian Linen Company Building. Now housing a grocery store, this modern-style structure is a remnant from the time when Yaletown served as the city's garment district. Heading one block east, at the corner of Davie and Homer, you'll encounter the Gray Block. Completed in 1912, this is just one of the Yaletown buildings built by brothers Donald and Russell Gray. The Gray Block is typical of many of the older Yaletown

structures, in both in architecture and in the fact that it has been converted into shops and residential lofts.

Continuing eastward along Davie, you'll find yourself descending a small hill. At the base is the Opus Hotel, Vancouver's first boutique inn and the hotel of choice for many in the film and music industries.

Continuing further along Davie, you'll pass by the Yaletown–Roundhouse Station. Opened in September 2009, it's part of the Canada Line, an automated light rail system that links the Vancouver International Airport to the downtown core.

The next intersection is Pacific Boulevard, a wide thoroughfare made possible by the lands cleared for Expo. As you cross Pacific, note a large glass pavilion displaying Canada's most historic locomotive. On May 23, 1887, Canadian Pacific Railway Engine 374 pulled the first transcontinental train into the city, thus completing the national dream. Appropriately, the pavilion is attached to the old CPR roundhouse, at which the locomotive was

Canada's most historic locomotive

serviced when in the city. The renovated roundhouse was used during Expo 86 as a pavilion and is now a community centre. The old turntable is still in place, forming the focal point of a large semi–circular courtyard. Directly across the street is Urban Fare, a gourmet food store that also features a cafeteria-style restaurant and a coffee shop. The tables

Time Top by sculptor Jerry Pethick

outside the store provide a favourite perch for people people-watchers.

The Seawall

The block ends in a roundabout, which is, in fact, the beginning of Davie Street. You'll notice an odd-looking structure displaying photographs from Vancouver's past. Each image becomes clear at a different angle — best remember to keep your eye on traffic as you cross the street. A description of each photo is engraved on the structure's concrete foundation. You are now on the seawall. Gazing to the left provides a nice view of Yaletown's new residential towers, a good indication of

False Creek

why renowned *Generation X* author Douglas Coupland refers to Vancouver as the "City of Glass." Straight-ahead is the Yaletown Aquabus ferry terminal, allowing pedestrians easy access to Granville Island and other destinations around False Creek.

Head to the right along the seawall. Be aware that the pedestrian portion of the route runs parallel to that set aside for cyclists and those on in-line skates. Although the lanes are clearly marked, it is easy to become sidetracked by the scenery.

You are now walking along False Creek, so named because it does not lead to Burrard Inlet, as early surveyors had expected. Once nearly five times larger than its present size, much of the creek was lost when sawmills, factories, and the railway moved into the area. In the past few decades, False Creek has become largely residential: more than 15,000 people now live along its shores.

Following the seawall brings you to David Lam Park. A real estate developer and philanthropist, Lam was the first Chinese-Canadian to serve as a lieutenant-governor. The park features tennis and basketball courts, and two children's playgrounds. It is dominated by a large playing field often used for soccer and ultimate Frisbee.

As you pass by the playing field, look to your right. Notice the twin waterfalls hugging what appears to be a glass-door garage. This is the False Creek Pump Station,

Time Capsule

which supplies water to Vancouver's fire hydrants. Anything but utilitarian in design, the pump station features two of the more welcoming public washrooms in the city.

Walking up the stairs on either side of the pump station leads to the roof, which affords a dramatic view of False Creek. You are now back on Homer Street, near the intersection of Homer and Pacific. Crossing Pacific, you'll come upon a series of red wedge-shaped structures. They are, in fact, time capsules. Unlike most time capsules, the contents are conveniently listed on each: "a woman's left boot, a woman's right boot (non-matching), not too many men's black plastic combs …" It is no coincidence that the capsules are interspersed with identically shaped trash receptacles.

Having passed all three capsules, you'll be at the corner of Homer and Drake, starting point of the Great Fire of Vancouver. On June 13, 1886, a fire set to clear brush ran out of control and swept toward the city. In less than an hour, the City of Vancouver, which had been incorporated just two months prior, was all but destroyed.

Old Yaletown

Cross the street and walk a short block east on Drake. You're now at the corner of Drake and Hamilton. Turning left on Hamilton leads to the older area of Yaletown. Once-neglected warehouses dominate this collection of narrow streets. Restored and converted to mixed use, they maintain their original elevated brick-paved loading docks. The large cantilever canopies, once unique to Yaletown, are emulated throughout the city.

Continue on Hamilton to Davie Street. Within two blocks is a rich, eclectic mix of clothing boutiques, furniture stores, hair salons, a microbrewery, and a Mini car dealership.

Yaletown's restored warehouses

The end of this retail strip is Nelson Street, historically the northern border of Yaletown. Turn right, walk a few dozen paces, and right again onto Mainland. Though the more attractive of the two streets, Mainland is otherwise a twin to Hamilton of each featuring unique and interesting shops. What's more, both offer a number of cafés and a wide variety of restaurants, one of which is certain to be the perfect place to rest your tired feet and eat a well-deserved meal.

Granville Island

Alma Lee

Granville Island today is one of the highlights of the city. Once a fish enclosure used by First Nations, it became an industrial site in the early twentieth century. From an area choked with sawmills and factories, Granville Island has risen to become a unique cultural oasis in the heart of the city.

In the early 1970s, federal Member of Parliament Ron Basford and a group of young maverick architects who saw the potential of the area brainstormed the redevelopment and spearheaded the transition. The industrial style is still prevalent in the look of the buildings, and Granville Island remains a place where people work. The Public Market is the hub and the centre of the island's activities. It is a

Granville Island Ferry

Downtown Vancouver

99

Granville Island Ferry

False Creek

English Bay

Aquabus Ferry

Granville Island Public Market

Granville Bridge

Creekhouse Gallery

Arts Club Theatre

Duranleau St.

GRANVILLE ISLAND

Johnston St.

Emily Carr University of Art & Design

Railspur Alley

Sea Village

Promenade

Anderson St.

Kids Only Market

Cartwright St.

Arts Umbrella

Entrance under bridge

Old Bridge St.

Granville Island Hotel

False Creek

Granville Island at night

huge draw for visitors, while locals, and especially local chefs, love shopping there. The market merchants are very knowledgeable about their products and it's worthwhile to indulge in a bit of chat with them. There's exotic fish from the southern hemisphere, fresh fruit from the Okanagan and fresh baked bread and bagels. "The butcher, the baker, the candlestick maker" comes to mind when one thinks of the Granville Island Public Market.

Island Offerings

If boats are your thing, there's a large maritime aspect to the island. There's everything from chandlers to boat repairs and kayak trips. If you have sailors or boaties in the family, this is the place to find an unusual gift. If you're a fan of plays, the theatres always have something interesting on their stages. In addition, there are the buskers — local, talented musicians and magicians who ply their trade on the island streets. Pottery, weaving, textiles, jewellery, leather, and exquisite glass are some of the unique crafts created by the large group of artisans who work on the island. Granville Island has stories to tell. These artisans will gladly stop what they are doing to speak with visitors and demonstrate what they are making — and encourage them to buy, of course. Many of them have been working on the Island for a long time and can certainly ply you with tales. Not only are there artisans and craftspeople on the island, it is home to recreation and cultural facilities, and educational and arts institutions.

Granville Island Pottery

A Tour of the Island

To make a circle of Granville Island, head east on Cartwright Street. You'll pass Arts Umbrella, a facility for young aspiring artists, dancers, and musicians. At the end of Cartwright is the Granville Island

Hotel, a boutique hotel with an excellent patio restaurant, a brew pub, and many charter boats moored close by. Walking west on Johnston Street, Sea Village on the north side is an eclectic mix of float homes with impressive container gardens on the decks. Continue along to the Emily Carr University of Art & Design. Drop in and see what's on at the Charles H. Scott Gallery. As you stroll on, you can't miss Ocean Cement, one of the island's last industrial tenants. The fabulous kinetic sculpture, created by ie creative, one of the island's most imaginative artisan workshops, shows how cement is made. You'll remember that the industrial nature of Granville Island still exists when you dodge cement trucks or pass a shop that makes nails. Many of the island's buildings are corrugated metal, retaining the industrial look. Next to Ocean Cement, the Creekhouse Gallery is home to a mix of shops, galleries, and offices. Nearby on Old Bridge Street is the New-Small and Sterling Glass Studio workshop and glass gallery. From the sidewalk, you can watch glass-blowing in progress.

Walk past the Granville Island Stage and the New Revue Stage, both run by the Arts Club Theatre, to the star of the site, the Granville Island Public Market. From the vivid bouquets of flowers outside to the locally grown fresh fruit and vegetables inside, it's a feast for the eyes and taste buds. Best advice: nibble your way through the market; there are often free samples.

Leaving culinary temptation behind, check out the Net Loft across the way. In the past, fishers repaired their nets here; today, it is yet another surprise of little shops. On the water nearby, Vancouver's love affair with the water continues with boat builders, boat repairers, chandlers, boat charter rentals, kayak rentals, fishing boats, and live-on moorages.

Kids' Market at
Granville Island

Granville Island visitors tour the world with the music of the buskers, whether they're flute players from the Andes or a chanteur from France. Stand-up comics and magicians entice you to take a break and laugh at their antics. You can watch artisans at work at Black Stone, David Clifford's hand press (1249 Cartwright); at Paper-YA, purveyor of handmade paper in the Net Loft; and in the Diane Sanderson Weaving Studio (15–1551 Johnston). Festivals are a year-round attraction, including Winterruption in February, the New Play Festival in May, a jazz festival in June, a folk music festival in July, a wooden boat festival in August, the Vancouver International Fringe Festival in September, and the Vancouver International Writers & Readers Festival in October. In December, the Christmas Carol Ships form a convoy to delight onlookers along False Creek with shimmering lights and music. As a visitor, you might want to plan a holiday to include one of these annual events.

Getting There

There are many ways to get to the island — by ferry, foot, bike, in-line skates, or car. From the north side of False Creek, you can take the False Creek Ferry from the Vancouver Aquatic Centre or the Aquabus Ferry from the foot of Hornby Street. The Aquabus has ferries that can accommodate bikes, so if you've been cycling in Stanley Park, you can cross over by water to the island for lunch, a coffee or a drink. Go Fish is a very popular outdoor café serving fish and chips or oysters. Free parking on the island

Art in the Public
Market

is limited but there is plenty of paid parking, both covered and uncovered. Traffic can get congested at times, so some people prefer to park off-island, in the lot where Lamey's Mill Road meets The Castings, and walk west along the seawall past the terraced houses along False Creek.

The cityscape and the mountains look spectacular from this location. The walk takes you north onto the island at the False Creek Community Centre, close to the children's water park.

Kitsilano

Trude LaBossiere Huebner

Cross Burrard Bridge from downtown and you are in a
world apart. High-rises are replaced by wood-framed
houses, business suits by bathing suits. The views from
the beaches strung along the south side of English Bay are
unmatched, especially at sunset. Often simply called
Kits, the area's name derives from the Squamish chief
Khahtsahlano. In 2005, Kitsilano celebrated its centennial.
Today, diversity is the essence of every aspect of the
neighbourhood.

**Kitsilano
neighbourhood**

4th Avenue, the Heart of Kitsilano

Once over the bridge, continue several blocks along
Burrard to 4th Avenue. Turn right and you are in the heart
of Kits, with its population of singles, families, and seniors
and an overall higher-than-average education level.
Housing ranges from small apartments to lovingly
refurbished heritage homes. Kitsilano is an outdoor
playground for its residents, who cycle, run, skateboard,
swim, and play tennis and beach volleyball.

Continue on 4th Avenue to Cypress Street. Turn left
and head south to 6th Avenue. At the intersection of
Cypress and 6th, one of the city's attractive community
gardens grows in abundance. Flowers and vegetables cover
the boulevard each summer. Turn right and continue west

Burrard Inlet

KITSILANO

Volunteer Park

1 Ave. West

Point Grey Rd.

Tatlow Park

4 Ave. West

Alma St.

Blenheim St.

Macdonald St.

Broadway West

Vanier Park cyclists

on 6th with the railway tracks on your right. The blue building at Maple Street is home to City Gardener, a non-profit organization that houses a demonstration organic garden.

Continue walking on 6th until you reach the Arbutus Real Food Market. This is a convenient spot for freshly baked goodies and a washroom break inside the market's rustic wood structure. Then head north along Arbutus, back to 4th Avenue. Cross 4th to Sophie's Cosmic Café, a popular, funky Kitsilano landmark since 1987.

Walk east along 4th Avenue back to Cypress Street, one of the city's designated bicycle routes. Turn left, check out the small village, then continue to Cornwall Avenue. Here you can begin to explore the famed Kitsilano waterfront.

Kitsilano Point

Cross Cornwall and continue south several blocks to Kitsilano Point. You'll reach it at the 30-metre (100-foot) totem pole, a replica of one given to Queen Elizabeth II in 1958 for B.C.'s centennial. Carved by Kwakiutl carvers, the totem is a reminder that this area was originally a Squamish village called Sun'ahk.

Totem pole in Haddon Park

Turn right at Whyte Street, cross Chestnut Street, and head to the Museum of Vancouver on your left. Pause to admire its Haida hat-shaped roof and the crab fountain sculpture in front. Inside are exhibits showcasing Vancouver's working and cultural history. Next door is the H. R. MacMillan Space Centre with its ever-popular space shows and musical offerings.

Head into Vanier Park. You can't get lost, as there are few trees on the site, which makes it ideal for kite-flying. Walk along the shoreline heading west. Vanier Park is the summer home to Bard on the Beach, an annual Shakespeare festival. More than 80,000 people attend the evening performances each year.

A few steps further west is the Vancouver Maritime Museum. Inside the A-frame building, you will discover explorer Captain

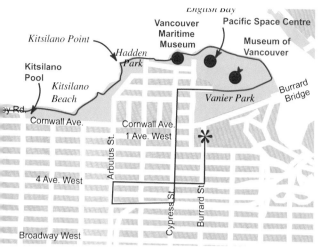

George Vancouver, after whom Vancouver is named. Displays detail the exploration of the Pacific Coast and the Orient. You are now in Haddon Park, named after millionaire property developer and philanthropist Harvey Haddon, who died in 1931.

Kitsilano Beach

Walking west along the shoreline, you approach Kitsilano Beach. Waist-high logs in orderly rows in the sand form ideal backrests for a multitude of sunbathers. The tower, situated where the sand meets the lawn, houses the city-wide lifeguard command centre for Vancouver's dozen beaches. Refreshments, washrooms, and fine dining at the new beachfront Watermark Restaurant are available here. It's no wonder that this is a favourite spot for Vancouverites — a great place to meet the locals.

Nearby is the 135-metre (450-foot) Kitsilano Pool, an outdoor summer classic overlooking the ocean. The pool opens early for brisk morning swims. The Kitsilano Showboat, an institution since 1936, is located above the pool. Amateur performers are showcased during the summer months at no charge. This is a wonderful spot to view the annual HSBC Celebration of Lights fireworks events on English Bay, which begin in late July.

Beyond Kitsilano Beach

From Kitsilano Beach, it's an easy walk along Cornwall to the foot of Macdonald Street. Two parks are located here. On the north side, Volunteer Park provides a path down to the rocky shoreline. On the south side, Tatlow Park is tucked in behind the tennis court. Cornwall Street becomes

Kitsilano Showboat

Tatlow Park

Bridge in Tatlow Park

Point Grey Road, leading to some of Vancouver's priciest waterfront homes.

Enter Tatlow Park with its picturesque wooden bridge. Beneath it is a salmon-spawning stream. Look closely: you may spot some fish. Beside it is an apartment complex built on the former palatial estate of Killarney, once the gathering place for the city's elite. Leaving Tatlow Park, walk along Macdonald Street to 4th Avenue. Cross to the south side, where you'll find the Naam Restaurant, founded in the 1960s. The food is vegetarian, the patio open-air, and the décor features West Coast cedar and plants.

Kitsilano has a variety of housing, with very few high-rises — a by-law prevents more. For typical Vancouver architecture, wander the neighbourhood streets and avenues. Streets run north and south, avenues run east and west. Many of the original stately homes have survived.

Shopping? In the 1960s, West 4th Avenue was known as a haven for hippies and artists. Today, the avenue bursts with eclectic shops and artisan bakeries from Burrard to Balsam.

Continuing south on Macdonald, head for Broadway Avenue (which is also 9th Avenue), five blocks away. In the early years, Kitsilano expanded southward to Broadway, a major east-west connector route. Today, it is a thriving residential and business district. Browse the jewellery stores, ethnic food outlets, clothing boutiques and bookstores (including Kidsbooks, the city's best children's bookstore). Stop for tea and mouth-watering fresh pastries at Notte's Bon Ton Pastry and Confectionary (3150 West Broadway), a favourite with locals since 1926. To sample renowned West Coast cuisine, choose from the many fine dining and casual restaurants, cafés and coffee shops.

The #99 B-Line express bus as well as the #9 regular bus run frequently along Broadway. If you're taking the bus, both connect to other bus routes as well as the SkyTrain's Broadway Station. The #22 Macdonald bus also goes downtown.

Somersault over Kitsilano Beach

UBC

Chris Petty

The University of British Columbia, Canada's third-largest university, is always abuzz with students, faculty, and staff. But you don't need to be registered in courses to take advantage of the university's many resources and attractions. Perched out on the end of Point Grey, some 20 minutes from downtown Vancouver, UBC boasts one of the prettiest

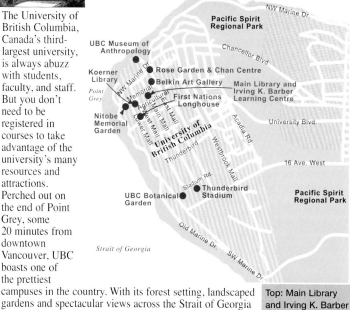

campuses in the country. With its forest setting, landscaped gardens and spectacular views across the Strait of Georgia and Howe Sound, visitors can often be heard to mutter, "How the heck do they get any work done around here?"

Almost a small city in itself, UBC has all the amenities: concert halls, restaurants (from greasy spoons to fine

Top: Main Library and Irving K. Barber Learning Centre

Forest Sciences Centre, UBC

dining), theatres, sports facilities, bars and shops. As a university, it has the vitality that goes along with a population skewed towards the younger end of the scale.

UBC is a walker's paradise. Visitors are drawn to the campus by its gardens, wide boulevards, outside eateries, stunning architecture, gorgeous viewpoints, and quiet, off-the-beaten-path spots for rest and reflection.

History

UBC became a degree-granting institution in 1915. It was originally housed in old warehouses and church basements near Vancouver General Hospital. The plan was to move UBC to Point Grey, but the First World War stopped construction. "The Great Trek" in 1922, in which students, faculty and alumni marched in demonstration from downtown to Point Grey, was the culmination of a noisy campaign to get the government of the day to resume building the campus. It worked. The Point Grey campus opened in 1925.

Those first buildings remain some of the most remarkable on campus and are quite wonderful examples of neo-Gothic architecture. Main Library, just off Main Mall, features superb stone masonry, stained-glass windows and brass fittings. Look for the two little stone monkeys on the front wall. Each holds a book, one saying "Funda," and the other, "Evolut," reflecting the Scopes Monkey Trial controversy that raged at the time. Main Library has one of the most spectacular study rooms in the country, called the Chapman Learning Commons. Have a seat in a comfortable leather chair and bask in the sunlight shining through 10-metre (30-foot) stained glass windows. Main Library was recently refurbished to strengthen the structure against earthquakes. Two wings have been replaced to form the Irving K. Barber Learning Centre, with an automated book retrieval system that is magical to watch in action.

Nitrobe Japanese Garden at UBC

A Tour of UBC

The university offers free walking tours daily from May to August, starting at the Student Union Building (SUB),

The Raven and the First Men, by Bill Reid, at the MOA.

with orientation to the main campus amenities and academic facilities. Or pick up a campus map and take a self-guided tour, starting at the Rose Garden. Drive onto the campus via Chancellor Boulevard (an extension of 4th Avenue), until you get to the Rose Garden parkade. You can park here all day for a few dollars. Take the elevator up from the parkade and look north towards the mountains. You're on the Flagpole Plaza above the actual Rose Garden. The view from the Rose Garden — Howe Sound and the North Shore's Coast Mountains fading off into the distance — stretches before you like a travel poster. The garden itself is spectacular and in bloom from early spring until well into fall.

As you contemplate the great view, remember that the world-class UBC Museum of Anthropology is just across the road and to the left. The museum, along with the Nitobe Memorial Garden and UBC Botanical Garden, should not be missed. With one of the top First Nations art collections in the world, the Arthur Erickson–designed building is a wonder on its own.

Main Mall

Main Mall stretches the length of the university from the Flagpole Plaza to Thunderbird Stadium. Short side trips from the mall bring you to virtually all the university's features. The Chan Centre is nearby (the big, round building that looks like a giant industrial widget), as are the Belkin Art Gallery, the Frederic Wood Theatre and the UBC School of Music. The Chan Centre auditorium, which seats 1,400, is said to have the best acoustics in town. Ticketed performances, free recitals by local and international performers, and

C. K. Choi Building

practices by the UBC School of Music are held here. For tickets, free tours, and free events, check with the box office. The Belkin Gallery just across the way shows travelling art exhibits as well as the university collection. It is open daily. Check, too, the schedule at the Frederic Wood Theatre, home to UBC's theatre program.

Continue along Main Mall to the huge library plaza and the Walter C. Koerner Library. Its architect calls the state-of-the-art building the "green jewel" of the campus. Locals think it's either beautiful or horrifying, but all agree that the Koerner stands out. Take the elevator to the top and look east to the Main Library and the Coast Mountains in the distance.

Koerner LIbrary at UBC

Sites of Interest

UBC has many great buildings. One of the most interesting is the C. K. Choi building west of the Koerner Library on West Mall. It's the most environmentally attuned building on campus and is built out of recycled materials from the Old Armouries (demolished a few years ago). It's also probably the only new building in Vancouver that has chemical toilets.

South on West Mall is another UBC wonder, the First Nations Longhouse. Built to house First Nations programs, it also serves as a gathering place for First Nations students. The interior features huge sculpted log poles and other pieces of First Nations art. Outside, follow the cool sounds of a waterfall to one of the most relaxing (and little-known) hideaways on campus.

From the longhouse, walk east on Agricultural Road, past Main Library to East Mall and the Student Union Building. That building and the nearby Aquatic Centre (indoor and outdoor pools), War Memorial Gym, and Student Recreation Centre make up the most active non-academic area of the campus. UBC has the largest intramural sports program in Canada. A visit to any of the latter three buildings shows why. The facilities are first-rate.

The UBC Bookstore, the largest university bookstore in Canada, is located kitty-cornered from the SUB. It has a huge selection of academic books and a well-stocked fiction and magazine section, as well as gifts, clothing, computers, art supplies, and electronics.

Back on Main Mall heading south, you'll come to the newest addition on campus. The Beaty Biodiversity Museum, open to the public as of early 2010, is home to UBC's impressive array of specimens — plants, insects, fish, vertebrates, fungi, and fossils — showcasing B.C.'s natural history. Centrepiece of this stunning collection is the 26-metre (85-foot) skeleton of a blue whale that was recovered, cleaned, and brought from P.E.I. where it had beached. Blue whales are the largest animals that have ever lived on earth.

UBC Bookstore

North Shore

Rochelle van Halm

It's the Coast Mountains that anchor Vancouver's majestic setting: the North Shore comprises a wilderness just 30 minutes from downtown Vancouver. Residents enjoy a beautiful community well-endowed with recreation opportunities, excellent shopping, and the beauty of nature best explored from the hiking trail. While some residents still see black bears and deer in their backyards, there are plenty of big-city attractions in the communities of West and North Vancouver.

Ambleside Park

Lighthouse Park

West Vancouver

After crossing the Lions Gate Bridge, the first exit takes you into West Vancouver, one of Canada's richest communities, evidenced by the visible presence of luxury import cars on the roads. Like its residents, the municipality takes pride in its appearance. Every year, it plants 30,000 spring-flowering bulbs, tends 180 hanging flower baskets and creates major floral displays. Follow Marine Drive between the two sides of Park Royal Shopping Centre, a home for fashion mavens. Next comes Ambleside Park, boasting beaches, a playground, skateboard park, duck pond, Ambleside Par 3 Golf Course, and an off-leash dog park. The West Vancouver Sea Walk along the shoreline is one of the community's best-used facilities. Dogs are relegated to their own path on the other side of the fence, between 18th and 24th streets. Seals bob in the distance, salmon leap, cruise ships pass nightly in summer, and in winter, savage storms toss logs onto the shore.

119

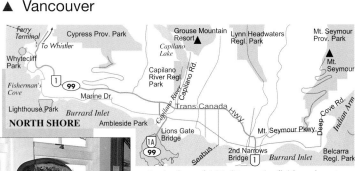

At the foot of 14th Street, the fishing pier at Ambleside Landing is used day and night. Ferry service began here in 1909 and ended in 1947.

The terminal, built in 1913, was renovated into the well-visited Ferry Building Gallery for community art exhibits. History lives nearby at the West Vancouver Museum and Archives, housed in an old ballast-stone house built in 1940 by Gertrude Lawson, daughter of John Lawson, who is known as the father of West Vancouver. The floral clock at the foot of 15th Street — considered ill-conceived by some residents — occasionally tells the correct time!

After strolling Bellevue Avenue, lined with fashionable shops, follow Marine Drive to West Vancouver's Memorial Library, which has the highest per capita circulation of any library in Canada. Across Marine Drive is Memorial Park, where large rhododendrons bloom each spring. Follow the path over the bridge to the playground by the stream, where the historic Village Walk begins. Nearby is the new geothermal-heated Aquatic Centre, with an ozone-treated leisure pool, waterslides and hydrotherapy.

In the 2400-block of Marine Drive, Dundarave Village blooms with hanging baskets and a summer flower boulevard. The shops include an old-style hardware store with whatever you might need, plus antiques, art, and gelato. Capers is the choice for an organic lunch on the deck overlooking the ocean. In late summer, the annual

Ferry Building Gallery

West Vancouver Museum

Lookout point at
Seymour Mountain

country-and-western hoedown fills the street with square
dancing and kids' pony rides.

Another pier at the foot of 25th Street marks the end of
the Sea Walk, along with playgrounds, an interesting
sculpture of a girl on a turtle, and a sandy beach for
swimming — plus a concession stand with architectural
merit and a stunning English Bay view. The Beach House
at Dundarave Pier offers upscale dining in a building finely
restored from its 1912 beginnings. The restaurant offers a
heater-warmed patio to allow diners to enjoy their meals
long after the sun sets into the Pacific. Marine Drive
meanders westward, past grand estates with multi-million-
dollar cliff-hanging homes and a few original seaside
cottages from the 1920s and 30s. In the 3700-block of
Marine Drive, the once-
treacherous Suicide
Bend, allows room to
pull over for a photo of
the ocean and Point Grey
beyond, and a close-up
look at freighters
anchored in the bay.
Explore local beaches
with their own natural
attractions at West Bay
(public access off
Radcliffe Avenue),
Sandy Cove (at Rose
Crescent), and Stearman
(off Ross Crescent).

Below: Sea Walk
Bottom: Memorial
Park

The government's
Fisheries and Oceans
laboratory (4100-block
of Marine Drive) now
studies salmon on the
site where the Great
Northern Cannery
packed fish from 1891
until 1967. Outside the
Cypress Park Market
(4360 Marine Drive),
historic photos show
the neighbourhood of
years ago. Watch for
Piccadilly Road South,
and take a left turn into
lower Caulfeild, the

Seaview Walk

English-style village designed by Francis Caulfeild in the 1920s. The neighbourhood celebrates on the village green in front of St. Francis-in-the-Wood Anglican Church, a favourite for weddings.

Returning to Marine Drive, turn left at Eagle Harbour Road to visit a small neighbourhood beach where you can watch local children learn to sail and see Eagle Island residents use a cable ferry to haul themselves and their groceries home, a stone's throw from the mainland.

From Marine Drive, turn north onto Cranley Drive for Seaview Walk, part of the TransCanada Trail. The path leads from Nelson Creek to the old rail bed, overlooking hundreds of boats moored in Fisherman's Cove and leading to the Gleneagles Golf Course. The municipally owned 18-hole course provides ocean views from the greens. Retrace your steps and continue west on Marine Drive, snaking up the rocky hillside.

North Vancouver

Follow the signs to Highway 1 East/Highway 99 South, known locally as the Upper Levels Highway, for a quick trip east with views of English Bay, Burrard Inlet, and Vancouver. When the skies are clear, you can see as far as Vancouver Island and Mount Baker. Take Exit 22 and follow Mount Seymour Parkway to the Parkgate Village Shopping Centre, then turn left at Mount Seymour Road.

Yachts in Deep Cove

Halfway up Seymour Mountain, you'll find a lookout point from which to view Simon Fraser University, Indian Arm, and the wilderness beyond. Hiking trails begin farther up, where the road ends in the top parking lot.

Returning downhill, turn left at Mount Seymour Parkway and watch for the close-up view of

Indian Arm, nestled among mountains shrouded in mist.

Turn left onto Deep Cove Road for the short drive into the forested cove. This franchise-free town offers unique cafés for lunch or coffee, where you'll meet the locals when you take a break from your sidewalk stroll. At the Deep Cove Cultural Centre, residents are invited to participate onstage or backstage. The Seymour Art Gallery features local artists. The Shaw Theatre, the Deep Cove Heritage Association, and Arts in the Cove provide opportunities for artists of all ages and aspirations. From Deep Cove Lookout at the foot of Gallant Avenue, see weekenders stocking up for a cruise up Indian Arm. Join them on a rental paddle from Deep Cove Canoe and Kayak Centre and view waterfront homes on Panorama Drive. A public footpath follows the shore to Panorama Park, where live music fills summer evenings. The Baden-Powell hiking trail begins just north of the park. This 48-kilometre (30-mile) trail links Deep Cove to Horseshoe Bay across the North Shore mountains.

North Vancouver is well-equipped for local culture. Live theatre is offered at Presentation House. Upstairs, the Presentation House Gallery is renowned for its photography exhibitions. North Vancouver Museum and Archives focuses on the local history of logging, shipbuilding, and early community development and features a walking tour of historic houses. Just down the hill is Lonsdale Quay Market where you can buy live crabs, salmon (whole or just a sandwich), fresh pasta, vegetables, flowers, and Italian deli specialties. Children can blow off steam in the upstairs ballroom. The Lonsdale Quay Hotel overlooks the Cates tugboat operation, and the SeaBus commuter ferry links Lonsdale Quay with downtown Vancouver. The Lower Lonsdale area is undergoing redevelopment from its shipyard past into a commercial and cultural hub.

Top: Lonsdale Quay market sign
Above: Lynn Canyon Park suspension bridge

Outdoor Fun

Lighthouse Park (off Beacon Lane at Marine Drive, West Vancouver) offers trails through an old-growth forest of giant Douglas firs, pines, hemlocks, and arbutus trees that look as if they're peeling rust-red bark. Stroll to Point Atkinson lighthouse, built in 1912 and still operating. When fog rolls in, the foghorn is very loud. The rocks are a great vantage point to view the freighters and sailboats in English Bay.

Seabus

Whytecliff Park offers rocky views to Bowen Island and the passing ferries, plus picnic sites and a climb up Whyte Islet, accessible at low tide. The stony beach is popular for divers, as marine life is protected in an underwater reserve.

Porteau Cove, 25 kilometres (15 miles)

123

north of Horseshoe Bay off Highway 99, is one of the few places you can camp alongside Howe Sound. An artificial reef of shipwrecks at the cove makes this a favourite dive area. Walking trails lead through the picnic area to a small hill with a lookout.

During winter, skiing and boarding are no more than 30 minutes away from downtown Vancouver at three different mountains. From Highway 1, take Exit 8 and follow Cypress Bowl Road to Cypress Provincial Park. Already a favourite for downhill and cross-country skiing, snowboarding, and snowshoeing, this facility has been improved for use as the freestyle skiing and boarding venue for the 2010 Winter Olympic Games. The 75-year-old rustic Hollyburn Lodge serves homemade chili, bakes its own bread and, during ski season, packs the house with Saturday night bluegrass or folk music. Whatever the season, the Highview Lookout provides a tremendous view of the City of Vancouver, the Fraser Valley, Richmond, the Strait of Georgia, and the Gulf Islands beyond. Summer hiking on Cypress Mountain ranges from Yew Lake Trail, an easy interpretive loop that is wheelchair- and stroller-accessible, to the rugged 30-kilometre (18-mile) Howe Sound Crest Trail.

Grouse Mountain offers excellent downhill skiing and snowboarding on 22 runs. Sleigh rides through alpine meadows, outdoor skating, snowshoeing, and the latest, snowshoe running, are also offered. Hiking in the summer includes the Grouse Grind, a steep climb under the Skyride. At the top, Grouse offers guided walking tours and paragliding for the ultimate view.

Mount Seymour provides natural terrain that's ideal for learning to ski or snowboard. There are snowshoe trails and snow tubing as well.

In North Vancouver, Lynn Canyon Park is a wilderness not far from civilization, with an informative Ecology Centre. The Lynn Canyon Suspension Bridge, less well-known than its well-promoted cousin, the Capilano Suspension Bridge, is just as spectacular in a more natural setting. Few, however, can resist the Capilano Suspension Bridge with its adrenaline-pumping, swaying pedestrian bridge across the deep Capilano River gorge.

Victoria

▲ Map of Victoria

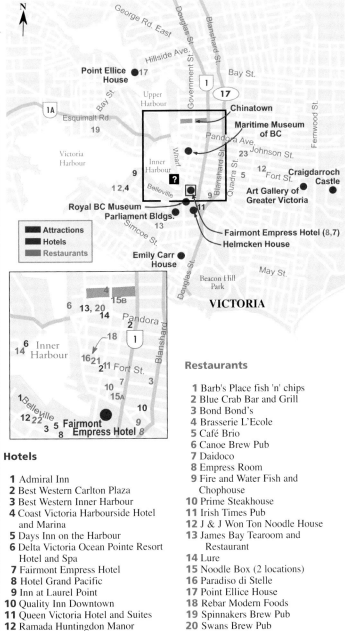

Hotels

 1 Admiral Inn
 2 Best Western Carlton Plaza
 3 Best Western Inner Harbour
 4 Coast Victoria Harbourside Hotel
   and Marina
 5 Days Inn on the Harbour
 6 Delta Victoria Ocean Pointe Resort
   Hotel and Spa
 7 Fairmont Empress Hotel
 8 Hotel Grand Pacific
 9 Inn at Laurel Point
10 Quality Inn Downtown
11 Queen Victoria Hotel and Suites
12 Ramada Huntingdon Manor
13 Swans Suite Hotel
14 Victoria Plaza Hotel

Restaurants

 1 Barb's Place fish 'n' chips
 2 Blue Crab Bar and Grill
 3 Bond Bond's
 4 Brasserie L'Ecole
 5 Café Brio
 6 Canoe Brew Pub
 7 Daidoco
 8 Empress Room
 9 Fire and Water Fish and
   Chophouse
10 Prime Steakhouse
11 Irish Times Pub
12 J & J Won Ton Noodle House
13 James Bay Tearoom and
   Restaurant
14 Lure
15 Noodle Box (2 locations)
16 Paradiso di Stelle
17 Point Ellice House
18 Rebar Modern Foods
19 Spinnakers Brew Pub
20 Swans Brew Pub
21 The Temple
22 Victoria Harbour House
23 Zambri's

Exploring Victoria

D. C. Reid

With the mildest climate in Canada, Victoria deserves its title as "the Garden City." In late February or early March, residents count the flowers, with annual totals always in the billions, for the benefit of the rest of the snowbound country. Every summer, it lines its streets with 3,000 overflowing hanging floral baskets.

Kabuki cab in front of the Empress Hotel

Compact and pretty, Victoria lies at the southern end of Vancouver Island. Vehicle traffic arrives at Swartz Bay's ferry terminal 30 minutes north of the city as well as at the Inner Harbour terminal, with scheduled ferry arrivals from Seattle and Port Angeles. Air travellers land at Victoria International Airport and take the scenic Pat Bay Highway. Others arrive on one of several daily helicopter flights from downtown Vancouver or the Vancouver International Airport, landing at the Helijet terminal within minutes of Victoria's city centre.

Victoria is a walker's delight, with many of the main attractions mere minutes from one another. For variety, hitch a ride in a human-powered Kabuki cab, or lounge in a horse-drawn carriage. Double-decker English buses whisk patrons to the world-famous Butchart Gardens. Historical interest trips leave from the Inner Harbour bound for Beacon Hill Park, Chinatown, and surrounding neighbourhoods. For something completely different, head to the Oak Bay Marina, where you can feed wild seals by the docks.

The centrepiece of the city lies at the corner of Belleville and Government streets. The ivy-covered Fairmont Empress Hotel opens onto the causeway and the Royal British Columbia Museum. Famed for its exhibits of natural history, Aboriginal lore, and gold-rush paraphernalia, the museum ranks high with visitors. Completing the corner are the grey granite Parliament Buildings with green-weathered copper domes. At night, the Parliament Buildings are spectacularly lit with 3,300 tiny lights.

A few blocks away, Bastion Square marks the site of the original Fort Victoria. On the square, the 1889 Supreme Court building, now home to the Maritime Museum of British Columbia, was the site of the city's first gallows and is said to be haunted. There are small ferries in the Inner Harbour, and you can take a pleasant walk along the Songhees boardwalk and by the Dungeness crab displayed at Fisherman's Wharf.

If you don't know where to begin, phone Tourism Victoria at 250 953-2033 or visit their office at 812 Wharf Street, across the street from the Fairmont Empress Hotel. Alternatively, there are several sightseeing companies in the city to take you on guided bus, carriage, or walking tours.

A Brief History

D. C. Reid

The Fairmont Empress Hotel

Amor de Cosmos

In 1843, James Douglas arrived aboard his ship, the *Beaver*, to become chief factor for the Hudson's Bay Company. His new Fort Victoria owed its origin to American territorial ambitions. At the time, Great Britain and the United States disputed control of the Pacific Northwest. Shrewdly judging that the 49th parallel ultimately would become the border between the two nations, the Hudson's Bay Company sent Douglas from its Columbia River depot to set up operations on Vancouver Island's southernmost tip, thereby solidifying trade in beaver and sea otter pelts.

Douglas wrote, "The place itself appears a perfect Eden in the midst of the dreary wilderness." Through the Hudson's Bay Company, he leased the entire area of Vancouver Island for a mere seven shillings a year. This move forestalled American expansionism.

The Gold Rush

The 1858 Fraser River gold rush transformed Victoria from a sleepy village of 500 inhabitants to a bustling, brawling settlement of 25,000 gold seekers. Seeking to keep Victoria ahead of Vancouver in development, Douglas declared the town a free port and taxed all traffic in goods.

Victoria's growing prosperity proved short-lived. The gold rush crash resulted in plummeting land values and the population shrank to 1,500 souls. Amor de Cosmos, the West's first radical newspaper baron, railed against the government, describing the law-and-order–prone James Douglas as a species of cockroach. When Arthur Kennedy succeeded Douglas as governor, de Cosmos won a seat in the House of Assembly.

First Peoples mask

Economic Change

Matching the theatricality of its new Legislature, Victoria's free port status conferred control over all B.C. trade in mining, lumbering, fishing, land sales, brewing, and shipbuilding. By 1900, Victoria's population had grown to 20,000 and business boomed. Francis Mawson Rattenbury, soon to become the province's most famous architect, designed the erroneously named British Columbia Parliament Buildings (in reality the Provincial Legislature) in 1898 and the Empress Hotel soon after.

But, again, the good times were short-lived. A fire during the First World War devastated the city core. The collapse of the seal hunt resulted in financial ruin for 80 per cent of Victorians. Salmon canneries and shipbuilding factories were moved to Vancouver. The Canadian government outlawed the opium trade. Victoria's economics changed from business and finance to government and tourism.

Tourism

Fortunately, Victoria's lingering financial demise received a restorative tonic: prohibition was declared in the United States. In the 1930s, whiskey from downtown factories moved through Smugglers Cove at night and sped to nearby American ports.

After the Second World War, retirees discovered Victoria, bringing with them over $50 million per year. Construction of new legislature wings, banks, law courts, power authorities, retail space, and the refurbished City Hall altered the skyline for good. Along with the arrival of old money came the stability of the government payroll and the expanding tourist trade.

Capitalizing on Victoria's tourist potential, the renowned Royal British Columbia Museum opened in the early 1970s. Its four impressive galleries now focus on what visitors love best about the province: its climate, forests and oceans, First Nations, and pioneer history.

Victoria's superlative weather and attractions do not go unnoticed: in 2007, *Travel and Leisure* magazine announced that readers had voted Victoria into the top ten list for cities in the U.S. and Canada. Vancouver Island was voted the top island in Continental U.S. and Canada.

Royal BC Museum

Top Attractions

Lesley Kenny

The Parliament Buildings

The Parliament Buildings

The name of this Victoria landmark overlooking the Inner Harbour is a misnomer. The only Canadian house of parliament is in Ottawa, the nation's capital. In Victoria, the Parliament Buildings (named after a bill that was passed in the 1890s) actually house the Provincial Legislature, where the members of the legislative assembly sit. Free 45-minute tours run every day in the summer. When the house is in session, visitors can sit in the galleries and watch the ad-libbed performances.

In 1856, Governor James Douglas, the first governor of the colony of Vancouver Island, issued a proclamation to elect the House of Assembly. Seven members were elected from four districts. Governor Douglas didn't believe that the common folk should have much to say about how they were governed, so he added a catch: all voters had to own at least 20 acres (8 hectares) of land. In the first so-called democratic election, only 40 people were allowed to vote for the seven representatives. All of the elected reps had ties to the Hudson's Bay Company. Three of them just happened to be enemies of Governor James Douglas.

The first Legislative Assembly had little power. The only source of money was through the sale of liquor licenses. The Hudson's Bay Company was the Legislative Assembly's rival for authority, with vast amounts of money at its disposal from trading profits and land sales. In the beginning, the assembly was basically a place for public criticism of the heavy-handed Douglas administration. The assembly didn't have money for much-needed roads, nor

Governor James Douglas

did it have the authority to levy taxes or give grants. Meanwhile, the downtown core of Victoria was expanding, largely because of the gold rush, which attracted immigrants from around the world.

The original government buildings were designed by a German immigrant, Herman Otto Tiedemann, and built between 1859 and 1864. They were dubbed the Bird Cages for their unusual design. After Confederation with Canada in 1871, the first parliament of British Columbia met in the Bird Cages. Most of these structures were demolished to make way for the stone and marble buildings of today.

The new Parliament Buildings were designed by Francis Mawson Rattenbury, a 25-year-old architect from Leeds, England. Building began in 1893 and ended in 1898, all for less than $1 million. The stones were cut locally. The slate for the roofs came from Jervis Inlet off Vancouver Island. Inside, the marble in the assembly hall was imported from Italy, while the marble in the rotunda was from Tennessee.

The diamond jubilee celebration of Queen Victoria was scheduled before the completion of the Parliament Buildings. To show its appreciation, the government honoured the anniversary by hooking up thousands of tiny lights to the outside of the buildings. The lights were used for special occasions until 1956, and since that time, the lights have been turned on every day at dusk and turned off at midnight. There are more than 3,300 bulbs outlining the buildings, giving them a Disneyesque look.

But there's more behind this manicured facade than meets the eye. Soon after he designed the Parliament Buildings, Francis Rattenbury became the Canadian Pacific Railway's architect in the West. He designed the Fairmont Empress Hotel and numerous banks and mansions in Victoria and Vancouver. But his affair with Alma Pakenham, 30 years his junior, resulted in rejection by polite society. He left his wife and moved to England with Alma. It was there that Alma's new lover, George Stoner, an 18-year-old chauffeur, bludgeoned the architect to death in 1935. Stoner was sentenced to death, but after a public outcry, received life in jail. Alma, thinking that her lover was going to be executed, committed suicide.

The Parliament Buildings at night

The Inner Harbour

The Inner Harbour and Fisherman's Wharf

Victoria's picturesque Inner Harbour is just a few steps from the Parliament Buildings. Walk down the steps either from Government or Belleville streets, and you'll find an eclectic group of buskers and artisans offering their talents and wares. After a day's shopping, sit on one of the benches or stone steps and watch the boats come into dock or see a small aircraft taxi along the water for a mid-harbour launch. Or enjoy a harbour view from the window at Milestone's restaurant on Wharf Street.

Walk around the dock and look at privately owned boats. On occasion, a meticulously restored sailboat or a reproduction of a historic explorer's ship is moored here. If the urge to get on the water overtakes you, try a Harbour Ferries tour or a shorter 10-minute ferry ride to the Westbay Marina in Esquimalt. From there, walk back along a boardwalk beside the ocean. You'll pass by Spinnakers, one of Victoria's fine microbreweries and pub, with patio seating that looks out at the Inner Harbour.

All around the Inner Harbour on Government and Belleville streets, horse-drawn carriage rides are available, as well as double-decker bus tours. Nearby, the *Coho* ferry docks on its way to and from Port Angeles, Washington, as well as a speedier catamaran destined for Seattle. On the Dallas Road end of the Inner Harbour is Fisherman's Wharf, a commercial fishing boat dock. Making the most of the fresh fish available here, Barb's Place Fish 'n Ships sells tasty lunches from a floating dock. No matter which way you face, the Inner Harbour is within a five-minute walk from major tourist attractions or the many boutiques along Government Street.

The Fairmont Empress Hotel

The Fairmont Empress Hotel

Probably one of the most-photographed Victoria landmarks, the Fairmont Empress

Gate of Harmonious
Interest

Hotel overlooks the Inner Harbour. The hotel was
originally one of a series of château-style luxury hotels
built by the Canadian Pacific Railway to attract cross-
country travellers. Designed by Francis Rattenbury
(architect of the Parliament Buildings), it was built in 1908
for $1 million. In the late 1980s, the hotel was restored
to the tune of $45 million, closed for six months and
completely gutted. The grand-style hotel, its towering brick
walls partly covered in ivy, has 477 rooms and 34 suites on
eight floors. There are 80 different room configurations,
some with vaulted ceilings, others with interesting nooks.
On a typical summer day, the Fairmont Empress Hotel
registers 1,000 visitors.

The Queen of England doesn't stay here, but she does
come for tea when she's in town. In fact, afternoon tea is
open to everyone willing to pay the rather hefty fee. In
summer, reservations are required for the five daily
seatings. After tea, consider a walking tour of the hotel's
public areas, including the archives with its collection of
pictures, menus, silver settings, and political cartoons.

Double-decker bus tours leave from the front of the
hotel on Government Street. Boutique shops in the
downtown core are just a block away. The concierges at the
front desk are well-versed in tours and travel plans.

Chinatown

The two blocks that make up Victoria's Chinatown may
seem small, but once you pass through the arched Gate of
Harmonious Interest at Fisgard and Government streets,
you could easily spend an entire afternoon browsing,
shopping, and eating. It is Canada's oldest Chinatown.
Until the late 1800s, it was the largest Chinese settlement
north of San Francisco. At one time, this "forbidden city"
covered several blocks and bustled with more than
100 businesses, three schools, a hospital, two churches,
five temples, and two theatres.

The elaborate red-and-gold-tiled archway was the first
permanent Chinese arch in Canada. In 1981, it was
dedicated to the spirit of co-operation between the two
cultures. Two hand-carved stone lions stand guard over the
entrance, a gift from Victoria's twin city, Suzhou, China.

Fan Tan Alley

Shrine at the Art Gallery of Greater Victoria

Modern Chinatown may be smaller today, but the variety of food and shopping still holds its appeal. Merchants are out early each morning, setting up their outdoor vegetable markets. That sudden craving you have for wonton soup can be satisfied at almost any hour of the day. Walk along this street carefully so you don't miss Fan Tan Alley. This narrow passage — some say the narrowest street in Canada — is home to several artist studios and boutiques. Its more exotic history was as a home to opium dens at the end of the nineteenth century.

An enjoyable way to spend a Sunday morning is having dim sum. This traditional Chinese brunch is served one delicious snack at a time. Wash them down with a pot of Chinese tea and you're ready for your walk back downtown.

The Art Gallery of Greater Victoria

The only Shinto shrine outside Japan sits in the Asian Garden of the Art Gallery of Greater Victoria. Walk up Fort Street from downtown for 1.5 kilometres (1 mile) to Moss Street. The art gallery is tucked in just around the corner.

The gallery's main base is Gyppeswick mansion, built by the Spencer family in 1889 and donated in 1951. Although the gallery has grown in size, the mansion is a significant part of the tour, from the tile painting of the Knights of the Round Table of Arthurian legend to the large dollhouse in the wooden hallway. This dollhouse is perfect in more ways than one: because it's under glass, there are no dusting chores for its tiny occupants. Outside the mansion, the Asian garden is a peaceful spot, more subtle than colourful. A wooden Shinto shrine lends a reflective quality. Found abandoned in Japan, the shrine was rescued in 1987 and brought to the gallery.

There are now seven galleries, including one entirely devoted to the work and writings of B.C. artist Emily Carr. Her passionate nature paintings are compared to those of Georgia O'Keeffe and Vincent van Gogh. A permanent exhibition entitled "In Her Own Words" features 20 works by Carr. Some seniors in Victoria remember that Emily Carr herself was

Exterior and interior of the Art Gallery of Greater Victoria

a visitor of the Spencer family, in the very mansion that is now part of the art gallery. Also in these galleries are the works of contemporary Canadian artists, North American and European historical artists, and traditional and contemporary Asian artists. One of the most recent gallery additions, the Lab, is devoted to original experimental projects. The gallery also hosts some 20 exhibitions per year.

The art gallery's permanent Asian collection of almost 17,000 items (the largest in the province) includes some of the finest examples of Japanese art in Canada. One of the permanent exhibitions is a fourteenth-century Buddha head. The City of Victoria's Ming dynasty bell was moved from Beacon Hill Park in 1990, perhaps because local kids of all ages figured out that if you curled your body up just right and placed your hands and feet just so, you could hide inside the dangling bell.

Once a year, in July, the art gallery turns itself inside out for the Moss Street Paint-In. From the art gallery on Moss Street, all the way down to the beach at Dallas Road, artists line the sidewalks with their palettes and easels. Thousands of people turn out to watch them at work.

Guided tours of the art gallery are available upon request and for special exhibitions. There are lecture series throughout the year as well as workshops, art appreciation programs for children, and a popular children's festival in September. Selected paintings are available for rent (private or business use), and some are for sale. There's also a gift shop with quality handmade decor items and jewellery. The gallery is open daily in the summer and extended hours on Thursday evening.

From here, it's a short walk to Craigdarroch Castle or the gardens at Government House (open to the public year-round).

135

HMS *Discovery*

The Royal British Columbia Museum

Adjacent to the Parliament Buildings, one of the most renowned museums in North America is open 363 days a year. The Royal British Columbia Museum, founded in 1886, sits on the corner of Belleville and Government streets. More than 120 staff and 450 volunteers work together to share the story of B.C. through the museum's seven million artifacts, specimens, and archival records. Only a fraction of these items are on display in the exhibition galleries at any one time. Archival records are often accessed for family history research, while natural history specimens are used for scientific research.

The Royal B.C. Museum is designed to allow you to experience the province through your senses. Of course, you can read the printed materials, or take the time to study all the accompanying display legends and documentation, but even if you just strolled through each room and hall, looking and listening, you would pick up much of it by osmosis. Perhaps a good gauge of the museum's success and popularity is the evidence at the entrance gate: thousands of Victoria locals return each year, alone, with guests, or with their kids to see the latest exhibits.

The museum's four featured galleries lead visitors through realistic walk-through scenarios. The First Peoples Gallery opened in 1970 with the support of the local First Nations community. In this mesmeric space, enlarged images of early photographs, along with artifacts, video, and audio, lead you through Aboriginal history. Spend a

Grizzly Bear; Living Land, Living Sea Exhibit

contemplative moment in the impressive house of Chief Kwakwabalsami, Jonathan Hunt, a Kwakwaka'wakw chief. His son, Henry Hunt, and grandsons Tony and Richard Hunt created the house and carvings for the exhibit. Their family maintains ceremonial rights to the house and it continues to be used for these occasions.

The Natural History Gallery introduces B.C.'s forests and ocean, and the history of settlement and development. The Modern History Gallery takes visitors on a tour of nineteenth-century Victoria, with a salmon cannery, authentic wood-cobbled street, Chinese herbalist's shop, and a dressmaker's studio. In the 20th Century Hall area, a living room scene has been replicated for each decade of the twentieth century, incorporating technological and design developments. Compare the history of the telephone, from a

big wooden box on the wall to a cordless phone. The Living Land, Living Sea Gallery explores the dynamic connections between the earth, its climate, and life forms. At the entrance to the gallery, the museum's famed woolly mammoth greets visitors in a naturalistic environment. The mammoth died in B.C. some 9,000 years ago.

From the tiny to the gigantic, the museum has something interesting or weird for everyone. For the bug collector, there are insect larvae and strange little critters that once roamed the territory where megastores now stand. Also fascinating is the tiny, intricately decorated Chinese slipper-shoe, once worn by a woman whose feet had been bound. The collection also includes iconic modern collectables such as John Lennon's 1965 psychedelic Rolls Royce. It's owned by the museum, though often on loan.

Top: Totem Gallery, First Peoples Gallery
Bottom: Giant Woolly Mammoth; Living Land, Living Sea Exhibit

The museum's National Geographic IMAX Theatre is a giant, six-storey screen adventure. The steeply pitched viewing room seats 400. The movies focus on family fare, such as nature or science, and run several times a day. A combined pass is available that includes the museum and the National Geographic IMAX Theatre.

Museum staff suggest you take three or four hours to experience all the galleries and exhibits available. After a trek through history, the café next door to the gift shop offers a respite.

The Maritime Museum of British Columbia

The Maritime Museum of British Columbia is on Bastion Square in the middle of downtown Victoria, between Government and Wharf streets. Located in Victoria's original 1889 provincial courthouse, the museum is home to a collection of

The Maritime Museum of British Columbia (above and below)

more than 5,000 artifacts that tell the story of the province's ocean-going history. Through its many precision-built models and antique nautical equipment, the galleries at this museum pay tribute to the Royal Canadian Navy from its early days. As well, they document the era of the elegant Empress steamship line, vessels of the same vintage as the *Titanic*. The economy-class version is represented in the paddle-wheelers that once steamed through the province's inland waterways.

Although most items are under glass, there are a few things to touch and operate. There's an 1864 torpedo and some other nasty hardware to play with (under supervision, of course). The old cage elevator, there since the building was the provincial courthouse, was installed for one of the rather portly judges. It seems that there was some doubt as to whether he could continue to walk up the three flights of stairs to his courtroom without risking a heart attack. Today, the elevator takes visitors to the third floor to watch a movie of a trip around Cape Horn from the perspective of a four-masted sailing vessel in a storm. When you return to either the second or first floor, you may have to take a small step up, or down, into the room, depending on the skill of the elevator operator.

The courthouse on the third floor is occasionally used for hearing cases when the new court on Broughton Street

gets jammed. The original gallows were just a short distance from the courthouse, and the executed were buried in paupers' graves in the courtyard. The remains of nine such unlucky citizens have been found during upgrading. It's believed that there are three graves underneath.

Museum staff have devised a treasure hunt for kids. Written clues are scattered throughout the building and the winners are rewarded with a treat. This is nice for kids, and great for parents.

The museum's bookstore offers a wide selection of maritime books on Vancouver Island, as well as the other items common to museum gift shops. After leaving the museum, walk across the square for a pint to talk about your own seafaring days, or wander towards the water to view the Inner Harbour in a new light. The museum is open seven days a week, with extended daytime hours in the summer.

First-floor galleries at the Maritime Museum

Emily Carr House

A few short blocks behind the Parliament Buildings, at 207 Government Street, you'll find Emily Carr House, built in 1864. Emily Carr, Canada's first independent artist and writer, was born here in 1871, just a few months after British Columbia became the newest Canadian province. At the time, the house was located in a rural setting. The architecture of the artist's very Victorian-era family home is described as both San Francisco Victorian and English gingerbread. Tour the restored rooms and see some of Carr's own pottery and sculpture, as well as some of the family's original possessions.

Later in life, Emily Carr was an ingenious housekeeper at her boarding-house residence just around the corner from the family home. Carr rigged up a rope-and-pulley system and tied it to her sitting room chairs. When she didn't want visitors, she'd haul the chairs to the ceiling. Imagine, as well, her household menagerie, including her beloved pet monkey, Woo, and her griffon dogs.

In contrast to the Victorian artifacts, a modern convenience has been added. A computer terminal is available in the house for guests to look up information about the life and work of Emily Carr. One of the rooms, called the People's Gallery, is used to present the works of local artists. These changing exhibits can be viewed from May to September. Parking in this area is cramped at best, so the 10-minute walk from downtown is your best bet.

Helmcken House

Helmcken House is the oldest house in British Columbia on its original site. It was built in 1852 for Dr. John Sebastian Helmcken, after he married the daughter of Governor Sir James Douglas. Dr. Helmcken was a surgeon with the Hudson's Bay Company who went on to become a statesman and helped negotiate the province's entry into Canada.

Originally, Helmcken House was a three-room log house. As the family grew, so did the house. Today, there are guided tours through the restored rooms, which are filled with many of the original Victoriana knick-knacks and furniture pieces to make the house feel lived in. Although there are velvet ropes keeping you out of most of the rooms, you can sit on the reproduction sofa in the parlour, formerly the room where ladies entertained. Upstairs in the attic, there are old trunks and books and wooden toys you can examine. Dr. Helmcken's original nineteenth-century medical kit is on display on the top floor in the newest part of the house, which was added in 1883.

Emily Carr House

Helmcken House is right beside the Royal British Columbia Museum and adjacent to Thunderbird Park, where you can sometimes watch totem poles being carved.

Point Ellice House

In the middle of an industrial area, in what seems like the heart of a wrecking lot, there is a little oasis called Point Ellice House. Caroline and Peter O'Reilly owned Point Ellice House in the late 1800s. Both emigrated from England in the 1850s — Caroline after having spent some time in India looking for a British officer to marry. Instead, she married Peter O'Reilly in 1863 and spent the next few years in Victoria and on the mainland. After the birth of her second child, Caroline wanted to settle in Victoria to be near her own family. When she and Peter established their home at Point Ellice House, she was the quintessential lady of the house, organizing dinner parties and social events. Point Ellice House quickly became the place to be for local schmoozers.

Helmcken House

Peter O'Reilly, after immigrating to Canada at the age of 31, was employed as a justice of the peace, a magistrate,

a gold commissioner, a collector of revenue, an assistant commissioner of lands, an Indian agent, and a coroner. From 1864 to 1881 he served on the British Columbia Legislative Council as a magisterial appointee. In 1881, he retired as a judge.

The gardens at Point Ellice House have been restored according to the meticulous notes kept by the couple's daughter Kathleen O'Reilly. Some of the heritage varieties of plants here are not often found in modern gardens. Today, the English-garden atmosphere is often used for private functions such as weddings, company parties, and special anniversaries.

140

Point Ellice House

Inside the house, more than 10,000 original O'Reilly items have been catalogued by conservators and are on display, touted as the largest collection of Victoriana in its original setting. There is an audio tour of the house narrated by the "house boy," which no doubt makes Caroline O'Reilly turn in her grave.

Point Ellice House is located at 2616 Pleasant Street. If you travel west over the Bay Street Bridge and turn north on Pleasant Street, you'll see the large Point Ellice House sign. You can also get there from the Inner Harbour by taking a harbour ferry across the water.

Craigdarroch Castle

The Gaelic translation of Craigdarroch is "rocky oak place." Certainly the Dunsmuir family, who built Craigdarroch, couldn't have imagined how apt this name would be.

Craigdarroch was built in the late 1880s. Robert Dunsmuir and his wife Joan emigrated from Scotland, but before moving to Victoria lived in Nanaimo (a 90-minute drive north of Victoria today). In Nanaimo, Robert Dunsmuir began to make what became his fortune in mining. As mine superintendent for the Hudson's Bay Company, Robert discovered his own coal seam and started a company to export the coal to San Francisco. In 1882, the family moved to Victoria, where Robert served as the representative for Nanaimo in the provincial Legislative Assembly.

The stone mansion designed for the Dunsmuir family was built on the highest point in Victoria. Originally gracing the estate were a lake, a bridge, streams, an orchard, tennis courts, a coach house, stables and a gazebo on the estate. All that's left today are the mansion, the south lawn and the original stone wall. Robert Dunsmuir died shortly before Craigdarroch was completed, but his wife moved in with some of her daughters (she had 11 children) and grandchildren. Presumably, they lived comfortably in the 39 rooms on four floors with 17 fireplaces. The mansion was equipped, even then, with gas lighting, electricity, plumbing, and the new telephones.

The interior white oak panelling and woodwork were prefabricated and sent from Chicago. Inside the mansion is the best collection of residential stained and leaded glass on the West Coast. In the grand entrance hall, the white oak

Craigdarroch Castle

staircase and sandstone fireplace greeted visitors after they parked their coaches under the porte-cochère. On the second floor, Joan Dunsmuir's sitting room and two of the bedrooms are restored to their Victorian state. In the Billiard Room, on the third level, stand on the Douglas fir floor and get a good view of the Strait of Juan de Fuca and the Olympic Mountain range in Washington State. But the best view is from the tower, with its blue dome ceiling and curved doors and windows, with circular stained-glass windows fitted above the doors. From here, you can have an unobstructed vista of the ocean and mountains.

Some years after Robert Dunsmuir died, his two sons began legal proceedings against their mother for control of their generous trust funds. When one son died, he left his estate to his brother, who continued to engage Mrs. Dunsmuir in a legal battle that made newspaper headlines. Some reports say that the formidable Joan Dunsmuir was a recluse during the last 18 years of her life, spending most of her time on the second floor of "rocky oak place." Craigdarroch Castle is open daily with extended hours in the summer. As the house is a historical museum, there are 87 stairs, but no ramps or elevator, and thus is not wheelchair accessible.

Dining room at Craigdarroch Castle

Butchart Gardens

Butchart Gardens is not a botanical garden; it's just for show, but what a show it is! Located 21 kilometres (13 miles) north of Victoria, halfway between the Swartz Bay ferry terminal and Victoria, the gardens began life as a rock quarry. Today, the 22 hectares (55 acres) of floral displays on the meticulously well-kept estate feature four main areas: the Sunken Garden,

Japanese Garden, Rose Garden, and Italian Garden. In 2004, the Canadian Government honoured Butchart Gardens with the designation of National Historic Site.

Original owner Robert Butchart was born in 1856, the oldest of 11 children in a Scottish family living in Owen Sound, Ontario. In his early twenties he formed a partnership with friends and began to manufacture Portland cement. The successful twist to his entrepreneurial idea was that Robert packaged and transported his cement in sacks, rather than the cumbersome barrels used at the time. As urban Canadian centres sprang up, the demand for cement increased, as did Robert Butchart's business. The young man went west.

The Sunken Gardens at Butchart Gardens

In 1902, Robert moved to Victoria, where a nearby limestone deposit at Tod Inlet provided him with the materials needed for his business: limestone, clay, fresh water, and transportation by sea. Shortly thereafter he established the Tod Inlet Cement Plant, on the grounds of what is now Butchart Gardens. His Toronto-born wife, Jeanette Foster Kennedy Butchart, and their two daughters moved to the site and set up their home.

Mrs. Butchart was a certified chemist and sometimes worked in the cement factory — presumably for love and not money. To hide the unsightly factory from view, Jennie (as she liked to be known) planted trees and shrubs. When their formal residence was complete, she turned her hand to the construction of a Japanese garden, with the help of Japanese landscape artist Isaboru Kishida.

In 1908, the limestone supply from the quarry was exhausted and it was abandoned. The story goes that an offhand comment made to Jennie Butchart by a friend — "Even you would be unable to get anything to grow in there" — inspired the now famous Sunken Gardens. Jennie had tons of topsoil brought from nearby farms, and she used a bosun's chair to lower herself down the sides of the quarry, where she tucked ivy into the crevices, knowing it would one day cover the bleak walls. Rock gardens were made with the unearthed stones. One part of the 1.4-hectare (3.5-acre) quarry was lined and filled with water from a natural spring, forming a deep lake. The Sunken Garden took nine years to make, and was completed in 1921.

The Italian Garden, the most formal of all the gardens, was completed in 1926. The bronze girl-and-dolphin statue

143

Butchart Rose Garden

in this garden was purchased by the Butcharts in Italy. The Rose Garden was completed in 1930, and here, too, the centrepiece wrought-iron wishing well was imported from Florence, Italy. As her gardens grew, Mrs. Butchart hosted hundreds and then thousands of curious guests, offering them tea and showing them around the gardens for free. In the 1930s, she and her husband were honoured with citizenship awards from the City of Victoria.

In 1939, 35 years after starting their garden work, the Butcharts gave the gardens to their grandson, Ian Ross, who continued to devote the same care to them until his death in 1997. It was Ian Ross who oversaw the illumination project in the 1950s to celebrate the gardens' 50th anniversary. At the time, it was one of the largest underground wiring projects in North America. Hundreds of miles of electrical cords were laid in the ground so that hidden lights would show off the gardens at night. Ross Fountain, at the far end of the gardens in the midst of a small lake, was built and named for Mr. Ross. The patterns made by the 21-metre (70-foot) fountain's spray continue for many hours before they are repeated.

Every year, approximately 250,000 new bulbs are planted by the 60 full-time gardeners. On summer nights, musical entertainment features actors, singers, and dancers, and on Saturdays, visitors take in a spectacular fireworks show choreographed to music. Teak benches are strategically placed for viewing the gardens. (Some of these benches were made from the decking of British sailing ships.) Enjoy afternoon tea or an evening meal in what was the original Butchart residence or in one of the other two restaurants on-site. If you prefer to eat and enjoy the scenery, pre-order a picnic basket for a lunch on the lawn. For a sweet tooth, there's the Gelateria ice cream takeaway in the Italian Garden.

If you're driving, follow Blanshard Street as it becomes Highway 17, and turn left on Keating Cross Road, about 21 kilometres (13 miles) north of Victoria. From there, follow the signs to the gardens. Public transit and private tour buses will also get you there.

Beacon Hill Park

Centrally located Beacon Hill Park is across from the greatest soft ice cream drive-through in town (the Beacon Drive-In on Douglas Street). The combination of soft ice cream and the oldest and largest park in Victoria is difficult to resist. When the city was granted Beacon Hill Park in trust in 1882, the council introduced bylaws regulating the use of the park. To this day, it is illegal to graze cattle or discharge firearms in the park. Nor is it legal to use the grass to clean your carpets.

Ming dynasty bell

Beacon Hill Park seems to be made up of different rooms, each one with an ambience of its own. Roll up your pant legs and splash at the water park on a hot day, or stroll through one of the more shady "rooms" and watch the ducks and swans from a wooden bridge arched over a stream. The swans have a royal pedigree; the first ones were shipped from the Royal Swannery on the Thames in the 1940s. About the park are exotic eucalyptus and palm trees and gnarled native Garry oaks.

Starting as early as February, daffodils and crocuses spring up everywhere. Their bright yellows and purples complement the blue-green plumage of the peacocks strutting on the walks. Bird watchers have recorded more than 150 species of birds in the park. Children enjoy the petting zoo (open in summer only) with goats and sheep, piglets, chickens, and a pony. In the bandshell, free outdoor concerts are held throughout the summer. On a Saturday morning cricketers, play on the outskirts of the park. Beacon Hill Park is a non-commercial zone, so bring your own picnic lunch.

From the hilltop, there's a great view of the Olympic Mountain range just south of the border. It was on this hill that two beacons were set up in the mid-1800s to guide ships. Their presence led to the naming of the park by the Hudson's Bay Company. On the other side of the hill, towards Dallas Road and the ocean, is the official "Mile 0" of the Trans-Canada Highway. Cross Dallas Road here and follow the scenic path along the cliffs or climb down the steps to one of the beaches. Driving, biking, or walking,

Japanese Garden

the route along Dallas Road is probably the most spectacular in Victoria. Scenic lookout points along the ocean and some prizewinning neighbourhood gardens are found along the way.

Walking north, back toward downtown, stroll through St. Ann's Academy and grounds (corner of Blanshard and Belleville). The

Fountain in Beacon Hill Park

Fort Street

former convent and girls' school was built in 1871 and recently restored, with the majority of the building now housing offices. A portion of St. Ann's is open to the public. For a donation, take a self-guided tour of the interpretive centre and chapel. The 150-year-old chapel is worth a visit. Patterned after Catholic churches in Quebec, it features a gilded altar, original oil paintings, exquisite gold-leaf detailing and a 1913 Casavant pipe organ. Now an interfaith chapel, St. Ann's hosts special events, including, of course, weddings.

Oak Bay

About three kilometres (two miles) east of downtown Victoria lies the village of Oak Bay. Follow Fort Street, veering right onto Oak Bay Avenue to this British-style shopping district. Bookstores, gift stores, and women's clothing stores, as well as a mews with various eccentric items on both sides of the street (from galleries to sweet shops), are found here.

At the corner of Oak Bay Avenue and Monterey, the Blethering Place is a cozy English-style teahouse. Amidst lace-covered tables and English memorabilia, treat yourself to a platter of crustless sandwiches, scones with cream and raspberry jam, and black (or herbal) tea. The price is a fraction of afternoon tea at the Empress, though the atmosphere is a tad more modest. Nearby is an Italian deli and café that serves coffee and homemade gelato ice cream. Half a block west is the Penny Farthing pub if a pint of beer is called for.

Along Oak Bay Avenue past the shops, curve to the right then take a left on Windsor Street to the Oak Bay Marina on Beach Drive. There's a decent coffee shop at the marina as well as a more posh restaurant. Either gives you a view of the boats in the harbour through the large windows.

If you walk along the path beneath the restaurants, you have a good chance of getting up close and personal with one of the many seals that hang around waiting for scraps of fish from the daily catch.

Willows Beach is a short drive east along Beach Drive from the marina (turn right when you leave the parking lot). This sandy beach and children's play area is lively in the summer, especially if you're young and have the latest in fashion swimwear. Admire the great view of Mount Baker, a mountain and extinct volcano in the State of Washington.

Shopping

Melaney Black

Downtown Victoria, or Old Town Victoria, can be covered on foot in about an hour — a little longer if you stop at one of the many world-famous attractions nestled among fine examples of turn-of-the-century architecture. Lucky for you, one of these buildings, the Fairmont Empress Hotel, is also a good place to start your shopping tour.

Bastion Square

The Fairmont Empress Hotel

For most shoppers, Victoria begins here. The Fairmont Empress, a historic Canadian Pacific hotel, holds centre stage in Victoria's signature Inner Harbour. This elegant setting tempts travellers with objets d'art and designer clothes in shopping areas throughout the upper and lower hotel reception areas. Pewter and porcelain collectibles, fine jewellery, and sculpture are all part of the Fairmont Empress shopping experience. Aboriginal art and masks can be found in the Art of Man Gallery at the back of the hotel where it joins the Victoria Convention Centre. On the upper level of the hotel, visit Collections by Madison Avenue, a retailer of fine furs, leathers, and designer accessories.

Fairmont Empress Hotel

Government Street and The Bay Centre

Both Government Street and The Bay Centre abound with treasures for the discriminating shopper. Rogers' Chocolates and Purdy's Chocolates are irresistible to those with a penchant for chocolate. Irish Linen Stores boasts a wide assortment of table linens and home goods, as well as a selection of women's clothing. Similarly, W&J Wilson Clothiers offers Burberry men's and women's apparel, among other world-famous lines.

Top: Roger's Chocolates
Above: Murchie's tea and coffee

Government Street

A major landmark in Old Town Victoria is the very contemporary Hudson's Bay (now called the Bay) Centre Mall, a four-tiered shopping area built around a central courtyard, fountain and clock, spanning an entire block of Government Street from Fort Street to View Street. Those

searching for the familiar will find it in La Senza Lingerie, Club Monaco, Aldo Shoes, Tabi International, Leather Ranch, Le Chateau Men's, and Body Shop.

Across the street from The Bay is historic Munro's Books, housed in a 1909 building. You'll find books for every interest. Next door is a B.C. icon, world-famous Murchie's Tea and Coffee, where you can buy Olde English and exotic teas, local coffee blends and gifts for caffeine connoisseurs. To complete the European flavour of the area, consider Crabtree & Evelyn for English toffee, soaps and scents, and the finer things in life.

Wharf Street, one block west, primarily features restaurants that appeal to a variety of palates.

Yates Street

Yates Street is the place for those with a sweet tooth for all things British. The British Candy Shoppe teases taste buds with British toffee, biscuits, and grocery items. A block farther up, you'll find the English Sweet Shop, offering a similarly tempting array of English chocolates and sweets. For lovers of fine British tweeds, British Importers has a complete selection of men's clothing and accessories.

First Nations art is very popular in Victoria and around the world. While the Art of Man Gallery at the Fairmont Empress Hotel deals in large-scale art works on canvas or soapstone sculptures, the Cowichan Trading Company features locally designed, authentic Cowichan sweaters, small carvings, and a wide assortment of less formal crafts. Hill's Indian Crafts sells gold and silver jewellery, as well as moccasins, carvings, and Inuit art.

Top: Shop on Fort Street
Above and Below: Art at Sa-Nuu-Kwa Gallery
Bottom: Sweaters at Cowichan Trading Post

Market Square

Market Square, a collection of specialty stores built around a heritage courtyard, has something for everyone. You'll find shops selling home decor, gift shops, and clothing stores, including Oqoqo for lululemon designs. It's easy to spend hours browsing Beadworld, where they have thousands of beads and findings, or Victoria Miniland, where they have just about everything in the world, only tinier. For decadent pleasures, there's Fat Phege's Fudge Factory. For more substantial meals, there are several cafés in Market Square, including creative vegetarian fare at Green Cuisine. There's even a store — Woofles, A Doggy Diner — for your favourite canine friend.

Chinatown

The Gates of Harmonious Interest at the corner of Government and Fisgard streets mark the entrance to Victoria's small but atmospheric Chinatown, which happens to be the oldest Chinatown in

Canada. Here you'll find an eclectic mix of east and west. Quonley's combines groceries and gifts in bamboo, wicker, and brass. In Fan Tan Alley, a hodgepodge of storefronts cater to more global interests. From musical instruments to artisan goods to African clothing and jewellery, these close quarters provide a unique shopping experience. Back on Fisgard beyond the alley is Fan Tan Gallery, a sensual array of textures and colours, batik, woods, glass, and folk art from around the world.

Bay Centre

Antique Row

Antique Row

Packed into two city blocks on Fort Street, Antique Row draws those who appreciate the beauty of history. Each vendor has a particular specialty. Among the offerings are period furniture found at Charles Baird and Faith Grant antique stores. Look for china, Depression glass or pottery, and a little bit of everything, at Recollections. Whatever you're looking for, Antique Row offers a rich assortment of pre-millennium artifacts.

Dining

Gary Hynes

Victoria is becoming known for its high concentration of quality restaurants, featuring cuisine based on the foodie mantra of "local, seasonal, and organic" — not surprising since the city is located within one of the best food-growing areas in Canada. All the ingredients a chef could want are close at hand, with a nearly year-round growing season, spectacular seafood from the surrounding ocean, and wild food from nearby forests and mountains.

The Victoria dining scene is generally more laid-back than its trendy Vancouver cousin. An influx of younger chefs over the last few years, however, is proving it has more to offer than the places on the Inner Harbour tourist beat. The city now offers many good restaurants, bistros, and cafés in every area. Neighbourhoods such as Cook Street Village and Antique Row offer choices from sophisticated to casual dining, in a village-like atmosphere.

Compared to other major Canadian cities, high-quality dining in Victoria is generally less expensive. Start your culinary tour in the city and take in the charms of the heritage buildings and colourful gardens. Then, if you're willing to take a drive into the country, you will find many top tables set amidst spectacular West Coast surroundings. Dine at the

Spectacular Vancouver Island dining: Sooke Harbour House

Fried yellow rockfish tail with stinging nettle spaetzle

Café Brio

Aerie Resort, high atop a mountain overlooking the long fiord-like Finlayson Arm, or make a pilgrimage to Sooke Harbour House, one of Canada's gastronomic treasures.

Fine Dining

Fine dining in Victoria in most cases means an emphasis on what is local and in season. The valleys and coastal areas of Vancouver Island are a haven for small farmers, many of them escapees from the big cities on the mainland. Many chefs scour the farm gates of the Cowichan Valley, Metchosin Valley, or Saanich Peninsula, trying to outdo their rivals in sourcing out the most flavourful blackberries or the rarest heirloom tomatoes. Throw in a catch from the sea, such as local spot prawns, Dungeness crab, sablefish, and a variety of wild salmon, and why would they want to cook with faraway global ingredients anyway?

In town, for four-star dining and impeccable service, there's Café Brio serving up some of the best food in town. The art-filled room may be noisy for some, but the kitchen sources its crispy salad greens from a local farm, the staff is warm and knowledgeable, and owner Greg Hays' wine list always features a rare find or two. The cooking is contemporary Pacific Northwest. For a real bargain, arrive before 6 p.m. for the chef's special three-course early dinners.

A new addition to the dining scene is the Rosemeade Bistro Dining Lounge. Located in the restored former home of architect Samuel McClure, stunning contemporary decor mixes with an edgy menu to create a dramatic and astonishing dining experience. "Elegant, yet relaxed" is the

The view from Ocean Pointe

best way to describe both the menu and the setting.

Downtown, the Temple is located in a historic bank building close to the waterfront. The restaurant — an award-winner, both for its architecture and its menu — serves beef tenderloin, lamb, and wild B.C. salmon (among other seafood). Within the Marriott Hotel, the Fire & Water Fish & Chophouse has garnered superlatives for its gentle handling of local seafood, strong relationships

Sooke Harbour House

with local farmers and producers, and a canny eye for just the right wine pairing, making this one of the highlights of the downtown dining scene. If you're having a light meal on a summer evening, try the outdoor patio. For classic continental cuisine served by black-tie waiters in a cottage-like setting, reserve for dinner at Victoria Harbour House, which offers a reliable, award-winning, and enduring menu of seafood, lamb, and steak; Dungeness crab is a specialty.

The most sumptuous restaurants, however, are to be found just outside of town. No one visiting Victoria should miss one of Canada's top restaurants, the Sooke Harbour House. Frederique and Sinclair Philip started this country inn in 1979 and have been receiving accolades ever since. Dazzlingly innovative and delightfully eccentric, the kitchen remains a crucible for modern Canadian regional cuisine. A close second is the SeaGrille at the Brentwood Bay Lodge and Spa. An award-winning wine list, a gorgeous West Coast–style dining room fashioned from native woods, and a menu filled with gastronomic treats make for a complete and exciting dining experience. Seafood is a restaurant specialty: Dungeness crab, wild salmon, sablefish, monkfish, Ahi tuna, Baja scallops, and swordfish all find a place on the menu.

Chef Edward Tuson at Sooke Harbour House

At the Aerie Resort, perched high up on the Malahat, diners feast on the regionally inspired creations of Chef Castro Boateng. His French techniques give a refined twist to the local

ingredients he adores. At the far tip of the Saanich Peninsula, near the ferries to Vancouver, the Deep Cove Chalet has been turning out some of the most sophisticated dishes to be found in the province. Deciding may be the most difficult part, with choices including pan-fried oysters, yellowfin tuna, breast of duck, civet of local rabbit, sautéed scallops and prawns, and Atlantic lobster.

Bistros, Cafés

Victorians are an outdoorsy lot and prefer not to dress up if they can help it. Therefore, the most popular destinations are the bistros and cafés springing up all over the city. A husband-and-wife team look after Paprika Bistro in the city's tony Oak Bay area. Here, George Szasz's Hungarian background combines with his ability to present light, yet vividly flavoured dishes to make a night out in this intimate room a pleasure. At Brasserie l'Ecole, chef Sean Brennan and wine sommelier Marc Morrison team up to present classic French bistro dishes using Vancouver Island ingredients. Devotees swear by the steak and frites, which are tossed with parmigiano and doused with truffle oil. The daily cheeseboard offerings are not to be missed. Casual modern restaurants are a hot category in Victoria, and no wonder. The prices are affordable, the food is well-prepared and contemporary, and the people-watching is the entertainment. At Rebar, a funky, quirky downtown café, health food never tasted so good. Here you'll find inventive, delicious meat-free meals. Completely guilt-free — and there's a wine list.

Victoria is also a city on the go, and the cafés that offer quick lunches and the best coffees to keep its denizens well-fuelled never lack patrons. Zambri's, located downtown in a tiny strip mall behind a London Drugs, holds the title as the best casual Italian restaurant. Order from Peter Zambri himself as he stands cooking at the stove in his small, open kitchen. He'll size you up and tell you what you should have. You can't go wrong with the illy espresso. There's Paradiso di Stelle on Bastion Square for gelato, soups, and sandwiches. Bond Bond's, the city's top bakery, serves simple, fresh lunches.

One popular trend is gourmet delicatessens that offer small meals. Great ambience can be found at the Ottavio in Oak Bay and at La Collina. As well, both offer large selections of fine cheeses, pastries, and other gourmet products. Of course, Barb's Place Fish 'n Ships at Fisherman's Wharf is the spot for reliable fish and chips, hauling in both Victorians and visitors to this funky dockside takeout.

Seafood

Good seafood used to be harder to find than you would think for a coastal city, but this is changing thanks to a number of small seafood companies that have recently

started supplying local restaurants. These days, most good restaurants offer well-prepared seafood. But four restaurants come to mind when the urge for fresh fish hits. The Blue Crab Bar & Grill in the Coast Harbourside Hotel is Pacific Northwest casual and has a great water view. Check out the blackboard for the specials of the day and don't skip the desserts here — they're delicious. The Marina Restaurant at the Oak Bay Marina, with a view that's as nautical as the food, is just the setting to sample the three-course meals, new each month. Lure, in the Delta Victoria Ocean Pointe Resort, offers a different, equally delightful, view — looking across the waters of the Inner Harbour at the city's skyline, including the Parliament Buildings. This sleek, contemporary room boasts a seafood-centric menu. Executive chef Craig Stoneman and restaurant chef Michael Weaver deliver plenty of wow with the freshest of local ingredients and innovative recipes. Twenty minutes outside the city, at Van Isle Marina in Sidney, the Dockside Grill expands the focus by including grilled meats as well as the freshest seafood. After dinner, meander around this lovely seaside town.

Top: The Empress dining room
Above: High tea at the Empress

Brew Pubs

Ever since Paul Hadfield got an act of parliament to allow pubs to brew their own beer, Victoria has been a leader in craft brewing in Canada. Popular brews at Hadfield's Spinnakerss Gastro Brew Pub include his light and lemony Hefeweizen wheat beer and a smoky Dunkleweizen. Their hot and sour soup, which is made from their own India Pale Ale malt vinegar, is worth a try. Other brew pubs worth a visit are Canoe, Irish Times, Penny Farthing, and Swans.

A Spot of Tea

For many, Victoria and English high tea are synonymous. The Fairmont Empress Hotel holds court as the queen of teas. It isn't cheap, but the chance to sit amid historic splendour while sipping on properly steeped and poured tea and munching on dainty sandwiches is worth the expense. Another fine spot for afternoon tea is Butchart Gardens, a short drive from town on picturesque Brentwood Bay. It is especially refreshing after a tramp around the spectacular garden, one of Victoria's top attractions.

For more cost-effective yet equally satisfying teas, Blethering Place in Oak Bay, James Bay Tea Room and

Restaurant a walk away from the Inner Harbour, and historic Point Ellice House overlooking the gorge are all recommended.

Ethnic Eateries

A growing trend is the large number of small, owner-run Asian restaurants that are springing up all over town. Best of the crop include the Daidoco Deli & Café, a small haiku of a room that excels at serving innovative small plates of cold and hot dishes cafeteria-style. Every bite seems to shimmer with freshness and clarity. Offerings include a cold salad of tiny bay scallops with organic asparagus, turnip, chickpeas, and garlic oil.

Blethering Place tea room

Victoria's Chinatown, with its colourful history and other Asian influences, is shoulder-to-shoulder with grocery stores overflowing with the exotic and restaurants often serving the freshest fish in town. The always busy J & J Wonton Noodle House, a simple noodle shop featuring tasty Chinese fare, is worth a visit. The Noodle Box began life as a street cart. Its spicy Asian takeaway dishes, famed for eight levels of heat, are now wok'd up at two locations, one near Chinatown and the other strategically placed on Douglas Street, a block from the Inner Harbour.

Musicians at Blethering Place tea room

156

Whistler

Constance Brissenden

Whistler landscape

Whistler, consistently voted North America's top ski and snowboard resort, didn't really need the 2010 Winter Olympic and Paralympic Games to be great. The resort's meteoric climb from rustic local celeb in 1966 to international superstar was already accomplished. By 1975, responding to tremendous growth, the Resort Municipality of Whistler, Canada's first resort designation, was created. This enlightened decision paid off. Recreational attractions, accommodations, restaurants, shops, spas, cultural events, and children's activities were already in place when the games (shared with Vancouver) were announced. Legacies from the Olympics are icing on the cake: upgrades to the 120-kilometre (75-mile) highway linking Whistler to Vancouver, the spacious Celebration Plaza public space, the Whistler Olympic Park, and Whistler Sliding Centre. The addition of these world-class sporting facilities will undoubtedly draw more national and international sporting competitions in the future that visitors can attend as spectators.

Today, Whistler is a four-season destination with over two million visitors annually. The resort's infrastructure now includes the Whistler Medical Centre, Whistler Public Library, Whistler Museum and Archives, banks, groceries, schools, public transit, and a recycling depot with thrift store. Spas are immensely popular, with some found in luxury hotels, others run independently. The Squamish

Peak 2 Peak gondola

Lil'Wat Cultural Centre, a glass-enclosed complex, offers an authentic view of First Nations culture with tours, an interpretive centre, and a museum. Million-dollar chalets abound, but Whistler is still a small-town community at heart, with year-round residents now numbering 10,000.

For eight months of the year, there's action on the side-by-side Whistler and Blackcomb mountains: skiing and snowboarding on the slopes from mid-December to early June (operating on only one mountain after mid-April),

and from early June to late July on Blackcomb's Horstman Glacier. With more than 3,280 skiable hectares (8,100 acres) between them, the dual mountains' lift systems are capable of carrying 65,507 skiers and riders per hour with 13 high-speed lifts in a 38-lift system. Five terrain parks, one super pipe and one snow cross track dazzle snowboarders with over 150 features. For the less experienced, skiing and snowboarding lessons for adults and children are offered on both mountains. Add in three glaciers and 12 alpine bowls, and the sky is the limit.

Various locations offer snowmobiling, heli-skiing, heli-snowboarding, dog-sledding, snowshoeing, and sleigh rides. Post-Olympics, the Whistler Olympic Park (15 kilometres or about nine miles south of Whistler) opens to the public for recreational Nordic skiing with a twist: visitors can try biathlon, including shooting rifles at the ranges. At the new Whistler Sliding Centre on Blackcomb Mountain, they can challenge their thrill levels with bobsleigh, luge, and skeleton.

In addition to accolades for its two mountains, Whistler Resort has been praised for best overall resort design, combining ski-in, ski-out convenience with nouveau European architecture. The original Whistler Village is now joined by Upper Village at the foot of Blackcomb Mountain and Village North off Lorimer Road. All are within walking distance of one another. Creekside, the original Whistler site 6 kilometres (3.7 miles) south of Whistler Village, has had a multi-million-dollar facelift. The result is a family-oriented alternative to the Village, with condo-style lodging, child-friendly restaurants, and quick access to children's and family zones on Whistler Mountain. A gas station and 1,200-stall complimentary parkade are conveniently located here.

Shopping at Whistler is part of the fun, with six shopping areas and over 200 shops in the Village alone

Whistler Village in the summer

Snowboarder

selling everything from handmade chocolates to locally made snowboards. Luxurious winter wear is a highlight. Nearly a dozen art galleries tempt visitors to take home a First Nations carving, a nature-inspired oil painting, or a finely designed piece of jewellery as a keepsake.

As befits an international resort, Whistler dining is exceptional. There are more than 90 restaurants, cafés and pubs. Live entertainment at clubs and lounges adds kick to after-hours activities.

Summer activities are a major draw, attracting even more visitors than winter adventures do. In 1914, Alex and Myrtle Philip opened the Rainbow Lodge and soon had visitors backpacking in to canoe and fish the five local lakes. Locals recommend the simple pleasures of picnics and swims at Alpha and Lost lakes. Three new and spectacular year-round attractions demand notice. Whistler Blackcomb's Peak 2 Peak is a 4.4-kilometre (2.7-mile) gondola ride between Whistler and Blackcomb mountains. From high above, the Coastal forests and unique Alpine terrain are breathtaking in their beauty. At Ziptrek Ecotours, daring visitors are harnessed to a steel line, then zipline over the landscape between Whistler and Blackcomb mountains. Skyline Eco-Adventures, at Cougar Mountain, seats visitors in a comfortable harness for an awe-inspiring cable line tour above old-growth forest. In late spring and fall, expect to find a quieter Whistler. Prices are at their best, with special hotel and dining offers.

You can get to Whistler by scheduled bus and air service as well as charter buses, taxis, limousines, and charter air service. The Whistler Mountaineer (mid-May to early October) offers a scenic three-hour train ride from North Vancouver. Its heritage observation car provides spectacular views of Howe Sound and the Coast Mountains. If you drive, take Highway 99 from Vancouver. Watch the speed limit; give yourselves 2.5 hours to make the trip. The resort offers two complimentary parking lots plus three large and many smaller paid parking lots.

Shops in Whistler Village

Check www.whistler.com for Whistler accommodations and central reservations. In the Village, drop by the Whistler Activity and Information Centre for personal advice. For contact information, see Listings under Excursions/Whistler.

Whistler Mountain

First opened in 1966, Whistler Mountain offers 1,925 hectares (4,757 acres) of skiable terrain. Consider for a moment the thrill of Whistler Mountain's longest run, a satisfying 11 kilometres (seven miles). Twenty per cent of runs are designed for beginners, 55 per cent for intermediate skiers and 25 per cent for advanced to expert skiers. Between the easy runs and double black diamonds, there's something for every level of skier or snowboarder.

Choice is the name of the game. Take the gondola from Whistler Village or Whistler Creekside. A third Whistler Mountain access point was added in 1999 with the Fitzsimmons Quad, installed between the Blackcomb Excalibur Gondola and Whistler Gondola. It connects with the new Garbanzo Express with the greatest vertical rise of any chair on either mountain. On your way to the top, don't forget to count the more than 100 marked runs below.

Whistler Mountain also attracts enthusiastic snowboarders. Get to the top via Symphony Express, Peak Chair, and Harmony Express. All have trails accessible to intermediate skiers. Ideal for newer riders, Habitat Terrain Park is now 10.5 hectares (25 acres) of snowboarding freedom. The Nintendo Habitat Terrain Park offers an area more than 335 metres (1,100 feet) long for intermediate to advanced.

To satisfy culinary cravings, check out Whistler Mountain's restaurants. Chic Pea at the top of Garbanzo Express is a cabin-like 230-seat restaurant that serves pizzas, soups, and huge cinnamon buns. Familiar spots include the renovated 1,740-seat Roundhouse Lodge, with a full fast-food menu, and Pika's, offering cafeteria-style food. Both eateries are at the top of the Whistler Express Gondola. Steep's Grill, located in the Roundhouse Lodge, offers casual seated dining. Raven's Nest, at the top of the Creekside Gondola, boasts a valley-view deck as well as hearty soups and stews. At the Whistler Creek Base (at the bottom of Creekside Gondola), Dusty's Bar & BBQ, home to the Canadian National BBQ Championships in August, takes you from breakfast to après-ski fun.

Downhill skier

Blackcomb Mountain

Blackcomb's nickname is the "Mile-High Mountain". Launched in 1980 as a brand-new facility, Blackcomb rivalled Whistler until the merger of both mountains in 1997 as Whistler Blackcomb. Total terrain on Blackcomb is an awe-inspiring 1,382 hectares (3,414 acres).

Blackcomb is serviced by three base areas: Excalibur Gondola in Whistler Village, Upper Village Blackcomb Base (known as the Daylodge), and Excalibur Base II Station. There are more than 100 marked runs. Fifteen per cent are designed for beginners, 55 per cent for intermediate skiers and 30 per cent for the advanced and expert group. The superb Excalibur gondola system features 97 eight-passenger sit-down cabins capable of carrying 2,600 skiers an hour. Combined with the Excelerator high-speed quad chair and the Glacier Express,

Kids at
Whistler Resort

Zipline at Whistler

skiers can climb from village to glaciers in 19 minutes.

Snowboarding has an impressive niche with three parks, one super pipe and one snow cross track. Like Whistler Mountain, Blackcomb has different parks aimed at different abilities. Terrain Garden is the place to start as an introduction to freestyle features. Work up to Highest Level Terrain Park, 525 metres (1,720 feet) long with a 148-metre (485-foot) vertical drop. Accessible by its own lift, the Catskinner Triple Chair, the park includes big table tops, hips, spines, rails, and jibs.

Dining on the mountain is a must. For a warm-up, enjoy freshly brewed coffee and deli choices in the Rendezvous at the top of Solar Coaster. Rustic Horstman Hut, at the top of 7th Heaven Express, serves hot food including soups, stews and macaroni and cheese. Crystal Hut, with a Canadiana theme, offers wood-oven prepared steak and salmon, waffles, and an evening fondue program. Glacier Creek, at the base of the Jersey Cream and Glacier Express quad chairs, is Blackcomb's largest dining facility. Upstairs is River Rock Grill, with multiple food areas ranging from Asian specialties to made-to-order sandwiches. Downstairs is Expressway, featuring bistro-style counter fare. For casual seated dining, head to Christine's in the Rendezvous with its view of Wedge Mountain and Armchair Glacier.

Home base for Blackcomb Mountain is Upper Village, a classy mix of hotels, shops, restaurants, and condominiums. The grand centrepiece is Fairmont Château Whistler, built in the impressive Canadian Pacific Railway style, with stone-clad fireplaces and domed ceilings painted with gold leaf. Just walking through is a vicarious pleasure. In 2004, the adjacent Four Seasons Hotel opened to complement the château.

Summer Activities

Black bear in Whistler

You can still canoe down the River of Golden Dreams in Whistler, a favourite of Alex Philip in the early 1900s. The

mountains, and the resort's five lakes (Alpha, Nita, Alta, Lost, and Green), are still there. What has changed, however, is the way you experience them. Mountain biking in Whistler Mountain Bike Park is hugely popular. Leisurely rides are found on the Valley Trail, a 30-kilometre (18-mile) circuit around the resort. Golf on four outstanding designer courses, all with mountain views. A unique tour is a three-hour jeep ride to active bear dens with bear researcher Michael Allen. Add in the new

Peak 2 Peak summer experience, opening new hiking trails on Blackcomb as well as incredible views for sightseers, plus summer skiing and snowboarding on Blackcomb, helicopter and float plane flights, glider rides, paragliding, bungee jumping, valley bus and four-wheel drive tours, in-line skating, horseback riding, whitewater rafting, jet boating, kayaking, fishing, and good old unadorned hiking.

The memorable Ancient Cedars Trail is an easy, 4-kilometre (2.4-mile) hike to a 1,000-year-old forest. Ride the lifts to sightsee on Whistler Mountain or experience the glaciers on Blackcomb Mountain. No matter what the weather below, always take a warm jacket, sunscreen, and good hiking shoes up with you.

Cultural Activities

When you need a break from all that healthy physical stuff, take in some culture. Street entertainers, band concerts, art shows, First Nations performances, jazz, blues, and even symphony concerts will entertain you and your family. Throughout the year, annual festivals add energy to the scene. Among the best are WinterPRIDE, February's gay and lesbian ski and snowboard week; TELUS World Ski & Snowboard Festival in mid-April; Canada Day celebrations on July 1; Kokanee Crankworx mountain bike festival in mid-August; Cornucopia, a food and wine extravaganza, in November; and the Whistler Film Festival, a four-day feast of 90 films in early December.

Especially for Children

Children get plenty of attention in Whistler. Ski and snowboard lessons, snowshoeing and snowcat adventures, dog sledding, and sleigh rides are just a few of the winter activities. The year starts with First Night Whistler, a family-oriented, non-alcoholic New Year's Eve event.

Summer features Blackcomb Base Adventure Zone with rock-climbing and activities such as Westcoaster Luge and the Spider Web climbing web. Swim or ice skate with the family at the Meadow Park Sports Centre. At the five local lakes, swimming, picnicking, fishing, and canoeing are options. Whistler Golf Club, Nicklaus North, and the Fairmont Château Whistler Golf Club offer free golf for children (10 to 18 years) with one paying adult per child. In addition to nature walks, families can enjoy the easygoing Valley Trail on rented bikes, while children's mountain-bike camps are a big draw on Whistler Mountain. First-run movies are shown at Village 8 Cinemas. Arts activities are found year-round, with the Whistler Children's Art Festival in July. For more child-friendly activities, contact the Whistler Visitor Centre.

Gulf Islands

Kathryn LeSueur

Mount Maxwell Ecological Reserve, Saltspring Island

Located off the West Coast, nestled in the Strait of Georgia, is a group of islands each with its own unique character and charm. British naval captain George Vancouver made his first sighting of these islands, home to several Coast Salish First Nations, in 1792. Mistakenly believing they were situated in a gulf, he named them the Gulf Islands. And the name stuck.

The Gulf Islands are well situated between British Columbia's mainland and Vancouver Island, and are easily accessible by B.C. Ferries, private vessels, or floatplane. The islands are beloved for their Mediterranean climate and multitude of activities for visitors.

Stopovers

B.C. Ferries offers scenic ferry passage to the six main Gulf Islands. Four of the most southerly — Mayne, Pender, Galiano, and Saturna — can be reached via a B.C. Ferries circle tour from Vancouver Island's Swartz Bay. To the north, Gabriola Island is a 20-minute ferry ride from Nanaimo. Accommodations are varied and include bed and breakfasts, hotels, cabins, resorts, provincial park campsites, and private campgrounds.

In the busy summer months, it's best to plan ahead. Although slightly more expensive, consider making ferry reservations where available. It's also wise to book accommodations ahead of time.

Activities abound, most revolving around the outdoors: hiking, golf, kayaking, sailing, swimming, and cycling. From May to October, many of the islands host Saturday morning outdoor markets selling the wares of residents. At these community events, discover eclectic goods such as glass beads, ceramic tiles, bird houses, specialty cheeses, and local organic produce.

Saltspring Island

The largest of the southern Gulf Islands, Saltspring (also known as Salt Spring) is named for its salty north-end mineral springs. The island is 27 kilometres (17 miles) long and has 10,000 winter residents. The number triples in the summer months.

The commercial centre of the island is the village of Ganges, easily explored on foot. Visitors spend leisurely afternoons browsing the many galleries, craft stores, and studios lining the main streets. Before leaving, stroll the Ganges seawalk to enjoy the views of the chain of small islands in the harbour and the yachts at anchor.

Drumbeg Provincial Park, Gabriola

If you prefer a hike, head to Baynes Peak at Mount Maxwell Provincial Park. From the summit, the views of the entire Pacific Northwest are exquisite.

Pender Island

After a 40-minute ferry ride from Vancouver Island's Swartz Bay, you'll arrive at Otter Bay on Pender Island. Pender is actually two islands, appropriately named North and South, with a connecting one-lane bridge. The two islands combined are about 34 kilometres (21 miles) long.

On the south island, a hike up Mount Norman rewards the hearty with spectacular views of the southern region from the highest point on "the Penders." Beaumont Marine Park has sandy beaches as well as provisions for boaters. On the north island, Roesland's 230 seaside hectares (568 acres) offers views of sunsets, harbour seals, and eagles. The original Roe family home, built in 1908, is now a museum detailing early life on the island. Prior Centennial Park is a small, forested spot for campers. Near Magic Lake is the Golf Island Disc Park, a popular 27-hole wooded course for disc golf players from as far away as California; all ages can join in. Craft stores, artist galleries, restaurants, and pubs are plentiful.

Rocky shore of Galiano Island

Galiano Island

With its shoreline ranging from high bluffs to sandy beaches, many consider Galiano the most scenic of the Gulf Islands. Nearly as long as Saltspring Island, Galiano is less than 9 kilometres (5 miles) at its widest, but boasts seven parks. Montague Harbour Provincial Marine Park features marine life and a lagoon that can be explored by an easy trail system. Birdwatchers delight in more than 120 species. At Sturdies Bay, on the south end, the Cabra Gallery Museum is dedicated to local artists and history, including the Spanish captain who gave the island its name.

Mayne Island

Mayne Island

Some 150 years ago Mayne Island was the stopping point for miners en route to B.C.'s goldfields. Its historical past attracts many visitors. Miners Bay, with its century-old buildings, is the commercial hub. Here, too, is the Springwater Lodge, one of the province's oldest hotels. There's the Plumper Pass Museum, and it's possible you might catch sight of a whale from Lighthouse Park on Georgina Point. A hike to the end of Campbell Bay offers expansive views of Mt. Baker in Washington State. On the east side of the island, discover one of the Gulf Islands' finest beaches at Bennett Bay. When heading to the ferry terminal, you may want to end your trip with a stroll through the magnificent Japanese garden at Dinner Bay Park.

Saturna Island

One of the more remote of the Gulf Islands, Saturna offers an appreciated tranquility. Wildlife and more than 180 species of birds add a pleasant dimension. Cycling and paddling past galleries of natural sandstone sculptures are popular. With 320 permanent residents, Saturna is the least populated of the Gulf Islands, as most of the land is protected within a National Park Reserve. East Point Park has a swimming beach ideally situated to view orcas, while Winter Cove features a tidal marsh popular among birdwatchers. On Canada's birthday, July 1, the entire island welcomes the world to the annual Saturna Lamb Barbecue.

Gabriola Island

Gabriola is an easy place to visit for a daytrip or overnight stay. The narrow island is 9 kilometres (5.5 miles) long. Although small, Gabriola offers a variety of places to stay, eat, and shop, as well as several provincial parks with picnic facilities, hiking trails, and beautiful views. The island community runs the Gabriola Museum, a compact spot with a historical collection that offers a glimpse of pioneer life. At Sands Provincial Park, the Malaspina Galleries is a series of outstanding natural limestone formations carved by the surf.

Vivid starfish on Gabriola Island

Sunshine Coast

Heather Conn

Amidst misty fiords, a gorgeous harbour, and a coastline savoured by cottagers, you'll find the town of Gibsons, which, with its high-facade restaurant Molly's Reach and surrounding Pacific waters, once formed the backdrop for Canada's longest-running TV drama series, *The Beachcombers*. This popular show ran from 1972 to 1990.

Sechelt from the air

Gibsons serves as the gateway to the Sunshine Coast, a spectacular recreational area on the mainland north of Greater Vancouver. It's accessible by way of a picturesque 40-minute ferry ride from Horseshoe Bay to nearby Langdale, followed by a 2-kilometre (1.2-mile) drive from the dock. Return fare is free with your ticket over.

The Sunshine Coast — it does indeed enjoy more yearly sun than Vancouver — makes a highly recommended day-trip at any time of year, along Highway 101, which winds past numerous seaside communities, including Roberts Creek and Sechelt. But you may find that you want to stay longer, to see it all. In winter months, take in stunning views from the uncrowded cross-country trails at Dakota Ridge, accessed from Field Road in Wilson Creek.

Downtown Gibsons

For summer visitors, the Sunshine Coast hosts many expansive beaches like Bonniebrook and Davis Bay, along with excellent hiking day-trails. Fishing, diving, canoeing, sailing, and kayaking attract visitors to both the Lower and Upper Sunshine coasts. You can also find a rich array of culture, from festivals of music and fibre arts to performing arts and history. Gibsons' Elphinstone Pioneer Museum honours the region's old-time lifestyles while the Tems Swiya Museum in Sechelt showcases the Shishalh (Sechelt) First Nation's culture, art and artifacts.

If you have a second day to spend, follow the highway up to the rocky shores of Jervis Inlet, and take yet another ferry to Powell River. Proceed to Lund, the northern terminus of the highway and while you're there, try the delightful Nancy's Bakery, a harbourfront gathering spot.

Sechelt and Surrounding Area

A few kilometres past Gibsons is Cliff Gilker Park, with an excellent network of trails adjacent to the challenging 18-hole Sunshine Coast Golf & Country Club. In Roberts Creek, turn left on Roberts Creek Road and drive to the

much-loved "heart of the Creek," a huddle of stores and services at the Lower Road junction. Both the iconic Gumboot Garden Café and the Gumboot Restaurant next door offer live entertainment and indoor/outdoor eating. For a lively evening, join a dance at Roberts Creek Hall near the corner of Roberts Creek Road and Highway 101.

Travelling northwest from "the Creek," you'll cross a series of rivers before arriving in the mid-coast town of Sechelt, a narrow isthmus separating the Strait of Georgia from Sechelt Inlet. Downtown edges along a sandy beach, with Snickett Park forming the western perimeter. Rockwood Lodge, a restored heritage house, hosts the annual Festival of the Written Arts in mid-August. The Sunshine Coast Arts Centre, at the corner of Trail and Medusa, exhibits local and off-coast visual arts. Authors, both from the Coast and across Canada, read from their works here. Note the centre's unusual log construction designed by pioneer builder Clarke Stebner. The front doors feature etched glass panels by local First Nations carver Bradley Hunt.

Farther up the road, Halfmoon Bay's rustic General Store, built in 1938, hails from an earlier time when steamers made daily stops at the pier to drop off mail and pick up passengers. Situated on a beautiful bay, it is reached from Redrooffs Road, which detours off the highway and winds past Sargeant Bay and Coopers Green (a great picnic spot) before meeting the highway a stone's throw from the bay itself. Homesite Road, farther along, features an old-growth forest and great hikes.

The coastline gets progressively rockier toward Secret Cove and finally Pender Harbour, where communities lie clustered in tiny coves linked by secondary roads and the meandering coastline. The Pender Harbour Jazz Festival, held in September, draws top-notch performers. Madeira Park, Garden Bay, and Irvines Landing lie centered around the waters of Pender Harbour itself. The Ruby Lake Resort, en route to Earls Cove, is ideal for boating, fishing, and bird-watching. Check out its wildlife and bird sanctuary and Iris Griffith Interpretive Centre.

If weather permits, take the Egmont turnoff just before Earls Cove and hike to Skookumchuk Rapids, where tidal forces churn placid waters into gigantic eddies and whirlpools. Check the tide table for the best viewing times. Gutsy kayakers can sometimes be seen playing in the frothing current.

Island Alternatives

Foot passengers arriving at the Langdale ferry dock can board the tiny pedestrian-only *Stormaway III* to visit Keats or Gambier islands across Howe Sound. Both offer day-trippers excellent trails, beaches and kayaking routes. Keats Island enjoys a commanding view of the Strait of Georgia. Gambier is home to a wonderful general store with home-baked goodies and a rugged mountain backdrop.

If boating, try to arrive at dusk when the harbours and coves are at their most exquisite. Keats Island has excellent moorage at Plumpers Cove on the northwest side.

Listings: Contents

Getting There

Vancouver

On the brink of the Pacific Ocean, at the foot of the Coast Mountains, Vancouver is well-served by air, land, and sea routes.

By Air

Vancouver International Airport (YVR) is located south of Vancouver, approximately 15 minutes away in Richmond. In 2008, YVR became the first official airport supplier in Olympic Games history. YVR serves 70 airlines including scheduled carriers, charters, code share, and cargo carriers to 110 destinations. General inquiries are taken at 604 207-7077. More information about YVR can be found at www.yvr.ca.

An Airport Improvement Fee (AIF) is levied from passengers departing from Vancouver: $5 when travelling within BC and the Yukon Territory, and $15 when travelling to all other destinations. Children under two and passengers on same-day connecting flights are exempt. The AIF is included in the ticket price.

Available from the airport are buses, rapid transit, shuttles, taxis, and limousines. TransLink, the city's public transit system (604 953-3333, www.translink.ca), provides a connection from the airport into Vancouver and suburbs ($2.50 to $5 depending on distance and time of day). Take the #424 from the airport for the five-minute ride to Airport Station and transfer to the limited-stop #98 B-Line into downtown Vancouver, 30 minutes away. Bus service to major downtown hotels is available via the Airporter ($13.75 one way, $21.50 return; 604 946-8866, 1-800-668-3141). Scheduled bus service is also available to Whistler, Victoria, Nanaimo, and Seattle, US. Rapid transit on the new Canada Line to Richmond and downtown Vancouver is operational as of Labour Day 2009.

Courtesy shuttles are available to many local hotels. Taxis and limousines (Limojet Gold, 604 273-1331) picking up at the airport are regulated by the airport and are on-site 24 hours per day. Black Top and Checker Cabs (604 731-1111), MacLure's Cabs (604 683-6666), Vancouver Taxi (604 871-1111), and Yellow Cab Company (604 681-1111, 1-800-898-8294) are the main taxicab companies. A typical trip downtown would cost $30 by taxi and $80 by limousine. Car rental companies operating from YVR include Avis, Alamo, Budget, Hertz, National, and Thrifty, plus several local enterprises.

By Sea

BC Ferries (1-888-223-3779 from anywhere in North America) offers year-round passenger and vehicle service from Vancouver Island, the Gulf Islands, and many other parts of BC. Vehicle reservations can be made for an additional fee of $17.50. Regular year-round fares (subject to change) are $13.50 adult, $6.75 child 5–11 years, $45 per car. See www.bcferries.com for information on sailing and fares.

By Car

Three major highways connect Greater Vancouver to the rest of British Columbia, Canada, and the United States. Highway 99 connects the north end of the city to Whistler before joining Highway 97, BC's main inland north-south highway. To the south, Highway 99 also connects Vancouver to Washington's Interstate 5 and Seattle. The Trans-Canada Highway (Highway 1) runs into Vancouver through the Lower Mainland and Fraser River Valley from the rest of Canada, where its feeders include Highway 97 and various connectors and highways from the US.

By Bus

Pacific Central Station (1150 Station St.) is Vancouver's bus station. Visitors from many US and Canadian cities can get to Vancouver on Greyhound buses (1-800-661-8747 in Canada, 1-800-231-2122 in the US). Seattle travellers can catch Quick

Shuttle Bus Service (604 940-4428 or 1-800-665-2122, www.quickcoach.com).

By Rail

Pacific Central Station is also the city's train station. VIA Rail (1-888-842-7245, www.viarail.ca) offers Canadian transcontinental service three days a week. Travellers from Seattle may choose Amtrak (1-800-872-7245, www.amtrak.com), which operates one round-trip per day between Seattle and Vancouver.

Victoria

Three main options are available to the traveller:
- fly to Victoria International Airport
- fly to Vancouver, then transfer to a plane or a bus plus a ferry
- fly to Seattle, then transfer to a plane or a ferry

By Air from Vancouver

Thirty-five-minute flights to Victoria from Vancouver are offered by the following:
- Harbour Air Seaplanes (250 384-2215 in Victoria, 604 274-1277 in Vancouver, 1-800-665-0212, www.harbour-air.com). Twin Otter seaplane service from downtown Vancouver and YVR to Victoria's Inner Harbour.
- Helijet International Incorporated (1-800-665-4354 for Vancouver or Victoria reservations, www.helijet.com). Helicopter service from downtown Vancouver or YVR to Victoria's Ogden Point, a five-minute drive from the Inner Harbour.
- West Coast Air (604 606-6888 in Vancouver, 1-800-347-2222, www.westcoastair.com). Float plane service from downtown Vancouver to Victoria's Inner Harbour.
- Air Canada (1-800-247-2262, www.aircanada.com). Flights on small planes from airport to airport.

By Air from Seattle

- Horizon Air (1-800-547-9308, www.horizonair.com). Flights to Victoria International Airport.

- Kenmore Air (425 486-1257 in Seattle, 1-800-543-9595 in the US and Canada). Fifty-five-minute seaplane flights from downtown Seattle (shuttles from Seattle-Tacoma Airport available in summer) to Victoria's Inner Harbour.

The Victoria International Airport is located near Sidney, about 30 minutes from the downtown area. From the airport, the AKAL Victoria International Airporter (250 386-2525) runs to all hotels, motels, and downtown on the half-hour, for $18 one way. Taxis are run by Victoria Taxi (250 383-7111), Yellow Cab (250 381-5577), and Blue Bird Cabs (250 384-1155). Fares are about $55. Cabs are usually waiting at the airport; there is no need to call ahead.

By Sea from Vancouver

BC Ferries (1-888-223-3779, www.bcferries.com) crosses the Strait of Georgia between Vancouver and Victoria. Ferries make the journey from Tsawwassen (Vancouver) to Swartz Bay (Victoria) in approximately 95 minutes. The drive into Victoria is 32 kilometres (20 miles). Board as a walk-on passenger ($13.50) or by car ($45 for car, passengers extra; all fares subject to change). Different rates apply to motorcycles, bicycles, and oversized vehicles. Pacific Coach Lines runs buses directly from YVR and downtown Vancouver onto the ferry and into downtown Victoria. Call 1-800-661-1725, 604 662-8074 (Vancouver), or 250 385-4411 (Victoria), or visit www.pacificcoach.com for rates and more information.

By Sea from Seattle and Port Angeles

- From Pier 69 in Seattle, Victoria Clippers' high-speed catamarans make the trip to Victoria in 2 to 2.5 hours. Rates and information can be found at 1-800-888-2535, 206-448-5000 (Seattle) and 250 382-8100 (Victoria), www.clippervacations.com.

- The Black Ball Ferry Line runs the MV *Coho* as a year-round, daily service between Port Angeles, Washington (360 457-4491), and Victoria (250 386-2202). For schedules, fares and online reservations see www.cohoferry.com.
- The Victoria Express Ferry runs the *Victoria Express* ferries from Port Angeles, Washington to Victoria, and Victoria to San Juan Island from May through September, reservations available. Call 250 361-9144 (Canada), 1-800-633-1589 or 360 452-8088 (US), www.victoriaexpress.com.

By Car

Driving to Victoria from any place off Vancouver Island involves taking a ferry. Allow extra time to make your selected sailing in peak season (reservations are extra). From the Swartz Bay Ferry Terminal (and the Victoria International Airport), take Highway 17 south into the city.

By Bus

Pacific Coach Lines runs buses directly from YVR and downtown Vancouver onto the ferry and into downtown Victoria. Call 1-800-661-1725, 604 662-8074 (Vancouver) or 250 385-4411 (Victoria), or visit www.pacificcoach.com for rates and more information.

Travel Essentials

Money

Canadian cash consists of $1 (loonie) and $2 (toonie) coins, 1-cent, 5-cent, 10-cent and 25-cent coins and differently coloured $5, $10, $20, $50, $100, and $1000 bills. Main branches of Canadian chartered banks can exchange foreign currency, although small local branches may not exchange currency other than US dollars directly. Several foreign banks have offices in Vancouver, and will handle some foreign currencies directly. Banking hours in general are 9:30 a.m. to 4:30 p.m., Monday to Friday, with extended hours and weekends at some branches. Most banks have automatic teller machines posted in locations around the city, accessible 24 hours a day with bank cards on international banking networks such as Cirrus, Plus, and Interac. Currency can also be exchanged at the many commercial money exchange outlets in each city.

Most businesses accept all major credit cards such as American Express, Diners Club, EnRoute, MasterCard, and Visa. Smaller businesses, however, may accept only one or two of these cards. Traveller's cheques can be cashed in major hotels, some restaurants, and large stores.

Passports

To enter Canada, citizens and permanent residents of the United States require a US birth certificate, US passport, or green card. (See also Customs, below, for departing to the US.) Proof of residence, such as a driver's licence, should also be carried. However, this is not accepted as proof of citizenship. All other international visitors must have a valid national passport and, in some cases, a visa. Check with the nearest Canadian Consulate or Embassy well in advance of travel.

Customs

Arriving

Travellers entering Canada must declare all goods. Reasonable amounts of personal effects and food are admitted free of duty. Special restrictions or quotas apply to certain specialty goods, especially to plant-, agricultural-, and animal-related materials. Each visitor over the age of 19 may bring into Canada, duty free, a total of 1.1 litres (40 ounces) of liquor and wine, or 8.5 litres (228 ounces or 24 bottles) of beer. Visitors over the age of 19 may also bring up to 50 cigars, 200 cigarettes, 7 ounces (200 grams) of tobacco, and 200 tobacco sticks. Revolvers, pistols, and fully automatic firearms are not allowed into Canada. All other weapons (such as hunting rifles and shotguns) must be declared. For more information contact:

Canada Customs – Pacific Region
Third Floor, 333 Dunsmuir Street
Vancouver, BC
V6B 5R4 Canada
Fax: 604 666-3144
1-800-461-9999 – automated in Canada
Outside Canada: 204 983-3500
8 a.m.to 4:15 p.m., Monday to Friday
Visit Canada Border Services Agency at www.cbsa.gc.ca.

Departing

Before visiting BC, contact a US Customs office, where copies of the US customs information brochure "Know Before You Go" are available, to find out customs rules for entering or re-entering the United States. Note new requirements to travel to the US under Western Hemisphere Travel Initiative (WHTI) are in effect June 2009. Visit the US Department of Homeland Security website, www.DHS.gov. Visitors from other countries should check their own customs regulations before leaving home as well.

Taxes

The Federal Goods and Services Tax (GST) of 5% is applied to most goods and services whether the buyer is a resident of Canada or a visitor. The previous Visitors Rebate Program was terminated in 2007. The new Foreign Convention Incentive and Tour Incentive Programs may be applicable to groups but are not available to individuals. For more information or assistance, call 902 432-5604 (outside Canada) or 1-800-565-9353 (within Canada) or visit www.cra.gc.ca/visitors.

A non-refundable provincial sales tax (PST) of 7% applies to all retail purchases except liquor, which is taxed at 10%.

Getting Acquainted

Time Zone

Vancouver and Victoria are in the Pacific Standard Time Zone.

Climate

These are the average high and low temperatures in Vancouver (source Environment Canada):

January	5.7°C to 0.1°C
	42°F to 32°F
February	8.0°C to 1.4°C
	46°F to 34°F
March	9.9°C to 2.6°C
	50°F to 37°F
April	12.7°C to 4.9°C
	55°F to 41°F
May	16.3°C to 7.9°C
	61°F to 46°F
June	19.3°C to 11.0°C
	67°F to 52°F
July	21.7°C to 12.7°C
	91°F to 55°F
August	21.7°C to 12.9°C
	71°F to 55°F
September	18.4°C to 10.1°C
	65°F to 50°F
October	13.5°C to 6.4°C
	56°F to 44°F
November	9.0°C to 3.0°C
	48°F to 37°F
December	6.1°C to 0.8°C
	43°F to 33°F

Average temperatures are:
12.0°C (54°F) in spring
16.3°C (61°F) in summer
6.5°C (44°F) in fall
4.7°C (40°F) in winter

Average annual rainfall:
1117.2 mm (44.0 inches)

Average annual snowfall:
54.9 cm (21.6 inches)

The average high and low temperatures in Victoria, near the water, are as follows (source Environment Canada, based on data from 1967 to 1990).

January	6.7°C to 1.6°C
	44°F to 35°

February   8.4°C to 2.4°C
            47°F to 36°F
March   10.1°C to 3.0°C
            50°F to 37°F
April   11.9°C to 4.3°C
            53°F to 40°F
May   14.2°C to 6.7°C
            58°F to 44°F
June   16.4°C to 8.8°C
            62°F to 48°F
July   18.2°C to 9.9°C
            65°F to 50°F
August   18.6°C to 10.1°C
            65°F to 50°F
September   17.1°C to 8.8°C
            63°F to 48°F
October   13.1°C to 6.2°C
            56°F to 43°F
November   9.3°C to 3.8°C
            49°F to 39°F
December   6.9°C to 2.0°C
            44°F to 36°F

Average temperatures are:
10.4°C (51°F) in spring
14.0°C (57°F) in summer
6.9°C (44°F) in fall
5.4°C (42°F) in winter

Average annual rainfall:
1197.7 mm (47.2 inches)

Average annual snowfall:
29.3 cm (11.5 inches)

Guides and Information Services

BC has established a Visitor's Info Network with Visitor Info Centres in many communities to assist travellers throughout the province. Tourism BC's official website can be found at www.hellobc.com. Visitors can call 1-800-435-5622 in North America, 604 435-5622 in Vancouver and 250 387-1642 internationally, for reservations and assistance with accommodations and other travel plans.

Vancouver
• Tourism Vancouver Visitors' Centre, Plaza Level, 200 Burrard St., Vancouver, BC V6C 3L6, 604 683-2000, fax 604 682-6839, www.tourismvancouver.com. Source for current information on the Greater Vancouver area, guides and maps. Visitors can make reservations for many accommodations, sightseeing, transportation, and outdoor adventures.

Victoria
• Tourism Victoria Visitor Centre, 812 Wharf St., Victoria, BC V8W 1T3, 250 953-2033, 1-800-663-3883, fax 250 382-6539, www.tourismvictoria.com. Source for current information on Victoria area, with guides, maps, and other travel services.
• Tourism Vancouver Island, Suite 501–65 Front Street, Nanaimo, BC V9R 5H9, 250 754-3500, fax 250 754-3599, www.hellobc.com/vi. Source for travel guides on Vancouver Island and Gulf Islands.

Getting Around

Public Transit

Vancouver

The TransLink public transit system is a network of buses, SeaBus ferries, and light rapid transit (SkyTrain). Fares for buses, SkyTrain, and SeaBus are the same: travel in one zone costs $2.50 for adults and $1.75 for concession (teenagers, children over five, and seniors), travel in two zones costs $3.75/$2.50, and in three zones, $5/$3.50. Discount fares (single-zone amount for all zones) apply after 6:30 p.m. weekdays and all day weekends and holidays. Day passes cost $9/$7. Faresaver books of 10 tickets ($19/one zone, $28.50/two zones, $38/three zones, $16/concession) are available at many convenience stores. Schedules can be found at the TourismVancouver Visitors' Centre, public libraries, SkyTrain stations, and City Hall.

Buses on most routes run until approximately 1 a.m., with some major routes running until 4 a.m. Drivers carry no change, so bring exact fare. A transfer is given as proof of payment and allows passengers to transfer between buses, SkyTrain, and

SeaBus until the time shown (90 minutes). Blue Buses serve West Vancouver and leave downtown at the corner of Granville and Georgia. The same fares and transfers apply. Call 604 985-7777 or visit www.westvancouver.ca for more information on the Blue Buses.

SkyTrain is an automated rapid-transit line with three lines (Expo Line, Millennium Line, and Canada Line) that run on mostly elevated tracks (underground in some areas) connecting downtown Vancouver with the Vancouver International Airport and the municipalities of Richmond, Burnaby, New Westminster, and Surrey. SkyTrain's newest link, Canada Line, is open as of Labour Day 2009. System maps are posted in all train cars, as well as in stations. These operate from downtown from approximately 5 a.m. to 1:15 a.m., Monday through Saturday and on Sunday to approximately 12:15 a.m. Tickets can be purchased or validated at machines in each station. SkyTrain carries bikes all hours except 7 to 9 a.m. Westbound, 4 to 6 p.m. Eastbound, and in North/South counterflow direction during peak hours for Canada Line.

SeaBus carries passengers (and bikes) only from approximately 6 a.m. to 1:20 a.m. Leaving Waterfront Station every 15 minutes (30 minutes in evenings), the ferry crosses Burrard Inlet and arrives 12 minutes later at Lonsdale Quay in North Vancouver. Connects to extensive network of North Shore buses.

Most buses (except for trolleys) are wheelchair lift–equipped or have low floors for easy access. SkyTrains, SeaBuses, and SeaBus terminals are wheelchair-accessible. All SkyTrain stations have elevators.

For route and schedule information, call TransLink at 604 953-3333, or visit www.translink.ca.

Victoria

The Victoria Regional Transit System has a single fare throughout the Greater Victoria region, Sooke to Sidney. Adult fares are $2.25 and concession fares for seniors, children over five years of age, and students are $1.40. Exact change must be given on buses. Transfers are proof of payment and permit passenger use of buses for up to 60 minutes. Sheets of 10 tickets may be purchased in advance from many stores. Day passes are also available.

The majority of the Victoria Regional Transit System buses are wheelchair-accessible with low-floor buses. For route and schedule information, call the 24-hour information line at 250 382-6161 or visit the website at www.bctransit.com.

Cars and Rentals

Most foreign drivers' licences are valid in British Columbia. Check with a BC Motor Vehicle Branch to find out specific requirements. Visiting motorists should bring registration documents and have insurance in place before driving. Insurance is available as an option in most car rental contracts, and Visitor to Canada Insurance can be purchased through the British Columbia Automobile Association (BCAA). United States motorists should have a Canadian Non-Resident Interprovince Motor Vehicle Liability Insurance Card, available only in the US For more information or to obtain a copy of BC's "rules of the road," contact Driver Services Centre, 221–1055 West Georgia St., Vancouver, BC, 604 661-2255, 1-800-950-1498 (within North America), www.icbc.com.

Speed limits within Vancouver and Victoria are 50 km/h (30 mph) unless otherwise posted. The use of seat belts, child restraints, and motorcycle helmets is mandatory. Vancouverites and Victoria residents believe in the pedestrian's right of way.

Distances, speed limits, and fuel measurements are indicated in metric units. To convert kilometres to miles, multiply by 0.6; to convert miles to kilometres, multiply by 1.6. One litre equals about 1/4 of an American gallon or 1/5 of an Imperial gallon.

Vancouver

- Avis, 757 Hornby St., 604 606-2869, Vancouver International Airport, 604 606-2847, 1-800-879-2847, www.avis.com.
- Budget Rent A Car, 416 West Georgia St., 604 668-7000, 1-800-268-8900, Vancouver International Airport, 604 713-3102, 1-800-268-8900, www.bc.budget.com.
- Hertz, 1270 Granville St., 604 606-4711, 1-800-263-0600, Vancouver International Airport, 604 606-3782, www.hertz.com.
- National Car Rental — Downtown, 1185 West Georgia St., 604 609-7150, Vancouver International Airport, 604 207-3730, 1-800-227-7368, www.nationalcar.com.

Victoria

- Avis, 1001 Douglas St., 250 386-8468, Victoria International Airport, 250 656-6033, 1-800-879-2847, www.avis.com.
- Budget Rent A Car, 757 Douglas St., 250 953-5300, 1-800-268-8900, Victoria International Airport, 250 953-5300, 1-800-268-8900, www.budget.com.
- Hertz, 2353 Douglas St., 250 360-2822, Victoria International Airport, 250 656-2312, 1-800-263-0600, www.hertz.com.
  Check the Yellow Pages for more listings under Automobile renting.

Tours

Vancouver

- AAA Horse and Carriage (Stanley Park horse-drawn tours). One-hour narrated, horse-drawn carriages from mid-March through October, Stanley Park, 604 681-5115, www.stanleyparktours.com.
- Accent Cruises. Yachts for charter cruises and special occasions. 100–1676 Duranleau St., 604 688-6625, www.dinnercruises.com.
- Gastown Business Improvement Society. Enquiries for walking tours of Gastown. 145–332 Water St., 604 683-5650, www.gastown.org.

- Harbour Cruises. Sunset dinner cruises, harbour tours, luncheon cruises, day trips. North foot of Denman St., 604 688-7246, 1-800-663-1500, www.boatcruises.com.
- Vancouver Trolley Company. A loop of 16 attractions (30 stops) in Vancouver with Hop-on/Hop-off privileges, pickups every 15 minutes. 875 Terminal Ave., 604 801-5515, 1-888-451-5581, www.vancouvertrolley.com.
- Walkabout Historic Vancouver. Walking tours of historic neighbourhoods. 604 720-0006.
- West Coast City and Nature Sightseeing. Tours of Vancouver, Grouse Mountain, Whistler, and Victoria in mini-coaches. 3945 Myrtle St., Burnaby, 604 451-1600, 1-877-451-1777, www.vancouversightseeing.com.

Victoria

- Gray Line of Victoria. Popular sightseeing tours include city tours, Butchart Gardens, and Whale Watching. Ticket kiosk in front of Fairmont Empress Hotel, 250 388-6539, 1-800-663-8390, www.graylinewest.com.
- Kabuki Kabs. Pedicabs with friendly and knowledgeable drivers. Generally downtown tours, but some operators have specialized tours. 526 Discovery St., 250 385-4243, www.kabukikabs.com.
- Tally-Ho Carriage Tours. Private, single horse-drawn carriage tours. 7450 Veyaness Rd., Saanich, 250-514-9257, 1-866-383-5067, www.tallyhotours.com.
- Victoria Bobby Walking Adventures. One-and-a-quarter hours of talk and touring of old-town Victoria. 414–874 Fleming St., 250 995-0233, www.walkvictoria.com.
- Victoria Harbour Ferry. Full tours of the Gorge and Inner Harbour, evening cruises, or short hops. Board at any one of 10 stops on the Inner Harbour, 250 708-0201, www.victoriaharbourferry.com.

Accommodation

In Vancouver and Victoria, a multitude of lodgings have evolved, both to accommodate the varied tastes of world travellers and to showcase the allure of the West Coast. The major and minor hotels and motels, most located in the downtown areas, put the traveller in each city's heart, while a host of charming bed and breakfasts beckon from quieter residential streets.

What follows is a cross-section of the hotels, bed and breakfasts, and budget establishments to be found in each city. Maps are provided at the beginning of this book. Prices indicated are approximate, based on the costs (excluding taxes) quoted at the time of publishing, for two people staying in a double room during peak season: $ = $50–90, $$ = $90–180, $$$ = above $180. Except for campgrounds and houseboats, rates quoted are subject to an 8% provincial hotel and motel room tax. Where approved, an additional 2% tourism tax is levied by the local municipal government. GST (5%) is also applied. Many establishments offer special Internet rates and online reservation services. HELLO BC (1-800-435-5622, www.hellobc.com) is a free service providing access to over 700 Tourism BC–approved lodgings and trip planning services.

Vancouver

Hotels: Vancouver International Airport

Most of Vancouver's hotels are within a short drive of the airport. The following, however, are considered the closest:

- Accent Inns, 10551 St. Edwards Dr., Richmond, BC V6X 3L8, 604 273-3311, fax 604 273-9522, www.accentinns.com. Well kept and comfortable. Exterior corridors, restaurant. Welcomes small pets. $$.
- Best Western Abercorn Inn, 9260 Bridgeport Rd., Richmond, BC V6X 1S1, 604 270-7576, 1-800-663-0085, fax 604 270-0001, www.abercorn-inn.com. Styled as a Scottish country inn, with antiques and fresh flowers. Spacious rooms, restaurant. Continental breakfast included. $$.
- Delta Vancouver Airport Hotel, 3500 Cessna Dr., Richmond, BC V7B 1C7, 604 278-1241, 1-800-268-1133, fax 604 276-1975, www.deltavancouverairport.com. Older hotel on nine landscaped acres overlooking the Fraser River. Heated pool. Welcomes small pets ($35). $$.
- Fairmont Vancouver Airport, 3111 Grant McConachie Way, Richmond, BC V7B 1X9, 604 207-5200, www.fairmont.com/vancouverairport. World-class hotel brings sophistication to the concept of airport accommodation. Rated as #1 Fairmont in the world in 2007. Globe@YVR Restaurant, Jetside Lounge, pool, fitness centre. Offers in-hotel airline check-in service. Welcomes pets. $$–$$$.
- Four Points by Sheraton Vancouver Airport, 8368 Alexandra Rd., Richmond, BC V6X 4A6, 604 214-0888, 1-888-281-8888, fax 604 214-0887, www.fourpoints.com/vancouver. Modern hotel in Richmond's shopping and entertainment district. Restaurant, lounge. $$.
- Hilton Vancouver Airport, 5911 Minoru Blvd., Richmond, BC V6X 4C7, 604 273-6336, 1-800-445-8667, fax 604 273-6337, www.vancouverairport.hilton.com. Restaurant, lounge, pool, fitness centre, tennis courts. $$.
- Holiday Inn Vancouver Airport, 10720 Cambie Rd., Richmond, BC V6X 1K8, 604 821-1818, fax 604 821-1819, www.hi-airport.bc.ca. Kid-friendly rooms include bunkbeds, video games. $$.
- Radisson Vancouver Airport Hotel and Suites, 8181 Cambie Rd., Richmond, BC V6X 3X9, 604 276-8181, 1-800-333-3333, fax 604 279-8381, www.radisson.com/vancouverca.

Home to Western-style and Chinese seafood restaurants. Heated pool, whirlpool. $$$.

Hotels: Downtown Vancouver

In downtown Vancouver, over 10,000 rooms, from budget hostels to luxury hotels, can be found amid a myriad of shops, restaurants, and a bustling business district:

- Best Western Downtown Vancouver, 718 Drake St., Vancouver, BC V6Z 2W6, 604 669-9888, 1-888-669-9888, fax 604 669-3440, www.bestwesterndowntown.com. Great views. Rooftop fitness centre, sauna, Jacuzzi. Complimentary downtown shuttle. $$$.
- Century Plaza Hotel & Spa, 1015 Burrard St., Vancouver, BC V6Z 1Y5, 604 687-0575, 1-800-663-1818, fax 604 682-5790, www.century-plaza.com. Oversized suites with panoramic, mountain, and city views. Day spa, steam room, pool. Beyond Restaurant, Beyond Café. Totally renovated, family-run. $$–$$$.
- Days Inn Vancouver Downtown, 921 West Pender St., Vancouver, BC V6C 1M2, 604 681-4335, 1-877-681-4335, fax 604 681-7808, www.daysinnvancouver.com. 1914 English-style heritage building, renovated 1998. Views restricted by neighbouring buildings. Restaurant, lounge. $$.
- Fairmont Hotel Vancouver, 900 West Georgia St., Vancouver, BC V6C 2W6, 604 684-3131, 1-800-411-1414, fax 604 662-1929, www.fairmont.com/hotelvancouver. Heritage landmark that is home to the renowned restaurant Griffin's. Beautiful guestrooms and suites. Indoor pool, healthclub, spa, business centre. $$$.
- Fairmont Waterfront, 900 Canada Place Way, Vancouver, BC V6C 3L5, 604 691-1991, fax 604 691-1999, www.fairmont.com. Waterfrontage, terraced gardens. Enclosed walkway links hotel to Vancouver Convention and Exhibition Centre and cruise ship terminal. Heated pool. Welcomes dogs. $$$.
- Four Seasons Hotel Vancouver, 791 West Georgia St., Vancouver, BC V6C 2T4, 604 689-9333, 1-800-268-6282 (Can.), 1-800-332-3442 (US), fax 604 684-4555, www.fourseasons.com/vancouver. Entrance off Howe St. Luxurious hotel atop the shops of Pacific Centre. $$$.
- Georgian Court Hotel, 773 Beatty St., Vancouver, BC V6B 2M4, 604 682-5555, 1-800-663-1155, fax 604 682-8830, www.georgiancourt. com. Intimate, European-style hotel, well-known William Tell Dining Room. Deluxe guestrooms and suites. Welcomes small pets. $$$.
- Hampton Inn & Suites — Vancouver Downtown, 111 Robson St., Vancouver, BC V6B 2A8, 604 602-1008, 1-877-602-1008, fax 604 602-1007, www.hamptoninnvancouver.com. West Coast–themed hotel. Breakfast buffet, daily newspaper, local calls, rooftop exercise facilities. $$$.
- Holiday Inn Hotel & Suites Vancouver Downtown, 1110 Howe St., Vancouver, BC V6Z 1R2, 604 684-2151, 1-800-663-9151, fax 604 684-4736, www.hivancouverdowntown.com. Offers some suites with extra-long beds. 24-hr. fitness centre, pool, and sauna. $$$.
- Hyatt Regency Vancouver, 655 Burrard St., Vancouver, BC V6C 2R7, 604 683-1234, 1-800-233-1234, fax 604 639-4829, www.vancouver.hyatt.com. Luxury tower connected to Royal Centre plaza. Restaurant, kosher kitchen, coffee bar, and two lounges; health club, outdoor pool. Multilingual staff. $$$.
- Listel Vancouver, 1300 Robson St., Vancouver, BC V6E 1C5, 604 684-8461, 1-800-663-5491, fax 604 684-7092, www.thelistel hotel.com. Features two Gallery floors showcasing original work by regional and international artists.

Restaurant and bar with live jazz nightly. $$$.

- Metropolitan Hotel, 645 Howe St., Vancouver, BC V6C 2Y9, 604 687-1122, fax 604 643-7267, www.metropolitan.com. Sumptuous surroundings, full-service rooms. Hosts elegant Diva at the Met Restaurant. Sports court. Welcomes pets. $$$.
- Opus Hotel, 322 Davie St., Vancouver, BC V6B 5Z6, 604 642-6787, 1-866-642-6787, fax 604 642-6780, www.opushotel.com. Modern, stylish hotel with French brasserie Elixir and eclectic Opus Bar. $$$.
- Pacific Palisades Hotel, 1277 Robson St., Vancouver, BC V6E 1C4, 604 688-0461, fax 604 688-4374, www.pacificpalisadeshotel.com. All-suite hotel. Kitchens in some suites, health club with pool, steam room. Welcomes small pets. $$$.
- Pan Pacific Hotel Vancouver, 300–999 Canada Place Way, Vancouver, BC V6C 3B5, 604 662-8111, 1-800-663-1515, fax 604 685-8690, www.panpacific.com. One of the city's best luxury hotels. Part of a complex shared by the cruise ship terminal, the convention centre, and the celebrated Five Sails Restaurant. Health club, harbour and mountain views, full service. Welcomes small pets. $$$.
- Quality Hotel Downtown, 1335 Howe St., Vancouver, BC V6Z 1R7, 604 682-0229, 1-800-663-8474, fax 604 662-7566, www.qualityhotel.ca. Santa Fe atmosphere. Heated outdoor pool, complimentary access to nearby fitness centre. Offers excellent "passport" featuring 50% savings at 35 Vancouver attractions, restaurants, and entertainment. $$–$$$.
- Renaissance Vancouver Hotel Harbourside, 1133 West Hastings St., Vancouver, BC V6E 3T3, 604 689-9211, 1-800-468-3571, fax 604 689-4358, www.renaissancevancouver.com.

Guestrooms and suites with harbour and city views. Restaurant, heated pool, conference space, pet-friendly. $$$.
- St. Regis Hotel, 602 Dunsmuir St., Vancouver, BC V6B 1Y6, 604 681-1135, 1-800-770-7929, fax 604 683-1126, www.stregishotel.com. A boutique-style hotel. Steakhouse, bar and grill, breakfast lounge. $$.
- Sheraton Vancouver Wall Centre Hotel, 1088 Burrard St., Vancouver, BC V6Z 2R9, 604 331-1000, fax 604 893-7200, www.sheratonvancouver.com. Luxurious guestrooms and suites, first-class service. $$$.
- Sutton Place Hotel, 845 Burrard St., Vancouver, BC V6Z 2K6, 604 682-5511, 1-800-961-7555, fax 604 642-2928, www.sutton place.com. Attentive staff, understated elegance. Home to award-winning Fleuri Restaurant. $$$.
- Sylvia Hotel, 1154 Gilford St., Vancouver, BC V6G 2P6, 604 681-9321, fax 604 682-3551, www.sylviahotel.com. A charming, ivy-covered heritage building immortalized by the children's book Mister Got To Go. Welcomes pets. $$.
- Wedgewood Hotel, 845 Hornby St., Vancouver, BC V6Z 1V1, 604 689-7777, 1-800-663-0666, fax 604 608-5348, www.wedgewoodhotel.com. Intimate and stylish European boutique hotel. Attentive staff, award-winning Bacchus Restaurant. Afternoon tea, weekends only, lounge. $$$.
- Westin Bayshore Resort & Marina Vancouver, 1601 Bayshore Dr., Vancouver, BC V6G 2V4, 604 682-3377, 1-800-228-3000, fax 604 687-3102, www.westin.com/bayshore. Luxury in a waterfront setting. Two restaurants, two lounges, whirlpool, masseur, pools, some environmentally friendly rooms. Welcomes small dogs. $$$.

Accommodation: Vancouver

- YWCA Hotel, 733 Beatty St., Vancouver, BC V6B 2M4, 604 895-5830, 1-800-663-1424, fax 604 681-2550, www.ywcahotel.com. Built in 1995 for women and men. Air-conditioning, private, shared or hall bathrooms, shared kitchen, laundry room. Complimentary access to off-site YWCA Health and Wellness Centre with pool, steam room, whirlpool, gym, fitness and aquatics drop-in classes. $–$$.

Bed and Breakfasts

Bedding down in one of Vancouver's bed and breakfasts gives travellers a glimpse of the enviable, everyday lifestyle of the West Coast.

Vancouver B&Bs include:

- Anthem House/O Canada House, 1114 Barclay St., Vancouver, BC V6E 1H1, 604 688-0555, 1-877-688-1114, fax 604 488-0556, www.ocanadahouse.com. Six rooms in a beautifully restored 1897 home, where the national anthem O Canada was written in 1909. Fans, designated smoking area, breakfast. $$–$$$.
- West End Guest House, 1362 Haro St., Vancouver, BC V6E 1G2, 604 681-2889, fax 604 688-8812, www.westendguesthouse.com. Seven period rooms in a pink Victorian-era home. Resident ghost, designated smoking areas, breakfast plan. $$–$$$.
- Windsor House, 325 West 11th Ave., Vancouver, BC V5Y 1T3, 604 872-3060, 1-888-872-3060, fax 604 873-1147. Ten rooms, simple decor. Outside designated smoking area, breakfast plan. $–$$.

Hostels and Educational Residences

Hostels offer spartan but economical alternatives for accommodation. In the summer, a few educational institutes open their residences to travellers as well.

- C & N Backpackers Hostel, 927 Main St. and 1038 Main St., Vancouver, BC V6A 2V8 and V6A 2W1, 604 682-2441 and 604 681-9118, 1-888-434-6060, fax 604 682-2441 and 604 681-9118, www.cnnbackpackers.com. A 1926 heritage building with renovated interior near public transit. Staff speak many languages. Fully equipped kitchen, several showers per floor, laundry facility. Internet, guest phones, fax. $.
- Cambie International Hostel, 300 Cambie St., Vancouver, BC V6B 2N3, 604 684-6466, fax 604 687-5618, www.thecambie.com. Gastown hostel features a pub, general store, and bakery/café. Full laundry, bike storage, email, and wireless Internet. $.
- Cambie International Hostel, 515 Seymour St., Vancouver, BC V6B 2H6, 604 684-7757, fax 604 687-5618, www.thecambie.com. Downtown location. Full laundry, bike storage, email, and Internet (wireless and kiosks). $.
- Hostelling International — Vancouver Central, 1025 Granville St., Vancouver, BC V6Z 1L4, 604 685-5335, 1-888-203-8333, fax 604 685-5351, www.hihostels.ca. Renovated hostel offering private and dormitory rooms. Popular pub The Royal on-site. $.
- Hostelling International — Vancouver Downtown, 1114 Burnaby St., Vancouver, BC V6E 1P1, 604 684-4565, 1-888-203-4302, fax 604 684-4540, www.hihostels.ca. Shared and private rooms with fully equipped kitchen. Internet (wireless and kiosks), TV room, game room, and organized activities. Library/reading room, laundry room, bike rental/storage, limited parking. $.
- Hostelling International — Vancouver Jericho Beach, 1515 Discovery St., Vancouver, BC V6R 4K5, 604 224-3208, 1-888-203-4303, fax 604 224-4852, www.hihostels.ca. Shared and private rooms with fully equipped kitchen. Internet (wireless and kiosks), laundry, licensed cafeteria. $.

Victoria

Hotels: Victoria International Airport

Because the Victoria International Airport is located on the Saanich Peninsula away from the city, Victoria itself has no "airport hotels." However, the towns bordering the airport extend a number of lodgings to serve travellers too tired to make the 30-minute drive to the core of Victoria:

- Victoria Airport Super 8, 2477 Mt. Newton X Road, Saanichton, BC V8M 2B7, 250 652-6888, 1-800-800-8000, fax 250 652-6800, www.super8.com. Modern comfort, economically styled. Welcomes pets. $$.
- Victoria Airport Travelodge, 2280 Beacon Ave., Sidney, BC V8L 1X1, 250 656-1176, 1-866-656-1176, fax 250 656-7344, www.airporttravelodge.com. Older but remodelled digs. Courtyard, heated outdoor pool. Welcomes small pets. $$.

Hotels: Downtown Victoria and Inner Harbour

Victoria's downtown and Inner Harbour hotels perfectly situate the traveller in the thick of the city's attractions:

- Admiral Inn, 257 Belleville St., Victoria, BC V8V 1X1, 250 388-6267, 1-888-823-6472, fax 250 388-6267, www.admiral.bc.ca. Well-equipped rooms and suites in a harbourside hotel-class accommodation. Complimentary local calls, parking, continental breakfast, and coffee. English and French-speaking staff. Welcomes pets. $$–$$$.
- Best Western Carlton Plaza, 642 Johnson St., Victoria V8W 1M6, 250 388-5513, 1-800-663-7241, fax 250 388-5343, www.bestwestern carltonplazahotel.com. Refurbishing has made for bright and spacious rooms. Air conditioning, De Dutch Pannekoek Restaurant. $$–$$$.
- Best Western Inner Harbour, 412 Quebec St., Victoria, BC V8V 1W5, 250 384-5122, 1-888-383-2378, fax 250 384-5113, www.victoriabestwestern.com. Spacious, renovated rooms, all with private balconies. Jacuzzi, sauna, heated seasonal outdoor pool. $$–$$$.
- Coast Victoria Harbourside Hotel and Marina, 146 Kingston St., Victoria, BC V8V 1V4, 250 360-1211, 1-800-663-1144, fax 250 360-1418, www.coasthotels.com. Waterfront with indoor/outdoor pools, health club. Award-winning Blue Crab Bar and Grill, lounge. $$$.
- Days Inn on the Harbour, 427 Belleville St., Victoria, BC V8V 1X3, 250 386-3451, 1-800-665-3024, fax 250 386-6999, www.daysinnvictoria.com. Restaurant, lounge, heated pool, whirlpool. $$–$$$.
- Delta Victoria Ocean Pointe Resort and Spa, 45 Songhees Road, Victoria, BC V9A 6T3, 250 360-2999, 1-800-667-4677, fax 250 360-1041, www.deltavictoria.com. Casually elegant with heated pool, sauna, whirlpool, racquetball and tennis courts, European spa. Home to The Lure Seafood Restaurant and Bar. Welcomes small pets. $$–$$$.
- Fairmont Empress Hotel, 721 Government St., Victoria, BC V8W 1W5, 250 384-8111, 1-866-540-4452, fax 250 389-2747, www.fairmont.com/empress. Elegance and service in a restored heritage setting as regal as the name implies. The Empress Room Restaurant and Bengal Lounge, world-famous Afternoon Tea. Fitness facilities. $$–$$$.
- Hotel Grand Pacific, 463 Belleville St., Victoria, BC V8V 1X3, 250 386-0450, 1-800-663-7550, fax 250 380-4475, www.hotelgrandpacific.com. Rooms all have private balconies, air conditioning. Pool, whirlpool, sauna, workout facilities, squash and racquetball courts. Chinese, English, French, German, Spanish, Punjabi spoken. $$$.

Accommodation: Victoria

- Inn at Laurel Point, 680 Montreal St., Victoria, BC V8V 1Z8, 250 386-8721, 1-800-663-7667, fax 250 386-9547, www.laurelpoint.com. Resort-style downtown hotel with indoor pool and fitness facility. Free local calls. Aura Restaurant, lounge, business centre. English, French, and Japanese spoken. $$$.
- Quality Inn Downtown, 850 Blanshard St., Victoria, BC V8W 2H2, 250 385-6787, 1-800-661-4115, fax 250 385-5800, www.victoriaqualityinn.com. Convenient, large rooms, small indoor pool, steam and fitness rooms. Smith's English-style Pub, Green Room Restaurant. $$.
- Queen Victoria Hotel & Suites, 655 Douglas St., Victoria, BC V8V 2P9, 250 386-1312, 1-800-663-7007, fax 250 381-4312, www.qvhotel.com. Pool, sauna, Samuel's by the Park Restaurant. $$–$$$.
- Ramada Huntingdon Manor, 330 Quebec St., Victoria, BC V8V 1W3, 250 381-3456, 1-800-663-7557, fax 250 382-7666, www.bellevillepark.com. Full-service hotel with English-style interiors. Sauna, whirlpool, aromatherapy. Hunter's Club Restaurant, bar and grill, ice-cream parlour. Home to Artisans Lane. $$–$$$.
- Swans Suite Hotel, 506 Pandora St., Victoria, BC V8W 1N6, 250 361-3310, 1-800-668-7926, fax 250 361-3491, www.swanshotel.com. Restored heritage building with art collection in Olde Towne. On-site brew pub, Wild Saffron Bistro, club, beer and wine store. $$.
- Victoria Plaza Hotel, 603 Pandora Ave., Victoria, BC V8W 1N8, 250 386-3631, 1-800-906-4433, fax 250 386-9452. Modern and clean rooms with fine service. $.

Bed and Breakfasts

More than any other, the bed-and-breakfast experience evokes the graciousness and hospitality of a bygone era.The following are but a few of the many bed and breakfasts that dot the Victoria area:

- Abigail's Hotel, 906 McClure St., Victoria, BC V8V 3E7, 250 388-5363, 1-800-561-6565, fax 250 388-7787, www.abigailshotel.com. Twenty-three rooms on four floors in a Tudor-style country bed and breakfast inn. Antique furniture, no elevator. Breakfast served, hors d'oeuvres in library. Won Best B&B in Victoria for nine years. $$$.
- Beaconsfield Inn, 998 Humboldt St., Victoria, BC V8V 2Z8, 250 384-4044, 1-888-884-4044, fax 250 384-4052, www.beaconsfieldinn.com. Six rooms, three suites in a four-storey 1905 manse. Edwardian atmosphere, beamed ceilings and leaded glass windows. Gourmet breakfast, afternoon tea, cookies, and sherry. No elevator, no pets, no smoking. $$$.
- Gatsby Mansion Boutique Hotel & Restaurant, 309 Belleville St., Victoria, BC V8V 1X2, 250 388-9191, 1-800-563-9656, fax 250 382-7666, www.bellevillepark.com. A collection of 19 suites in Belleville Park in a restored Queen Anne mansion dating back to 1877 and smaller house, with ocean views. Main house has antiques and large verandah. Licensed lounge, restaurant, gift shop. Full breakfast. No smoking, no pets. $$–$$$.
- Heathergate House B&B, 122 Simcoe St., Victoria, BC V8V 1K4, 250 383-0068, 1-888-683-0068, fax 250 383-4320, www.heathergatebb.com. Quiet, elegant, immaculate rooms with private baths as well as a two-bedroom cottage in a delightful garden setting. Full English breakfast served. No smoking, no pets. $$
- Humboldt House Bed and Breakfast, 867 Humboldt St., Victoria, BC V8V 2Z6, 250 383-0152, 1-888-383-0327, fax 250 383-6402, www.humboldthouse.com. Six romantic rooms in authentic Victorian-era house. Large

whirlpool, wood-burning fireplaces. Sherry served in sitting room. Gourmet champagne breakfast delivered to rooms. No smoking. $$$.

- Orchard House Bed and Breakfast, 9646 Sixth St., Sidney, BC V8L 2W2, 250 656-9194, www.orchardhouse.com. Four rooms in a historic house built in 1914 by Sidney founding family. Close to airport and Vancouver ferries. Full breakfast served. Smoking outdoors, no pets. $.

- Rosewood Victoria Inn, 595 Michigan St., Victoria, BC V8V 1S7, 250 384-6644, 1-800-335-3466, fax 250 384-6117, www.rosewoodvictoria.com. Seventeen rooms in a 1930s residence. Relaxed elegance, country antique items, charming library/lounge with open-log fire. No elevator, no pets, no smoking. Breakfast served. $$–$$$.

Hostels and Educational Residences

For the budget-conscious traveller not looking for pampering, hostels are the accommodation of choice:

- Hostelling International Victoria, 516 Yates St., Victoria, BC V8W 1K8, 250 385-4511, 1-888-883-0099, fax 250 385-3232, www.hihostels.ca. Shared and private rooms. Equipment storage, self-service kitchen, laundry room. Hostel-based activities and tours. Games/TV room, Internet (wireless and kiosks). $.

- Ocean Island Backpacker's Inn, 791 Pandora Ave., Victoria, BC V8W 1N9, 250 385-1788, 1-888-888-4180, fax 250 385-1750, www.oceanisland.com. Spacious dorms with kitchen facilities. Licensed café, music room, Internet (wireless and kiosks). $.

Dining

Vancouver and Victoria restaurants take full advantage of their setting,

poised on the edge of an ocean and surrounded by wilderness. Fresh flavours incorporating indigenous ingredients mark each restaurant, as do the creativity of each chef and the diverse origins of the people they serve. Smoking in Vancouver and Victoria restaurants is prohibited by law. Please smoke in designated areas only. Tips are not usually added to a restaurant bill. Tipping a server is standard practice, at the rate of 15% to 20%. The following lists a select number of the multitude of restaurants in each city. Each listing includes the approximate price range for dinner for two, including a bottle of wine (where served), taxes, and gratuity: $ = under $45, $$ = $45–80, $$$ = $80–120, $$$$ = $120–180, $$$$$ = over $180. Keep in mind that many fine restaurants make a wide selection of wines available by the glass as well. Meals served are indicated as: B = breakfast, L = lunch, D = dinner, G = grazing, T-O = take-out, Late = open past midnight. The credit cards accepted by each establishment are also listed: AX = American Express, V = Visa, MC = Mastercard, DC = Diners Club.

Vancouver

Asian

Chinese

Most restaurants represent the Cantonese and Mandarin regions. Many other styles, however, are showing up at diverse locations. Dim sum is available at most establishments, with the exception of noodle houses.

- Floata Seafood Restaurant, 400–180 Keefer St., 604 602-0368. Sets a standard for good food and strong service in a huge venue. L/D/T-O, $$$, AX/V/MC/DC.

- Hon's Wun-Tun House, 1339 Robson St., 604 685-0871. An institution for fast, cheap rice and noodles, potstickers, wun-tun, and vegetarian dim sum. Multiple locations: 108–268 Keefer St.,

604 688-0871; 310–3025 Lougheed Hwy., Coquitlam, 604 468-0871; 408 6th St., New Westminster, 604 520-6661; 101–4600 #3 Rd., Richmond, 604 273-0871. L/D/T-O, $, AX/V/MC/DC.

- Imperial Chinese Seafood Restaurant, 355 Burrard St., 604 688-8191. Elevated Chinese Dining. L/D, $$$$, V/MC/DC.
- Kirin Mandarin Restaurant, 102–1166 Alberni St., 604 682-8833. Refined dining from China's northern regions. L/D, $$$$, AX/V/DC.
- Pink Pearl Chinese Seafood Restaurant, 1132 East Hastings St., 604 253-4316. Come early for the dim sum, come late if you want to see a Chinese wedding banquet. L/D/T-O, $$$, AX/V/MC/DC.
- Red Star Chinese Restaurant, 2200-8181 Cambie Rd., 604 270-3003. A hotel restaurant in Richmond's Asia West serving authentic Chinese fare. Additional location at 829A Granville St., 604 261-8389. L/D, $$$, AX/V/MC.
- Shanghai Chinese Bistro, 1124 Alberni St., 604 683-8222. Chinese food, Shanghai-style and a dinner show in the form of noodle-pulling demonstration. L/D/Late, $$, AX/V/MC.
- Sun Sui Wah Seafood Restaurant, 3888 Main St., 604 872-8822. Every visiting food writer makes this stop for seafood and dim sum. Additional location in Richmond at 102–4940 #3 Rd., 604 273-8208. L/D, $$$–$$$$, AX/V/MC.
- Szechuan Chongqing Seafood Restaurant, 1668 West Broadway Ave. (upstairs), 604 734-1668. Showcases Szechuan cuisine. L/D, $$–$$$, AX/V/MC.
- Won More Szechuan Cuisine, 201–1184 Denman St., 604 688-8856. Mainly spicy dishes in a crowded, upstairs space. D, $$, AX/V/MC.

Japanese

- Ezogiku Noodle Café, 5–1329 Robson St., 604 685-8606. For ramen in all its forms (and more). An additional location is under the Rosedale Hotel at 270 Robson, 604 685-9466. L/D/T-O, $, V/MC.
- Gyoza King, 1508 Robson St., 604 669-8278. Gyozas galore: meat-based, vegetable-based, seafood-based. Noodle and rice dishes, too. D/Late, $, AX/V/MC.
- Kamei Royale Japanese Restaurant, 1030 West Georgia St., 604 687-8588. An impressive second-floor setting with experienced, creative sushi chefs. L/D, $$$, AX/V/MC/DC.
- Oishii Sushi Japanese Restaurant, 780 Denman St., 604 687-0634. The West End's answer to sensibly priced sushi. L/D, $, V/MC.
- Tojo's Restaurant, 1133 West Broadway Ave., 604 872-8050. The ultimate in sushi springs from the hands of chef Hidekazu Tojo. Closed Sunday. D, $$$$, AX/V/MC.
- Yuji's Japanese Tapas, 2059 West 4th Ave., 604 734-4990. Appetizer dishes, sashimi, sushi. Open nightly and weekends, closed Monday. D, $$, V/MC.

South Asian

- Maurya, 1643 West Broadway Ave., 604 742-0622. Modern fine dining. Indian. L/D/T-O, $$$, AX/V/MC.
- Vij's Restaurant, 1480 West 11th Ave., 604 736-6664. Expect lineups (no reservations are taken) for Vij's BC-influenced Indian dishes. Next door at Rangoli, Vij markets frozen and refrigerated, ready-to-eat Indian dishes. L/D/T-O, $$$, AX/V/MC/DC.

Thai and Vietnamese

- Montri's Thai Restaurant, 3629 West Broadway Ave., 604 738-9888. Authentically hot, in every sense of the word. Closed Monday. D, $$$, V/MC.
- Phnom Penh, 244 East Georgia St., 604 682-5777. A Vietnamese-Cambodian-Chinese mix of dishes in a family-run establishment. L/D, $$, AX/MC.

French, Italian, Mediterranean

- Bistro Pastis, 2153 West 4th Ave., 604 731-5020. Satisfying bistro classics. Closed Monday. L/D, $$$, AX/V/MC.
- Café de Paris, 751 Denman St., 604 687-1418. Both the setting and fare bring to mind the classic Paris bistro. L(weekdays)/D, $$$, AX/V/MC.
- CinCin Ristorante and Bar, 1154 Robson St., 604 688-7338. Wood-fired Italian-inspired cucina, voted best Italian and Ambience. $$$, D, AX/V/MC.
- Cioppino's Mediterranean Grill, 1133 Hamilton St., 604 688-7466. Light, fresh dishes melding Italian, French, and Spanish flavours. Closed Sunday. D, $$$–$$$$, AX/V/MC.
- Il Giardino di Umberto, 1382 Hornby St., 604 669-2422. A seaside villa recreated, serving excellent pasta and game. Closed Sunday, no lunch Saturday. L/D, $$$$, AX/V/MC/DC.
- La Régalade, 103–2232 Marine Dr., West Vancouver, 604 921-2228. Country French at bistro prices. Closed Sunday, Monday. L/D, $$, V/MC.
- Le Crocodile, 909 Burrard St., 604 669-4298. Offers the full, real Alsace experience. Closed Sundays, no lunch Saturday. L/D, $$$$, AX/V/MC.
- Quattro on Fourth, 2611 West 4th Ave., 604 734-4444. Additional location at Gusto di Quattro, 1 Lonsdale St., North Vancouver, 604 924-4444, L(weekdays)/D. Mosaic and mahogany and marvellous food. D, $$$–$$$$, AX/V/MC/DC.
- Smoking Dog Bistro, 1889 West 1st Ave., 604 732-8811. Simple French fare in the perfect people-watching place. Weekend brunch. L/D, $$–$$$, V/MC.
- Villa Del Lupo, 869 Hamilton St., 604 688-7436. Generous and contemporary cooking in a charming old house. D, $$$$, AX/V/MC/DC.

Pacific Northwest

- The Beach House, 150 25th St., West Vancouver, 604 922-1414. Strong on seafood. By Dundarave Pier, it's a great spot for Sunday brunch à la carte. L/D, $$$$, AX/V/MC.
- Blue Water Café and Raw Bar, 1095 Hamilton St., 604 688-8078. Local seafood plus a master sushi chef at the Raw Bar. Fabulous deserts and an excellent champagne list. D, $$$, AX/V/MC.
- The Cannery Seafood Restaurant, 2205 Commissioner St., 604 254-9606. Promises good seafood, and delivers. Weekend brunch. L(except Monday)/D, $$$$, AX/V/MC/DC.
- The Fish House in Stanley Park, 8901 Stanley Park Dr., 604 681-7275. Bold and creative seafood and Oyster Bar. Weekend brunch. L/D, $$$–$$$$, AX/V/MC.
- Glowbal Grill & Satay Bar, 1079 Mainland St., 604 602-0835. The open kitchen conjures up award-winning regional dishes with a flourish. Try the great patio. L/D, $$$, AX/V/MC.
- The Pear Tree, 4120 East Hastings St., Burnaby, 604 299-2772. Inventive food, reasonable prices. Closed Sunday/Monday. D, $$$, AX/V/MC.
- Provence Marinaside, 1177 Marinaside Crescent, 604 681-4144. Meals from pasta to fresh seafood, plus afternoon tea by reservation and picnic baskets on order. Weekend brunch. B/L/D, brunch on weekends, $$$, AX/V/MC.
- Raincity Grill, 1193 Denman St., 604 685-7337. Ever-changing menu based on what's fresh. Weekend brunch. L/D, $$$$, AX/V/MC/DC.
- Rodney's Oyster House, 405–1228 Hamilton St., 604 609-0080. Oysters are the main attraction here, but other seafoods are popular too. L/D, $$$, AX/V/MC/DC.
- Seasons in the Park Restaurant,

Queen Elizabeth Park, Cambie St. and West 33rd Ave., 604 874-8008. Good, conservative food in an intoxicating garden setting. Weekend brunch à la carte. L/D, $$$–$$$$, AX/V/MC.

- The Teahouse Restaurant, Ferguson Point, Stanley Park, 604 669-3281. Fresh, local seafood and inventive salads. One of the best sunset views of the Pacific. Weekend brunch. L/D, $$$$, AX/V/MC.

Fine Dining and Hotel Dining

- Bacchus Restaurant, Wedgewood Hotel, 845 Hornby St., 604 689-7777. Small, exclusive room with unfailingly good food. Afternoon tea served, weekends only. B/L/D/Late (lounge), $$$$, AX/V/MC/DC.
- Bishop's Restaurant, 2183 West 4th Ave., 604 738-2025. Flawlessly prepared food, understated elegance and superb service. No lunch on weekends. L/D, $$$$, AX/V/MC/DC.
- C Restaurant, 2–1600 Howe St., 604 681-1164. Intriguing fish dishes and a million-dollar marina view. L(weekdays)/D, $$$$–$$$$$, AX/V/MC/DC.
- DB Bistro Moderne, 2563 West Broadway Ave., 604 739-7115. An up-tempo contemporary urban French bistro and bar. Weekend brunch. L(Tuesday to Sunday)/D, $$$, AX/V/MC/DC.
- Diva at the Met, Metropolitan Hotel, 645 Howe St., 604 602-7788. Airy space with multi-tiered seating and stylish food preparation. Weekend brunch. B/L/D, $$$$, AX/V/MC/DC.
- Five Sails Restaurant, Pan Pacific Hotel, 300–999 Canada Place Way, 604 844-2855. Imaginative orchestration of flavours and breathtaking views. D, $$$$, AX/V/MC/DC.
- Fleuri Restaurant, Sutton Place Hotel, 845 Burrard St., 604 642-2900. A hidden treasure. Afternoon tea; jazz brunch every Sunday. Chocoholic Bar (Thursday to

Saturday nights). B/L/D, $$$$, AX/V/MC/DC.
- Lumière, 2551 West Broadway Ave., 604 739-8185. Provocative blend of European sophistication, modern French sensibilities, and West Coast innovation. Closed Monday and Tuesday. D, $$$$–$$$$$, AX/V/MC/DC.
- Market by Jean-Georges, Shangri-la Hotel, 1128 West Georgia St., 604 695-1115 or 604 661-3336 for reservations. Fresh regional cuisine of the Pacific Northwest. Closed Sunday. L(weekdays)/D. $$$. AX/V/MC.
- Salmon House on the Hill, 2229 Folkestone Way, West Vancouver, 604 926-3212. High in the North Shore hills, this classic spot is romantic and traditional. Wild salmon is the specialty. Weekend brunch. D, $$$$, AX/V/MC.
- West Restaurant, 2881 Granville St., 604 738-8938. Regional, seasonal fare. L/D. $$$$, AX/V/MC.
- Yew Restaurant, Four Seasons Hotel, 791 West Georgia St., 604 689-9333. Casual front lounge and contemporary dining room. B/L/D, $$$$–$$$$$, AX/V/MC/DC.

Specialty

Heritage

- Hart House on Deer Lake, 6664 Deer Lake Ave., Burnaby, 604 298-4278. The Tudor-style setting embraces both traditional and more daring fare. L/D, $$$–$$$$, AX/V/MC.

Vegetarian

- Café Deux Soleils, 2096 Commercial Dr., 604 254-1195. Vegetarian food, music, and spoken word events. B/L/D, $, V.
- Planet Veg, 1941 Cornwall Ave., 604 734-1001. A warning: lineups form fast for the Indian, Mexican, and Mediterranean vegetarian fast foods. L/D/T-O, $, V/MC.

Tapas

- Bin 941 Tapas Parlour, 941 Davie

St., 604 683-1246. Generously filled tasting bowls. D/Late, $$–$$$, V/MC.

- Bin 942 Tapas Parlour, 1521 West Broadway Ave., 604 734-9421. Much like Bin 941, but bigger. D/Late, $$–$$$, V/MC.

Casual Dining and Bakeries

- Addis Café, 2017 Commercial Dr. Ethiopian. $.
- Au Petit Chavignol, 845 East Hastings St., 604 255-4218. Delightful cheese, charcuterie, and fondues. D. $$. V/MC.
- Dockside, 1253 Johnston St. in the Granville Island Hotel, 604 685-7070. Casual restaurant, micro-brewery, smashing patio. B/L/D, $$, AX/V/MC/DC.
- Earls Restaurants, 1601 West Broadway Ave., 604 736-5663. Fresh and healthy food that's fast. Good place to take children. Other locations: 901 West Broadway Ave., 604 734-5995; 1185 Robson St., 604 669-0020; 905 Hornby, 604 682-6700. L/D, $$, AX/V/MC.
- Falconetti's East Side Grill, 1812 Commercial Dr. Popular with carnivores. $.
- Go Fish, 1505 West 1st Ave., 604 730-5040. Mostly take-out, with a few canopied tables by the waterside. Halibut, salmon, and cod are cooked fresh from the dock. Closed Monday. L/D (noon to 6:30 p.m.), $, V/MC.
- Harambe Restaurant, 2149 Commercial Dr., 604 216-1060. Ethiopian food. L/D. $.
- Havana Restaurant, 1212 Commercial Dr., 604 253-9119. West Coast with a hint of Cuban and Latin American. Brunch/L/D, $, V/MC.
- The Irish Heather, 212 Carrall St., 604 688-9779. As Irish as they come: pub food from bangers 'n' mash to feature desserts. New cheese and charcuterie plates. Over 195 single malts and Irish whiskeys served. B/L/D, $$$, AX/V/MC.
- Juicy Lucy's Café, 1420 Commercial Dr.,

604 254-6101. Juice bar and café. B/L (to 7 p.m.), $.
- Les Amis du Fromage, 1752 West 2nd Ave., 604 732-4218. Wide selection of cheese take-out at Vancouver's best cheese shop. T-O, $, AX/V/MC.
- Little Nest, 1716 Charles St. Good food for young families. $.
- Memphis Blues Barbeque House, 1465 West Broadway Ave., 604 738-6806. Additional locations, 1342 Commercial Dr., 604 215-2599; 1629 Lonsdale St., 604 929-3699. Southern baah-be-cue with all the Memphis favourites. L/D/T-O, $, AX/V/MC.
- Milestone's on the Beach. The original Milestone's at 1210 Denman St., 604 662-3431. Cozy Kobe beef meatloaf, slow-roasted prime rib, and award-winning salads. Brunch/L/D, $$, AX/V/MC/DC.
- Patisserie Lebeau, 1728 West 2nd Ave., 604 731-3528. Fine Belgian waffles, jewel-like pastries, and French breads, freshly baked. Closed Sunday and Monday. Eat-in or take-out. V/MC.
- Solly's Bagelry, 189 East 28th Ave., 604 872-1821. Additional locations, 2873 West Broadway Ave., 604 738-2121; 368 West 7th Ave., 604 675-9750. Bagels, kosher lunches and Vancouver's best cinnamon buns. B/L/G/T-O, $, V/MC.
- Steamworks Brewing Company, 375 Water St., 604 689-2739. Some say the best beer in town is found in Steamworks' on-site brewery. B/L/D/Late, $$, AX/V/MC/DC.
- Subeez, 891 Homer St., 604 687-6107. Popular industrial-style bistro. Brunch, L/D, $$–$$$, AX/V/MC.
- Tomato Fresh Food Café, 2486 Bayswater, 604 874-6020. Distinctively healthy and colourful comfort food. B/L/D, $$$, AX/V/MC.
- Urban Fare, 177 Davie St., 604 975-7550. Other locations, 305 Bute St., 604 669-5831; 1133 Alberni St., 604 648-2053. Café and gourmet supermarket. B/L/D/T-O, $,

AX/V/MC.
- Waazubee Café, 1622 Commercial Dr., 604 253-5299. Casual and upbeat spot on The Drive. B/L/D, $$, AX/V/MC.
- White Spot, 580 West Georgia at Seymour, 604 662-3066. Nat Bailey's famous fare features salads, fries, milkshakes, and Vancouver's favourite burgers with legendary Triple O sauce. Many Vancouver locations. B/L/D/T-O, $, AX/V/MC.

Victoria

Fine Dining
- Aerie Resort and Spa, 600 Ebadora Lane, Malahat, 250 743-7115. French class and quality well worth the price. B/L/D, $$$$–$$$$$, AX/V/MC.
- Café Brio, 944 Fort St., 250 383-0009. Contemporary Italian creations in a lively, art-filled room. D, $$$–$$$$, AX/V/MC.
- Deep Cove Chalet, 11190 Chalet Road, Deep Cove, Sidney, 250 656-3541. Exceptional French cuisine, specializing in local seafood. Closed Monday and Tuesday. L/D, $$$$, AX/V/MC.
- Fire & Water Fish and Chophouse, Victoria Marriott Inner Harbour Hotel, 728 Humboldt St., 250 480-3800. Regional cuisine in a serene atmosphere, with all-seasons patio. $$$. B/L/D, AX/V/MC.
- Prime Steakhouse, Magnolia Hotel and Spa, 625 Courtney St., 250 386-2010. A steak-lover's paradise with the finest cuts of Alberta beef. L/D, $$$–$$$$, AX/V/MC.
- SeaGrille, 849 Verdier Avenue, 250 544-2079. Fine dining, West Coast regional food such as Haida Feast Platter on hand-carved yellow and red cedar ceremonial dishes. B/L/D. $$$. AX/V/MC.
- Sooke Harbour House, 1528 Whiffen Spit Rd., Sooke, 250 642-3421. Innovative, even eccentric, one of Canada's gastronomic treasures. D, $$$$$, AX/V/MC.
- The Temple Restaurant, 525 Fort St., 250 383-2313. Contemporary regional cuisine in 1890s heritage building. L/D, $$$, AX/V/MC.
- Victoria Harbour House, 607 Oswego St., 250 386-1244. Old-style elegance, Continental dining. D, $$$, V/MC.

Bistros and Cafés
- Barb's Place Fish 'n Ships, Fisherman's Wharf, Downtown Victoria, 250 384-6515. Look inside the blue-painted shack for authentic halibut fish and chips. Closed November to March. L/D/G/T-O, $, AX/V/MC.
- Bond Bond's Bakery, 1010 Blanshard St., 250 388-5377. The city's top bakery makes lunch items, too. Closed Sunday. G/T-O, $, no credit cards.
- Brasserie l'Ecole, 1715 Government St., 250 475-6260. Classic hearty French bistro dishes using Vancouver Island ingredients. D, $$$, AX/V/MC.
- Fresh Bakery and Bistro, 3115 Cedar Hill Rd., 250 595-2624. Italian bakery featuring fine pastries, breads; small dinner menu in summer. B/L, $–$$, V/MC.
- La Collina Bakery, 1286 McKenzie Ave., 250-477-1663. Italian bakery featuring fine pastries, bread, and event catering. $$, V/MC.
- Ottavio Gastronomia, 2272 Oak Bay Ave., 250 592-4080. Italian bakery and café specializing in cheese, pastries, organic gelato, and sandwiches. L, $, V/MC.
- Paprika Bistro, 2524 Estevan Ave., 250 592-7424. Vivid, locally inspired menu with French and Italian influences. Closed Sunday and Monday. D, $$$, AX/V/MC.
- Paradiso di Stelle, 10 Bastion Sq., 250 920-7266. The place to go for a gelato fix. Open 7 days. V/MC.
- Rebar Modern Foods, 50 Bastion Sq., 250 361-9223. Inventive, delicious, healthy food. Kid-friendly. B/L/D, $$, AX/V/MC.
- Rosemeade Bistro Dining Lounge, The English Inn, 429 Lampson St., Esquimalt, 250 412-7673.

Seasonally inspired salads, meats, and seafood fare. Kitchen tours. Closed Sunday and Monday. D, $$–$$$, V/MC.

- Zambri's, 110–911 Yates St., 250 360-1171. Best Italian café and bistro in town. L/D, $$, AX/V/MC.

Seafood

- Blue Crab Bar & Grill, Coast Harbourside Hotel, 146 Kingston St., 250 480-1999. Look for Pacific Northwest casual and look out for dessert. B/L/D, $$$, AX/V/MC/DC.
- Dockside Grill, Van Isle Marina, 2320 Harbour Rd., Sidney, 250 656-0828. Zeroes in on beef, lamb, pork, and the freshest seafood in Sidney. L/D, $$$, V/MC.
- Lure, Delta Victoria Ocean Pointe Resort and Spa, 45 Songhees Rd., 250 360-2999. Sleek and contemporary seafood restaurant with impeccable service. B/L/D, $$$$, AX/V/MC/DC.
- Marina Restaurant, 1327 Beach Dr., 250 598-8555. A nautical setting for seafood and continental fare. Sunday Brunch. L/D, $$$–$$$$, AX/V/MC.

Brew Pubs

- Canoe Brew Pub, Marina and Restaurant, 450 Swift St., 250 361-1940. Historic waterfront brew pub with modern food. L/D, $$–$$$, AX/V/MC.
- Irish Times Pub, 1200 Government St., 250 383-7775. Lots of wood timbers and fireplaces in this historic former bank dating from 1900. Live Celtic music nightly. L/D/T-O/Late. $–$$. AX/V/MC.
- Penny Farthing Olde English Pub, 2228 Oak Bay Ave., 250 370-9008. Lively gastropub with stylized pub food. L/D, $$–$$$, AX/V/MC.
- Spinnakers Gastro Brew Pub, 308 Catherine St., 250 384-2739. Traditional brewery, sausage kitchen, and bakery. L/D, $$, AX/V/MC/DC.
- Swans Brew Pub, Swans Hotel, 506 Pandora St., 250 361-3310. In-house brews and reasonably priced food

make this a popular hangout. B/L/D/Late, $$, AX/V/MC/DC.

Tea

While in Victoria, one must have tea. Keep in mind that many places make a distinction between "afternoon" or "light" tea — small sandwiches, scones, clotted cream, jam, berries, and coffee or tea — and high tea, a more substantial tea usually including meats and trifles, and more of the above.

- Blethering Place Tea Room and Restaurant, 2250 Oak Bay Ave., 250 598-1413. A cozy place in Oak Bay Village. B/L/Tea/D, $$, AX/V/MC.
- Butchart Gardens, 800 Benvenuto Ave., Brentwood Bay, 250 652-8222. Tea in the garden, a fine idea. Afternoon Tea (L/D seasonal), $$, AX/V/MC.
- Empress Room, Fairmont Empress Hotel, 721 Government St., 250 384-8111. Tea served as it should be. Reserve ahead. Dress code in Tea Lobby. Afternoon Tea, $$$$, AX/V/MC/DC.
- James Bay Tea Room and Restaurant, 332 Menzies St., 250 382-8282. A favourite for friendliness and prices. Breakfast all day, Afternoon Tea, High Tea Sunday, $, AX/V/MC.
- Point Ellice House, 2616 Pleasant St., 250 380-6506. Tea served out on the lawn, complete with white wicker, against a heritage house setting overlooking the Gorge. Light Tea, Afternoon Tea, $$ per person. V/MC.

Ethnic

- Daidoco, 633 Courtenay St., 250 388-7383. Japanese homestyle small plates. Go early as they sell out fast. Closed Saturday and Sunday. L/T-O (10 a.m.–2 p.m.), $, V/MC.
- J & J Wonton Noodle House, 1012 Fort St., 250 383-0680. Savoury noodles, soups, mein, fun, simply served. L/D, $, AX/V/MC.
- The Noodle Box, 818 Douglas St., 250 384-1314. Southeast

Asian–styled wok-cooked take-out with eight levels of heat. A local favourite. Also at 626 Fisgard St.. L/D/T-O, $, AX/V/MC.

Top Attractions

Vancouver

The list that follows gives the sights that define Vancouver to the rest of the world. Travellers who spend even a weekend here, however, will agree there's much more to see and do.

- Capilano Suspension Bridge and Park. A structure of sturdy steel cables sways high above the forested Capilano River canyon. New Treetops Adventure canopy walk. 3735 Capilano Rd., North Vancouver, 604 985-7474, www.capbridge.com.
- Dr. Sun Yat-Sen Classical Chinese Garden. A serene garden set in the heart of Chinatown reflects perfect equilibrium in all elements, from design through use. 578 Carrall St., 604 662-3207, www.vancouverchinesegarden.com.
- Gulf of Georgia Cannery National Historic Site of Canada. Impressive former fish cannery harking back to the 1890s when salmon was king. 12138 4th Ave., Richmond, 604 664-9009, www.gulfofgeorgiacannery.com.
- H. R. MacMillan Space Centre. Space comes to Earth with the Space Centre's hands-on galleries, interactive computer displays, multimedia and laser shows and live demonstrations, while the H. R. MacMillan Planetarium snares the stars on a 20-metre dome. 1100 Chestnut St., 604 738-7827, www.hrmacmillanspacecentre.com.
- Museum of Vancouver (MOV). Fronted by Vancouver's pet stainless steel crab, this odd structure encloses Vancouver's past. Also hosts visiting and temporary exhibits. 1100 Chestnut St., 604 736-4431, www.vanmuseum.bc.ca.
- Grouse Mountain/The Peak of Vancouver. Hike up Grouse or take the Skyride aerial tram for panoramic views, fine and casual dining, and winter and summer sports at the top. 6400 Nancy Greene Way, North Vancouver, 604 984-0661, www.grousemountain.com.
- IMAX Theatre at Canada Place. Five white sails hover over the Canada Place convention centre with its wraparound outdoor walkway and stunning views of Vancouver Harbour. Included is the IMAX Theatre where the steeply pitched amphitheatre seating, a five-story screen and six-channel IMAX Digital wraparound sound make film-viewing an intense experience. 999 Canada Place Way, 604 682-4629, www.imax.com/vancouver.
- Science World at Telus World of Science. Science and entertainment merge in creative, hands-on exhibits inside the mirrored geodesic dome. The OMNIMAX Theatre runs documentaries to tremendous effect. 1455 Quebec St., 604 443-7440, www.scienceworld.ca.
- Stanley Park. One thousand acres of urban wilderness. While its rim has been adapted for recreation, its centre is untamed. 604 257-8400, www.vancouverparks.ca.
- UBC Museum of Anthropology (MOA). Research and teaching museum-cum-gallery, with artifacts from around the world and one of the world's finest collections of Northwest Coast First Nations art. Free outdoor sculpture garden with totem poles and Haida houses. 6393 NW Marine Dr. (UBC campus), 604 822-5087, www.moa.ubc.ca.
- Vancouver Art Gallery. The neo-classical building is a permanent home to a collection of works by Emily Carr, among others, and hosts touring exhibitions, demonstrations, and lunch-hour concerts. 750 Hornby St., 604 662-4719, www.vanartgallery.bc.ca.
- Vancouver Aquarium. Canada's largest aquarium and home to over 70,000 animals from the Arctic to Amazon. Featuring a newly

expanded Arctic exhibit, 4D theatre, and daily animal shows in the heart of beautiful Stanley Park. 845 Avison Way, 604 659-3474, www.vanaqua.org.

- Vancouver Maritime Museum. A historic ship, Heritage Harbour, the Children's Maritime Discovery Centre, and permanent as well as temporary exhibits pay tribute to Vancouver's seagoing heritage. 1905 Ogden Ave., 604 257-8300, www.vancouvermaritimemuseum.com.

Victoria

- Art Gallery of Greater Victoria. 1889 mansion attracting internationally renowned exhibits and housing contemporary BC and other Canadian art, North American, European, Japanese, and Chinese works. Moss Street Paint-In festival every August. 1040 Moss St., 250 384-4101, www.aggv.bc.ca.
- Chinatown. Two crammed blocks' worth of browsing, shopping, and eating almost hides narrow Fan Tan Alley, current home to artist studios and boutiques, former haven for opium dens. Fisgard and Government Streets.
- Craigdarroch Castle. Monumental Dunsmuir family stone mansion. No wheelchair access. 1050 Joan Cres., 250 592-5323, www.craigdarrochcastle.com.
- Emily Carr House. Ministry of Tourism, Culture and the Arts Heritage building. Artist and writer Emily Carr's family home, restored and updated with computerized information centre and Canadian artists' gallery. 207 Government St., 250 383-5843, www.emilycarr.com.
- Fairmont Empress Hotel. Grand, chateau-style heritage hotel. Famed Afternoon Tea. 721 Government St., 250 384-8111, www.fairmont.com/empress.
- Helmcken House at the Royal British Columbia Museum. Oldest house in BC still on its original site (since 1852). 675 Belleville St. adjacent to Museum, 250 356-7226, 1-888-447-7977,

www.royalbcmuseum.bc.ca/RBCM_Cult_Pre/Helmcken_Hse.aspx.

- Inner Harbour and Fisherman's Wharf. Outdoors, where buskers and artisans offer their talents against a view of the harbour. On one side is Fisherman's Wharf, where commercial fishing boats dock. In front of the Fairmont Empress Hotel and Parliament Buildings.
- Parliament Buildings. The seat of the Provincial Legislature. Free tours and a live "performance" when the house is in session. 501 Belleville St., 250 387-3046, 1-800-663-7867, www.leg.bc.ca.
- Point Ellice House. Meticulously restored house and garden with unusual collection of Victoriana. 2616 Pleasant St., 250 380-6506, www.bcheritage.ca.
- Royal British Columbia Museum. Three permanent galleries — Natural History Gallery, Open Ocean Gallery, and the First Peoples and Modern History Gallery — plus multiple exhibits and the National Geographic IMAX Theatre. 675 Belleville St., 250 356-7226, 1-888-447-7977, www.royalbcmuseum.bc.ca.
- Maritime Museum of British Columbia. Original 1889 provincial courthouse houses artifacts documenting the province's oceangoing history. Treasure hunt for kids. 28 Bastion Square, 250 385-4222, www.mmbc.bc.ca.
- Ocean Discovery Centre. Vancouver Island's newest attraction. Massive aquarium habitats of living marine life of the Salish Sea from giant octopus to microscopic plankton. 9811 Seaport Place, Sidney, at the foot of Beacon Ave. in the Sidney Pier building, 250 665-7511, www.oceandiscovery.ca.

Galleries and Museums

Vancouver

Vancouver's galleries number more than 100 and cover a wide range

Galleries and Museums

of expressions: historic art, contemporary, avant garde, and traditional. The art is made by First Nations people, Canadians, Asians and Europeans. Check the Thursday editions of *The Georgia Straight* and *WestCoast Life* guide in the *Vancouver Sun* for details of current shows. *Preview: The Gallery Guide* listings and maps are also useful. An online version can be found at www.preview-art.com.

Galleries

- Access Gallery. New art installations. 206 Carrall St., 604 689-2907.
- Artspeak. Phototext and interactive video. 233 Carrall St., 604 688-0051.
- Bau-Xi Gallery. Contemporary art. 3045 Granville St., 604 733-7011.
- Buschlen Mowatt Galleries. International art. 1445 West Georgia St., 604 682-1234.
- Catriona Jeffries Gallery. Emphasis is on contemporary art. 274 East 1st Ave., 604 736-1554.
- Centre A. Shows of Asian art. #2 West Hastings St., 604 683-8326.
- Charles H. Scott Gallery. Located in the Emily Carr University of Art and Design. 1399 Johnston St., Granville Island, 604 844-3800.
- Circle Craft Co-op. Works by BC craft artists. 1–1666 Johnston St., Granville Island, 604 669-8021.
- Contemporary Art Gallery. Vanguard works. 555 Nelson St., 604 681-2700.
- Crafthouse Gallery. BC crafts. 1386 Cartwright St., Granville Island, 604 687-7270.
- Douglas Udell Gallery. Western contemporary. 1558 West 6th Ave., 604 736-8900.
- Douglas Reynolds Gallery. Northwest Coast art. 2335 Granville St., 604 731-9292.
- Dundarave Print Workshop. Limited edition prints. 1640 Johnston St., Granville Island, 604 689-1650.
- Equinox Gallery. Contemporary Canadian works. 2321 Granville St., 604 736-2405.

- Gallery of BC Ceramics. Talented local potters. 1359 Cartwright St., Granville Island, 604 669-3606.
- Heffel Gallery. Group of Seven and 19th-century artists. 2247 Granville St., 604 732-6505.
- Helen Pitt Gallery. Contemporary artist-run. 102-48 Alexander St., 604 681-6740.
- Inuit Gallery. Museum-quality Inuit art. 206 Cambie St., 604 688-7323.
- Lattimer Gallery. Northwest Coast artists. 1590 West 2nd Ave., 604 732-4556.
- Malaspina Printmakers Gallery. Limited edition prints. 1555 Duranleau St., Granville Island, 604 688-1827.
- Marion Scott Gallery. Inuit art. 308 Water St., 604 685-1934.
- Monte Clark Gallery. Contemporary photography. 2339 Granville St., 604 730-5000.
- Morris and Helen Belkin Art Gallery at the University of British Columbia. Exhibitions of international and Canadian art. 1825 Main Mall, 604 822 2759.
- New-Small and Sterling Glass Studio. Hot glass blowing and glass works. 1440 Old Bridge St., Granville Island, 604 681-6730.
- The Or Gallery. Conceptual art. 555 Hamilton St., 604 683-7395.
- Spirit Wrestler Gallery. First Nations works. 47 Water St., 604 669-8813.
- Uno Langmann Gallery. Antiques. 2117 Granville St., 604 736-8825.
- Vancouver Art Gallery. Traditional and contemporary Canadian and European art. 750 Hornby St., 604 662-4719.
- VIVO Media Arts Centre. Contemporary artist-run. 1965 Main St., 604 871-0173.
- Western Front. Contemporary artist-run. 303 East 8th Ave., 604 876-9343.
- Winsor Gallery. Contemporary. 3025 Granville St., 604 681-4870.

Museums

- BC Sports Hall of Fame and Museum. Chronicles BC's professional and amateur sports and recreation history through displays, hands-on exhibits and multimedia. Gate A, BC Place Stadium, 777 Pacific Blvd. S. 604 687-5520, www.bcsportshalloffame.com.

- Burnaby Village Museum. A turn-of-the-century town with authentically costumed "residents" and restored 1912 carousel called the "Carry-Us-All." May to September. 6501 Deer Lake Ave., Burnaby, 604 293-6501.
- Chinese Cultural Centre Museum and Archives. Temporary exhibits Chinese artists, archive of Chinese history in BC. 555 Columbia St., 604 658-8880.
- Hastings Mill Store Museum. A charmingly cluttered museum inside Vancouver's oldest building shelters items such as rifles, Native baskets, period clothes, clocks, a handsome cab and artifacts of the Great Fire. 1575 Alma St., 604 734-1212.
- Museum of Vancouver. Vancouver's past plus visiting and temporary exhibits. 1100 Chestnut St., 604 736-4431, www.vanmuseum.bc.ca.
- UBC Museum of Anthropology (MOA). Research and teaching museum-cum-gallery, with artifacts from around the world and Northwest Coast First Nations art. Outdoor sculpture garden with totem poles and Haida houses. 6393 NW Marine Dr. (University of BC campus), 604 822-5087, www.moa.ubc.ca.
- Vancouver Maritime Museum. A historic ship, Heritage Harbour, the Children's Maritime Discovery Centre and permanent as well as temporary exhibits pay tribute to Vancouver's seagoing heritage. 1905 Ogden Ave., 604 257-8300, www.vancouvermaritimemuseum.com.
- Vancouver Police Museum. Crime and crime-fighting paraphernalia, including old photos, gambling displays, artifacts and accounts of ancient unsolved murders. 240 East Cordova St., 604 665-3346, www.vancouverpolicemuseum.ca.

Victoria
Museums
- Maritime Museum of British Columbia. The original 1889 provincial courthouse houses artifacts documenting British Columbia's oceangoing history. Treasure hunt for kids. 28 Bastion Sq., 250 385-4222, www.mmbc.bc.ca.
- Royal British Columbia Museum. Three permanent galleries (Natural History Gallery, Open Ocean Gallery, and the First Peoples and Modern History Gallery) plus multiple exhibits and the National Geographic IMAX Theatre. 675 Belleville St., 250 356-7226, 1-888-447-7977, www.royalbcmuseum.bc.ca.
- Royal London Wax Museum. Wax figures of famous and infamous characters in history, show business, and literature. 470 Belleville St., 250 388-4461, www.waxmuseum.bc.ca.

Vancouver Entertainment

In addition to a well-known film and television production industry, entertainment in Vancouver can be found live at clubs, theatres, and arts centres around town. Alliance for Arts and Culture (www.allianceforarts.com) is a valuable resource, and The Georgia Straight publishes weekly events listings as well. Ticketmaster sells tickets for a wide range of events (604 280-4444). Tickets Tonight is a day-of half-price ticket outlet (main ticket booth at Tourism Vancouver Visitors Centre, Plaza Level, 200 Burrard St., 604 684-2787, daily 10 a.m.–6 p.m.). Note that those under 19 years of age are not allowed in nightclubs serving alcohol.

Theatre
- Bard on the Beach Shakespeare Festival, Vanier Park, 604 739-0559. Annual Shakespeare festival in a semi-outdoor setting.
- Firehall Arts Centre, 280 East Cordova St., 604 689-0926.

Entertainment

Converted fire station specializing in alternative theatre, performance art, and dance.

- Granville Island Stage, 1585 Johnston St., 604 687-1644. An Arts Club Theatre venue on Granville Island; Western Canada's largest regional theatre and a local institution.
- Metro Theatre Centre, 1370 Southwest Marine Dr., 604 266-7191. Attracts a loyal, mature audience looking for British comedy.
- New Revue Stage, 1601 Johnston St., Granville Island, 604 738-7013. Home to the hilarious Vancouver TheatreSports League's improv shows.
- Norman Rothstein Theatre, 950 West 41st Ave., 604 257-5111. State-of-the-art theatre in the Jewish Community Centre.
- Presentation House Theatre, 333 Chesterfield Ave., North Vancouver, 604 990-3474. Terrific community theatre.
- Queen Elizabeth Theatre. 600 Block Hamilton St., 604 665-3050. Glitzy, glamorous Broadway-style productions.
- Stanley Industrial Alliance Stage, 2750 Granville St., 604 687-1644. The Arts Club's third stage in a former vaudeville venue and movie theatre.
- Vancouver East Cultural Centre (The Cultch), 1895 Venables St., 604 251-1363. In its 35th season, BC's most diverse performance space, hosting contemporary theatre, dance, and music.
- Vancouver International Fringe Festival, Granville Island, 604 257-0350. The Island is overrun with 400+ shows each September.
- Vancouver Playhouse. 600 Block Hamilton St., 604 873-3311. One of the best regional theatres in Canada.
- Waterfront Theatre, 1412 Cartwright St., Granville Island, 604 685-1731. Big stage in a small theatre where many Canadian works debut.

Music and Dance

- Ballet British Columbia, Queen Elizabeth Theatre, 604 732-5003. Exceptional performers, the company also hosts some of Canada's leading ballet companies.
- The Cellar Restaurant and Jazz Club, 3611 West Broadway, 604 738-1959. Mellow jazz in a neighbourhood setting.
- Chan Centre for the Performing Arts, 6265 Crescent Rd., UBC, 604 822-2697. Best acoustics in town.
- Commodore Ballroom, 868 Granville St., 604 739-7469. Hosts an eclectic range of artists.
- Judith Marcuse Dance Projects, 778 782-8559. Ambitious, long-time local company performs at various locations.
- Kokoro Dance, 604 662-7441. Small, innovative company performs at various locations.
- O'Doul's Restaurant and Bar, Listel Hotel, 1300 Robson St., 604 661-1400. Popular live jazz venue.
- Orpheum Theatre, 800 Block Seymour, 604 665-3050. Old-time, elegant home of the Vancouver Symphony Orchestra.
- Scotiabank Dance Centre, 677 Davie St., 604 606-6400. Showcases BC and international performers.
- Vancouver Opera, Queen Elizabeth Theatre, 604 683-0222. A range of classical and modern operas.
- Vancouver Symphony Orchestra, Orpheum Theatre, 604 876-3434. Offers a marvelous assortment of music under conductor Bramwell Tovey as well as international and Canadian stars.
- Vogue Theatre, 918 Granville St., 604 688-1975. Hosts top musical acts and guest speakers, plus film screenings during the Vancouver International Film Festival.
- The Yale Hotel, 1300 Granville St., 604 681-9253. Now and always the best rhythm and blues bar.

Clubs

- AuBAR, 674 Seymour St., 604 648-2227. Popular, chic dance club.
- Backstage Lounge 1585 Johnson

St., 604 687-1354. Live world-beat music, casual meeting place for after-theatre drinks and snacks.

- Celebrities Night Club Vancouver, 1022 Davie St., 604 681-6180. Caters to a gay clientele.
- Fabric Nightclub, 66 Water St., 604 683-6695. Weekly events, drink specials, underground, and urban sounds.
- Gérard Lounge, Sutton Place Hotel, 845 Burrard St., 604 682-5511. Attracts celebrities and a moneyed crowd.
- Honey Lounge, Lotus Hotel, 455 Abbott St., 604 685-7777. Elegant mixed club that is lesbian friendly.
- Libra Room Café, 1608 Commercial Dr., 604 255-3787. Intimate crowded room, jazz combos.
- Lick, Lotus Hotel, 455 Abbott St., 604 685-7777. Women only.
- Numbers Cabaret, 1042 Davie St., 604 685-4077. Four split-levels and a pair of bars are crammed with a regular gay clientele..
- Oasis Ultra Lounge, 1240 Thurlow St. (above Denny's), 604 685-1724. Mixed, lounge, patio, food, piano.
- 1181, 1181 Davie St., 604 687-3991. Mixed, lounge.
- Opus Bar, Opus Hotel, 322 Davie St., 604 642-6787. Stylish and hip, a luscious bar in one of Vancouver's top customer-rated hotels.
- Pulse Nightclub, 1138 Davie St., 604 669-2013. Mixed, dance.
- Pumpjack Pub, 1167 Davie St., 604 685-3417. Gay club.
- Railway Club, 579 Dunsmuir St., 604681-1625. Intimate and hip, music ranging from indie to rootsy.
- Richard's on Richards, 1036 Richards St., 604 687-6794. Posh club with local bands, international recording acts, and DJ dance music.
- Score on Davie, 1167 Davie St., 604 632-1646. Mixed, pub, patio, food, TV sports.
- The Cellar Restaurant and Jazz Club, 3611 West Broadway, 604 738-1959. Mellow jazz in a neighbourhood setting.

Parks and Gardens

Mild in climate and outdoors-oriented, Vancouver and Victoria are rife with gardens. The following lists a few that shouldn't be missed:

Vancouver

- Century Gardens at Deer Lake Park, 6344 Deer Lake Ave., Burnaby, 604 297-4422, www.city.burnaby.bc.ca/visitors. Rhododendrons are Burnaby's official flower, flourishing on the grounds of the Burnaby Art Gallery.
- Dr. Sun Yat-Sen Classical Chinese Garden, 578 Carrall St., 604 662-3207, www.vancouverchinesegarden.com. Authentic, full-scale classical Chinese garden offering tours and a popular summertime evening concert series.
- Park & Tilford Gardens, 440–333 Brooksbank Ave., North Vancouver, 604 984-8200, www. parkandtilford.ca.. A garden oasis on the edge of a shopping centre.
- Queen Elizabeth Park and Bloedel Floral Conservatory, West 33rd Ave. and Cambie St., 604 257-8570, www.vancouverparks.ca. Quarry garden atop Little Mountain offers showy natural surroundings and a view of the city. The Conservatory, Canada's largest triodetic dome, encloses tropical birds and plants as well as desert and exotic plants.
- Riverview Lands Arboretum, 500 Lougheed Hwy., Coquitlam, 604 290-9910. Free spring to fall tours are offered by the Riverview Horticultural Society of the more than 1,800 trees on the Riverview Hospital grounds.
- Stanley Park's gardens. Stanley Park, 604 257-8400 or 604 257-8544 for nature walks, www.vancouverparks.ca. Gardens flourishing in heavily forested Stanley Park include the Rose Garden and the Ted and Mary Grieg Rhododendron Garden.
- UBC Botanical Garden, 6804 SW Marine Dr., 604 822-9666, www.ubcbotanicalgarden.org.

A living teaching and research library spread over 30 hectares (74 acres). UBC also includes Alpine, Asian, Japanese Nitobe Memorial, and B.C. native gardens with unusual and new locally developed plants. Parking is free.

- VanDusen Botanical Garden, 5251 Oak St., 604 878-9274, www.vandusengarden.org. Themed gardens on 22 hectares of former golf course include Asian, Children's, Fragrance, Meditation, and Canadian Heritage gardens, a maze, and a fern dell.

Victoria

- Beacon Hill Park, bounded by Dallas Rd. and Douglas, Southgate and Heywood streets, 250 361-0600, www.beaconhillpark.com. Victoria's oldest and largest park with wading pool, swans, ducks, English-style rose garden, and exotic trees.
- Butchart Gardens, 800 Benvenuto Ave., Brentwood Bay, 250 652-4422, www.butchartgardens.com. Twenty-two hectares of lush gardens on the historic site of a former rock quarry.
- Hatley Park & Royal Roads, 2005 Sooke Road, on Hwy. 1A, in Colwood. 250 391-2666, 1-866-241-0674, www.hatleypark.ca. Victoria's best-kept secret is 25 minutes west of downtown. On the ocean, Hatley Park National Historic Site features 229 hectares of forest, meadows, trails, gardens, and an Edwardian castle.

Activities and Spectator Sports

Vancouver is host to professional and amateur sports, as well as a wide range of year-round outdoor activities.

Sports

- BC Lions Football. Canadian Football League franchise. BC Place Stadium, 777 Pacific Blvd., 604 661-7373 or 604 589-7627, www.bclions.com.
- BC Sports Hall of Fame and Museum. Gate A, BC Place Stadium, 604 687-5520, www.bcsportshalloffame.com.
- Fraser Downs Racecourse. Harness racing from October to April. 17755–60th Ave., Surrey, 604 576-9141, www.fraserdowns.com.
- Hastings Racecourse. Thoroughbred racing live or via satellite. Located in Hastings Park, off Renfrew, Gate 6. 604 254-1631, www.hastingsracecourse.com.
- Rio Tinto Alcan Dragon Boat Festival. Colourful dragon boats compete internationally as part of this Festival in False Creek, 604 688-2382, www.dragonboatbc.ca.
- Vancouver Canadians Professional Baseball Club. Minor league affiliate of Oakland Athletics. Nat Bailey Stadium, 4601 Ontario St., 604 872-5232, www.canadiansbaseball.com.
- Vancouver Canucks. National Hockey League franchise. General Motors Place, 800 Griffiths Way, 604 899-4610, www.canucks.com.
- Vancouver Giants. Western Hockey League team. Pacific Coliseum, 100 North Renfrew St., 604 444-2687, www.vancouvergiants.com.
- Vancouver Whitecaps/Whitecaps Women Football Club. Professional men's and women's soccer, Swanguard Stadium, Central Park, Burnaby, 604 669-9283, www.whitecapsfc.com.
- Western Lacrosse Association. 604 421-9755, www.theboxrocks.com. Seven BC teams (five local) compete in this fast-paced, all-Canadian game at several venues in the Lower Mainland.

Outdoor Activities

Cycling, hiking, swimming, and lying on the beach can be done at will, almost anywhere. Beaches and parks in the city are the responsibility of the Vancouver Board of Parks and Recreation (604 257-8400, www.vancouverparks.ca).

The following list provides useful

information for some other recreational activities.

Cycling

- Cycling British Columbia, 201–210 West Broadway, 604 737-3034, www.cyclingbc.net. Information on BMX, road and track, and mountain biking competitions.

Skiing and Snowboarding

- Cypress Mountain. Great place for toboggans and inner tubes, with groomed trails for skiing. West Vancouver. Snow Phone: 604 419-7669. Programs: 604 926-5612. www.cypressmountain.com.
- Grouse Mountain. Sleigh rides and outdoor ice-skating as well as downhill and cross-country skiing and snowboarding. 6400 Nancy Greene Way, North Vancouver. Snow reports: 604 986-6262. Programs: 604 984-0661. www.grousemountain.com.
- Mt. Seymour. Backcountry and downhill skiing, toboggans, and inner tubes. 1700 Mount Seymour Rd., North Vancouver. Snow Phone, programs and special events: 604 986-2261. www.mountseymour.com.

Birdwatching

- Nature Vancouver. Founded in 1918, the society offers year-round birding walks and other nature walks and hikes around the Lower Mainland. Events line: 604 737-3074. www.naturevancouver.ca.
- Reifel Migratory Bird Sanctuary, 5191 Robertson Road on Westham Island, Ladner, 604 946-6980, www.reifelbirdsanctuary.com. Wetlands environment is especially attractive to shorebirds and migrating birds.

Canoeing, Kayaking, Windsurfing

- Canoeing, whitewater kayaking, and sea kayaking information is available from the Outdoor Recreation Council of British Columbia, 47 West Broadway Ave., 604 873-5546, www.orcbc.ca.

Golfing

- Fraserview Golf Course. A busy south Vancouver course rated as "Best Public Course in Canada." 7800 Vivian Dr., 604 257-6923 (Pro Shop). Tee Time bookings online at www.vancouverparks.ca.
- Furry Creek Golf and Country Club. For water views and a course carved from a mountainside. 150 Country Club Rd., Furry Creek, 604 896-2224, www.golfbc.com.
- Langara Golf Course. Popular city golf course. 6706 Alberta St., 604 713-1816 (Pro Shop). Tee Time bookings online at www.vancouverparks.ca.
- Mayfair Lakes Golf & Country Club. Challenges the golfer with many water hazards. 5460 #7 Rd., Richmond, 604 276-0585, www.golfbc.com.
- Queen Elizabeth Park Pitch & Putt. Scenic park setting. 33rd Ave. and Cambie St., 604 874-8336, www.vancouverparks.ca.
- Stanley Park Pitch & Putt. City-operated course in park setting. 2099 Beach Ave., 604 681-8847 (seasonal), www.vancouverparks.ca.
- University Golf Club. Beautiful, well-maintained course on the UBC grounds. 5185 University Blvd., 604 224-1818, www.universitygolf.com.

Swimming

- Kitsilano Pool. Gigantic outdoor saltwater pool at Kitsilano Beach. Open mid-May to mid-September. 2305 Cornwall Ave., 604 731-0011, www.vancouverparks.ca.
- Vancouver Aquatic Centre. 1050 Beach Ave., 604 665-3424, www.vancouverparks.ca.
- Vancouver beaches, www.vancouverparks.ca.

Kids' Stuff

Indoors

- H. R. MacMillan Space Centre. Hands-on galleries, interactive computer displays, multimedia and laser shows and live demonstrations

Kids' Stuff

bring space and the stars down to Earth. 1100 Chestnut St., 604 738-7827, www.hrmacmillanspacecentre.com.

- IMAX Theatre, Canada Place. Film-viewing becomes an intense experience with big sound and bigger screens. Check with staff to determine if the film is too intense for young children. 999 Canada Place Way, 604 682-4629, www.imax.com/vancouver.
- OMNIMAX Theatre, Science World at Telus World of Science. Runs documentaries to tremendous effect. 1455 Quebec St., 604 443-7440, www.scienceworld.ca.
- Science World at Telus World of Science. Science and entertainment merge in creative, hands-on exhibits inside the mirrored geodesic dome. 1455 Quebec St., 604 443-7440, www.scienceworld.ca.
- Vancouver Aquarium. Home to over 70,000 animals from the Arctic to Amazon. With daily animal shows, feedings, a new 4D theatre, children's play area and expanded Arctic Exhibit, there is always something new to see and do. It's amazing! 845 Avison Way, Stanley Park, 604 659-3474, www.vanaqua.org.

Outdoors

- Capilano Suspension Bridge. Hang high above the forested Capilano River canyon on a swaying structure of sturdy steel cables; visit the Treetops Adventure canopy walk. 3735 Capilano Rd., North Vancouver, 604 985-7474, www.capbridge.com.
- Greater Vancouver Zoo. Home to 115 animal species. 5048–264th St., Aldergrove, 604 856-6825, www.gvzoo.com.
- Lynn Canyon Park. Begin a hike in Lynn Headwaters Regional Park with a visit to the Ecology Centre, and brave the suspension bridge high above the rapids of Lynn Creek. Lynn Canyon entrance on Peters Rd., 604 990-3755, www.dnv.org/ecology.

- Maplewood Farm. Petting farm of 200 domestic farm animals and birds with seasonal special events and weekend pony rides. 405 Seymour River Pl., North Vancouver, 604 929-5610, www.maplewoodfarm.bc.ca.
- Pacific Spirit Regional Park. Experience BC's coastal cedar and fir forests firsthand with an easy hike through the many trails. Visitor Centre, 4915 West 16th Ave. at Blanca, 604 224-5739, www.metrovancouver.org.
- Playland at the PNE. Outdoor amusement park rides, midway games, and cotton candy. Open from April to Labour Day. Pacific National Exhibition Park, 604 253-2311, www.pne.ca.
- Reifel Migratory Bird Sanctuary. Feed the birds or view a wetlands ecosystem. 5191 Robertson Rd. on Westham Island, Ladner, 604 946-6980, www.reifelbirdsanctuary.com.
- Stanley Park. Kids' attractions include the Children's Farmyard and Miniature Railway, and the totem poles at Lower Brockton Oval. 2099 Beach Ave., 604 257-8400, www.vancouverparks.ca.
- VanDusen Botanical Garden. Themed gardens on 55 acres include Children's Garden and Heritage and Elizabethan Hedge Maze. Many popular special events. 5251 Oak St., 604 878-9274, www.vandusengarden.org.

Waterplay

- Canada Games Pool and Fitness Centre. Olympic-size pool and teaching/toddler pool. 65 East 6th Ave., New Westminster, 604 526-4281, www.nwpr.bc.ca.
- Eileen Dailly Leisure Pool and Fitness Centre. Burnaby's best indoor pool and community centre. 240 Willingdon Ave., Burnaby, 604 298-7946.
- Granville Island Water Park. Wet adventure playground with water cannons, spouts, waterslide, and wading areas. Near Sutcliffe Park, Granville Island, 604 666-5784.

- Kitsilano Pool. Gigantic outdoor saltwater pool. Open May to August. 2305 Cornwall Ave., 604 731-0011.
- Newton Wave Pool. Metre-high waves for bodysurfing and waterslides. 13730–72nd Ave., Surrey, 604 501-5540.
- Second Beach Pool. Features three small waterslides. Open mid-May to mid-October. Stanley Park, 604 257-8371.
- Splashdown Park. Twisting waterslides, hot tubs, and smaller-sized equipment for little kids. 4799 Nulelum Way, Tsawwassen, 604 943-2251, www.splashdownpark.ca.
- Stanley Park Water Park. Wet adventure playground with equipment suitable for children with physical disabilities. Near Lumberman's Arch, Stanley Park, 604 257-8400, www.vancouverparks.ca.
- Vancouver Aquatic Centre. Olympic-size indoor and outdoor pools and toddler pool. 1050 Beach Ave., 604 665-3424, www.vancouverparks.ca.
- Vancouver beaches. Second and Third Beach, English Bay, Sunset Beach, Kits Beach, Jericho Beach, Locarno Beach, and Spanish Banks. Beach information: 604 665-3418, mid-May to mid-September.

Children's Culture

- Global ComedyFest Vancouver. Free and funny street entertainment and some ticketed family-oriented events in mid-September. Granville Island, 604 685-0881, www.comedyfest.com.
- Vancouver East Cultural Centre (The Cultch). Events for children and youth are often on the program. 1895 Venables St., 604 251-1363, www.thecultch.com.
- Vancouver International Children's Festival. Week-long event featuring quality performances, roving entertainers, face painters, and a multicultural community stage. Vanier Park, 1100 Chestnut St., 604 708-5655, www.childrensfestival.ca.

- Vancouver International Writers and Readers Festival. Mid-October writers festival has three days of children's events. Granville Island, 604 681-6330, www.writersfest.bc.ca.
- Vancouver Kidsbooks. Readings, book launches, and book signings complement the huge variety of children's books. 3083 West Broadway Ave., 604 738-5335, www.kidsbooks.ca.
- Vancouver Public Library. Children's floor has CD-ROM stations, videos, books, and displays of children's art. 350 West Georgia St., 604 331-3600.

History

- BC Sports Hall of Fame and Museum. BC's past professional and amateur sports and recreation history. Displays, a Participation Gallery and multimedia. Gate A, BC Place Stadium, 777 Pacific Blvd. South, 604 687-5520, www.bcsportshalloffame.com.
- Burnaby Village Museum and Carousel. Recreation of a 1920s village with hands-on activities, restored carousel, and special events. May to September. 6501 Deer Lake Ave., Burnaby, 604 293-6501.
- Fort Langley National Historic Park. Sample life as it was in the last century in this reconstructed Hudson's Bay Company post. 23433 Mavis Ave., Fort Langley, 604 513-4777, www.pc.gc.ca/fortlangley.

Vancouver Annual Events

January

- Brackendale Winter Eagle Festival and Count. Just after the New Year begins, an eagle count is taken, and related events are hosted all month. Squamish-Brackendale area, 604 898-3333, www.brackendaleartgallery.com/Eagles.
- Chinese New Year's Festival.

Vancouver Annual Events

Chinatown greets the first day of the lunar year (in January or February) with festivals and events, 604 273-1655. NB: cancelled due to 2010 Olympic restrictions; plans to resume in 2011, venue pending.
- Polar Bear Swim. A New Year's Day plunge into the Pacific Ocean on English Bay. Vancouver Aquatic Centre, 604 665-3418.

February
- BC Home and Garden Show. The largest consumer home show in Western Canada. BC Place Stadium, 604 639-2288 (Market Place Events).
- Vancouver International Boat Show. Consumer show featuring the latest in boating. BC Place Stadium, Coal Harbour Marina, 604 678-8820.

March
- CelticFest Vancouver. Western Canada's biggest annual five-day Celtic festival, celebrating the best of Celtic music, dance, spoken word, film, food, and St. Patrick's Day Parade. Downtown Vancouver, www.celticfestvancouver.com.
- Festival du Bois. Maillardville celebrates voyageur traditions and French-Canadian music, dance, and food. Maillardville, Coquitlam, 604 515-7070, www.festivaldubois.ca.
- Vancouver Cherry Blossom Festival. City-wide events based on the beauty of cherry trees. 604 257-8120, www.vcbf.ca.

April
- Vaisakhi Parade. An ancient harvest festival of religious significance to Hindus and Sikhs, to mark the beginning of a new solar year and new harvest season. Main St. and 49th Ave. ("Little India'); also in Surrey. Organized by Khalsa Diwan Society, 604 324-2010, www.sikhpioneers.com.
- Vancouver Playhouse International Wine Festival. Week-long fund-raising celebration of good wine and food. Vancouver Convention and Exhibition Centre, 604 872-6622, www.playhousewinefest.com.
- Vancouver Sun Run. Canada's biggest and best community run with a record 59,179 Sun Runners in the 24th year of the event (2008). Downtown Vancouver, 604 689-9441, www.sunrun.com.

May
- BMO Vancouver International Marathon. Canada's largest marathon. 604 872-2928, www.bmovanmarathon.ca.
- Vancouver International Children's Festival. A week of quality performances, roving entertainers, face painters, and a multicultural community stage, all for kids. Vanier Park, 604 708-5655, www.childrensfestival.ca.

June
- Bard on the Beach. Shakespeare is staged in a backless tent to take advantage of the magical natural backdrop. Shows from June through September. Vanier Beach, 604 739-0559 or 737-0625, www.bardonthebeach.org.
- Rio Tinto Alcan Dragon Boat Festival. Dragon boats race in the largest dragon boat festival in North America. False Creek, 604 688-2382, www.dragonboatbc.ca.
- Vancouver International Jazz Festival. Something for every jazz lover in the 400 or so performances held downtown, 604 872-5200, www.jazzvancouver.com.

July
- HSBC Celebration of Light fireworks. Pyrotechnicians from different countries set fireworks to music in a four-day competition from late July to early August. English Bay, www.celebration-of-light.com.
- Vancouver International Folk Music Festival. Hugely popular annual celebration of folk music. Jericho Beach Park, 604 602-9798, www.thefestival.bc.ca.

August
- Abbotsford International Airshow. Aerial displays and aerobatics.

Abbotsford Airport, 604 852-8511, www.abbotsfordairshow.com.

- MusicFest Vancouver. Two-week-long festival in August featuring an array of classical, jazz, and world music. Various venues throughout the city, 604 688-1152, www.musicfestvancouver.ca.
- Pacific National Exhibition. Demolition derby, petting farm, exhibits, midway games, and amusement park rides. Win a house, win a car, eat candy floss and corndogs. Pacific National Exhibition Park, 604 253-2311, www.pne.ca.
- Powell Street Festival. A celebration of Japanese-Canadian history and traditional Japanese food, music and entertainment. Powell St., Oppenheimer Park, 604 683-8240, www.powellstreetfestival.com.
- Squamish Nations Pow Wow, Aboriginal Cultural Festival. Traditional dancing, drumming, and cuisine. Capilano Reserve, Squamish Territory, North Vancouver, www.squamish.net.

September

- Chilliwack Bluegrass Festival. Camp out for the bluegrass performances held at Chilliwack Heritage Park, 604 792-2069, www.chilliwackartscouncil.com.
- Global ComedyFest Vancouver. Performances from a diverse mix of comic artists. Granville Island, 604 685-0881, www.comedyfest.com.
- Vancouver International Fringe Festival. Alternative theatre performances by emerging and established companies, 604 257-0350, www.vancouverfringe.com.

October

- Cranberry Harvest and Festival. Celebration of the local harvest of the nutritious red berries. Enjoy everything cranberry, from bread to chutneys to sausages to wines. Fort Langley, www.fortlangley.com/events.
- Diwali Festival of Lights. The largest Diwali-themed South Asian performing arts festival in the Lower Mainland. Begins with the new moon between mid-October and mid-November to signify the victory of individuals' good over evil. Various locations, www.vandiwali.ca.
- Vancouver International Film Festival. Over 250 innovative and accessible films from around the world. Various venues, 604 685-0260, www.viff.org.
- Vancouver International Writers & Readers Festival. One week of readings, talks, and other events featuring local and international writers. Granville Island, 604 681-6330, www.writersfest.bc.ca.

December

- Carol Ships Parade of Lights. Carolers sail on ships decked out with lights. Vancouver Harbour, 604 878-8999, www.carolships.org.

Excursions

Whistler

- Canadian Snowmobile Adventures offers tours of Whistler and Blackcomb. P.O. Box 701, Whister, BC V0N 1B0, 604 938-1616, 1-877-938-1616, www.canadiansnowmobile.ca.
- Intrawest Central Reservations. Accommodations and activities centre, also books customized vacation packages. 1-866-387-8491 (North America); 0-800-731-5983 (UK), www.whistlerblackcomb.com.
- Whistler Visitor and Activity Centre. 4010 Whistler Way, Whistler, BC V0N 1B4, 604 938-2769, 1-877-991-9988, www.tourismwhistler.com.
- Whistler Visitor Information Centre. 4230 Gateway Dr., Whistler, 604 935-3357.
- Whistler.com, Whistler's official source for visitor reservations and information. 1-800-944-7853 in Canada and the US, 604 932-0606 direct, fax 604 932-0204, www.whistler.com.

The Gulf Islands

- Tourism Vancouver Island, 501–65 Front St., Nanaimo, BC V9R 5H9, 250 754-3500, fax 250 754-3599, www.hellobc.com/vi.

The Sunshine Coast

- For Lower Coast visitor info, Big Pacific (www.bigpacific.com), 604 885-0662; Sechelt region, 604 885-1036 (1-877-885-1036) or 604 885-0662; Upper Coast Visitor Info, 604 485-4701. For information on B&Bs see www.bbsunshinecoast.com.
- Additional information on accommodations, dining and entertainment: www.sunshinecoast.ca, www.sunshinecoast-bc.com.

Shopping

Vancouver

Neighbourhoods

Georgia and Granville

- The Bay, Georgia & Granville Streets, 604 681-6211.
- Bentall Centre, Burrard and Dunsmuir Streets, 604 661-5000.
- The Gallery Store, 750 Hornby St., 604 662-4706.
- Pacific Centre, 700 West Georgia St., 604 688-7235.
- Royal Centre, 1055 West Georgia St., 604 689-1711.

Robson Street

- Banana Republic, 1098 Robson St., 604 331-8285.
- The Gap, 1125 Robson St., 604 683-0906.
- Mexx, 1119 Robson St., 604 801-6399.
- Roots, 1001 Robson St., 604 683-4305.
- Rootskids, 1153 Robson St., 604 684-8801.

Gastown

- Deluxe Junk, 310 West Cordova St., 604 685-4871.

- Hill's Native Art, 165 Water St., 604 685-4249.
- Inuit Gallery, 206 Cambie St., 604 688-7323.
- Osake, Artisan Sake Maker, 1339 Railspur Alley, 604 685-7253.
- Salmagundi West, 321 West Cordova St., 604 681-4648.

Granville Island

- Beadworks, The Net Loft, 604 682-2323.
- Edie Hats, The Net Loft, 604 683-4280.
- Granville Island Public Market, 1689 Johnston St., 604 666-6477.
- Kids Only Market (Kids Market), 1496 Cartwright St., 604 689-8447.
- Paper-YA, The Net Loft, 604 684-2531.

Activewear

- A. J. Brooks Outdoor Outfitters, 147 West Broadway Ave., 604 874-1117.
- Eco Outdoor Sports, 202 West Broadway Ave., 604 875-6767.
- Lululemon Athletica, 2113 West 4th Ave., 604 732-6111. Other locations: 1148 Robson St., 604 681-3118; 318–4800 Kingsway, Burnaby, 604 430-4659; 18–910 Main St., West Vancouver, 604 921-6125.
- Mountain Equipment Co-op, 130 West Broadway Ave., 604-872-7858.
- Taiga Works Wilderness Equipment, 301 West Broadway Ave., 604 875-6644.

Antiques and Collectibles

- Baker's Dozen, 3520 Main St., 604 879-3348.
- Farmhouse Collections, 2915 Granville St., 604 738-0167 and 1098 SW Marine Dr., 604 261-3681.
- Folkart Interiors, 3720 West 10th Ave., 604 731-7576.
- Second Time Around, 4428 Main St., 604 879-2313.

Bookstores

- Banyen Books and Sound, 3608 West 4th Ave., 604 732-7912.
- Barbara-Jo's Books to Cooks, 1740 West 2nd Ave., 604 688-6755.
- Book Warehouse, 632 West

Broadway Ave., 604 872-5711; 1068 Homer St., Yaletown, 604 681 5711; and numerous other locations.

- Chapters, 788 Robson St., 604 682-4066. Additional locations: 4700 Kingsway, Metrotown, Burnaby, 604 431-0463; 2505 Granville St., 604 731-7822; 8171 Ackroyd Rd., Richmond, 604 303-7392.
- Duthie Books, 2239 West 4th Ave., 604 732-5344.
- Kidsbooks, 3083 West Broadway Ave., 604 738-5335 and 3040 Edgemont Blvd., North Vancouver, 604 986-6190.
- Little Sister's Book Store, 1238 Davie St., 604 669-1753, 1-800-567-1662.
- Once Upon a Huckleberry Bush, 4387 Main St., 604 876-4010.
- Oscar's Art Books, 1533 West Broadway Ave. at Granville, 604 731-0553.

Canadian Clothing Designers

- Club Monaco, 701 West Georgia St. in Pacific Centre, 604 687-5550; 1034–1042 Robson St., 604 687-8618.
- Dorothy Grant, 138 West 6th Ave., 604 681-0201. By appointment.
- JC Studio, 46 West 6th Ave., 604 688-5222.
- Margareta Design, 2448 West 41st Ave., 604 264-4625.
- Max Mara, 700 West Georgia St. in Pacific Centre, 604 257-2370.
- Tilley Endurables, 2401 Granville St., 604 732-4287.
- Zonda Nellis Design, 2203 Granville St., 604 736-5668.

Children's Stores

- Bobbit's for Kids, 2935-A West 4th Ave., 604 738-0333.
- Isola Bella Design, 5692 Yew St., 604 266-8808.
- Kaboodles Toy Store, 4449 West 10th Ave., 604 224-5311 and 1496 Cartwright St., Granville Island, 604 684-0066.
- Kidsbooks, 3083 West Broadway Ave., 604 738-5335 and 3040 Edgemont Blvd., North Vancouver, 604 986-6190.

- Kids Only Market, 1496 Cartwright St., Granville Island, 604 689-8447.
- Please Mum, 2951 West Broadway Ave., 604 732-4574. Also in many malls.
- Rootskids, 1153 Robson St., 604 684-8801.
- The Toybox, 3002 West Broadway Ave., 604 738-4322.
- Toys R Us, 1154 West Broadway Ave., 604 733-8697.

China and Crystal

- Atkinson's, 1501 West 6th Ave., 604 736-3378.
- Chintz and Company, 950 Homer St., 604 689-2022.
- W. H. Puddifoot Ltd., 2375 West 41st Ave., 604 261-8141.

Designer Boutiques

- Bacci, 2788 Granville St., 604 733-4933.
- Boboli, 2776 Granville St., 604 257-2300.
- Chanel, 900 West Hastings St., 604 682-0522.
- Dyanna Fine Clothing for Women, 355 Howe St., 604 685-4225.
- Edward Chapman Woman, 2596 Granville St., 604 732-3394. Other locations: 750 West Pender St., 604 688-6711; Oakridge Centre, 604 261-8161.
- Enda B Men and Women, 4346 West 10th Ave., 604 228-1214.
- Gianni Versace Boutique, 757 West Hastings St., 604 683-1131.
- Leone, 757 West Hastings St., 604 683-1133.
- Plaza Escada, 757 West Hastings St., 604 688-8558.

First Nations Art and Jewellery

- Hill's Native Art, 165 Water St., 604 685-4249.
- Inuit Gallery, 206 Cambie St., 604 688-7323.
- Lattimer Gallery, 1590 West 2nd Ave., 604 732-4556.
- Marion Scott Gallery, 308 Water St., 604 685-1934.
- Museum of Anthropology, 6393 NW Marine Dr. (UBC campus), 604 822-5087.

Gift Shops

- Bookmark — Vancouver Public Library Gift Shop, 350 West Georgia St., 604 331-4040.
- Chachkas Design, 2423 Granville St., 604 688-6417.
- Circle Craft Co-op, 1–1666 Johnston St., Granville Island, 604 669-8021.
- Clamshell Gift Shop, Vancouver Aquarium, Stanley Park, 604 659-3413, 1-800-663-0562.
- The Gallery Store, Vancouver Art Gallery, 750 Hornby St., 604 662-4706.
- Moulé, 1994 West 4th Ave., 604 732-4066.
- The Museum Shop, Museum of Anthropology, UBC, 604 822-5087.
- Ten Thousand Villages, 1204 Commercial Dr., 604 323-9233.

Home Furnishings

- Bernstein and Gold, 1168 Hamilton St., 604 687-1535.
- Country Furniture, 3097 Granville St., 604 738-6411.
- Industrial Revolution, 2306 Granville St., 604 734-4395.
- Jordan's, 1470 West Broadway Ave., 604 733-1174.
- Koolhaus, 1 Water St., 604 875-9004.
- Sofa So Good, 1401 West 8th Ave., 604 879-4878.
- Upholstery Arts Showroom, 2430 Burrard St., 604 731-9020.

Malls

- Aberdeen Centre, 4151 Hazelbridge Way, Richmond, 604 273-1234.
- Arbutus Village Square, 4255 Arbutus St., 604 732-4255.
- Bentall Centre, Burrard and Dunsmuir Streets, 604 661-5000.
- Brookfield Royal Centre, 1055 West Georgia St., 604 689-1711.
- Central City Shopping Centre, 102 Ave. and King George Hwy., Surrey, 604 588-6431.
- City Square, 555 West 12th Ave., 604 876-5165.
- Guildford Town Centre, 2695 Guildford Town Centre, Surrey, 604 585-1565.

- Lonsdale Quay Market, 123 Carrie Cates Crt, North Vancouver, 604 985-6261.
- Lougheed Town Centre, 9855 Austin Ave., Burnaby, 604 421-2882.
- Metropolis at Metrotown, 4700 Kingsway, Burnaby, 604 438-4715.
- Oakridge Centre, 650 West 41st Ave., 604 261-2511.
- Pacific Centre, 700 West Georgia St., 604 688-7235.
- Park Royal Shopping Centre, 2002 Park Royal South, West Vancouver, 604 925-9576.
- Richmond Centre, 6551 #3 Rd., Richmond, 604 713-7467.
- Royal Centre, 1055 West Georgia St., 604 602-4800.
- Sinclair Centre, 757 Hastings St.
- Vancouver Centre, 650 West Georgia St.
- Yaohan Centre, 3700 #3 Rd., Richmond, 604 231-0601.

Men's Clothing

- Boboli, 2776 Granville St., 604 257-2300.
- Boys' Co., 1044 Robson St., 604 684-5656. Also at Oakridge Centre, 604 266-0388; Metropolis, 604 484-0024; Richmond Centre, 604 303-0374.
- Eddie Bauer, Oakridge Centre, 604 261-2621 and Park Royal Centre, 604 925-0858.
- Enda B Men and Women, 4346 West 10th Ave., 604 228-1214.
- Harry Rosen Men's Wear, 700 West Georgia St., 604 683-6861 and Oakridge Centre, 604 266-1172.
- Holt Renfrew, 737 Dunsmuir St., 604 681-3121.
- Hugo Boss, Pacific Centre, 700 West Georgia St., 604 683-6861.
- Leone, 757 West Hastings St., 604 683-1133.
- Mark James, 2941 West Broadway Ave., 604 734-2381.
- Roots, 1001 Robson St., 604 683-4305; Rootskids, 1153 Robson St., 604 684-8801 and other locations.
- S. Lampman, 2126 West 41st Ave., 604 261-2750.
- Tilley Endurables, 2401 Granville St., 604 732-4287.

Shoe Stores

- Broadway Shoe Salon, 2809 West Broadway Ave., 604 731-1410.
- Freedman Shoes, 1151 Robson St., 604 331-4700. Other locations: 2867 Granville St., 604 731-0448; 2171 West 41st Ave., 604 261-2921.
- Ingledew's, 535 Granville St., 604 687-8606.
- John Fluevog Boots and Shoes, 837 Granville St., 604 688-2828.
- Walk with Ronsons, Pacific Centre, 700 West Georgia St., 604 682-0795. Other locations: 2717 Granville St., 604 731-4550; 2955 West Broadway Ave., 604 733-2973.

Victoria

Fairmont Empress Hotel

- Art of Man Gallery, 721 Government St., 250 383-3800.
- Collections by 5th Avenue, Upper Lobby, Fairmont Empress Hotel, 250 382 3166.

Government Street Area and The Bay Centre

- The Bay Centre, 1150 Douglas St., 250 952-5690, www.thebaycentre.ca. Variety of shops.
- Crabtree & Evelyn, The Bay Centre (off Fort St.), 250 388-0102.
- Irish Linen Stores, 1019 Government St., 250 383-6812.
- Munro's Books, 1108 Government St., 250 382-2464.
- Murchie's Tea & Coffee, 1110 Government St., 250 383-3112.
- Purdy's Chocolates, The Bay Centre, 250 361-3024.
- Rogers' Chocolates, 913 Government St., 250 384-7021.
- W&J Wilson Clothiers, 1221 Government St., 250 383-7177.

Yates Street Area

- British Candy Shoppe, 638 Yates St., 250 382-2634.
- British Importers, 960 Yates St., 250 386-1496.
- Cowichan Trading Company, 1328 Government St., 250 383-0321.
- English Sweet Shop, 738 Yates St., 250 382-3325.

- Hill's Native Art, 1008 Government St., 250 385-3911.

Market Square

- Beadworld, 63–560 Johnson St., 250 386-5534.
- Fat Phege's Fudge Factory, 134–560 Johnson St., 250 383-3435.
- Green Cuisine, 5–560 Johnson St., 250 385-1809.
- Oqoqo (Lululemon), 120–560 Johnson St., 250 380-6310.
- Victoria Miniland, 168–560 Johnson St., 250 995-1226.
- Woofles Barking Boutique 106–560 Johnson St., 250 285-9663.

Chinatown

- Fan Tan Gallery, 541 Fisgard St., 250 382-4424.
- Quonley's, 1628 Government St., 250 383-0623.

Antique Row

- Charles Baird Antiques, 1044A Fort St., 250 384-8809.
- Faith Grant Antiques, 1156 Fort St., 250 383-0121.
- Vanity Fair Antiques and Collectibles, 1044 Fort St., 250 380-7274.

Whistler

Accommodations
Whistler

For two people staying in a double room (excluding taxes) during peak season: $ = $50–90, $$ = $90–180, $$$ = $180–250, $$$$ = above $250. Rates quoted are subject to a 5% federal tax and a 10% hotel tax.

Whistler Village

- Adara Boutique Hotel, 4122 Village Green, Whistler, BC V0N 1B4, 604 905-4009, 1-866-502-3272, fax 604 905-4665, www.adarahotel.com. Smaller hotel, Modern-style, some rooms with lofts/dens. Full kitchens. Hot tub, pool. $$$.
- Coast Whistler Hotel, 4005 Whistler Way, Whistler, BC V0N 1B4, 604 932-2522, 1-800-663-5644, fax 604-932-6711,

www.coastwhistlerhotel.com. Value and location are very good. Free buffet-style breakfast. Covered pool, hot tub, sauna, exercise room. $$.

- Crystal Lodge, 4154 Village Green, Whistler, BC V0N 1B4, 604 932-2221, 1-800-667-3363, fax 604 932-2635, www.crystal-lodge.com. Casual, friendly, renovated. Short walk to Whistler Mountain gondolas, good price. Tuck shop, three restaurants on site (Ric's Grill, Mix by Ric's, and The Old Spaghetti Factory), plus Crystal Lounge. Up to three bedrooms available. Pool, hot tub. $$–$$$.

- Hilton Whistler Resort & Spa, 4050 Whistler Way, Whistler, BC V0N 1B4, 604 932-1982, 1-800-515-4050, fax 604 966-5093, www.hiltonwhistler.com. Luxury hotel with big rooms, big beds, great mountain views. Some rooms with double Jacuzzis, dry saunas. Health Club, pool, hot tub, spa. Cinnamon Bear Grille, Cinnamon Bear Lounge. Pet-friendly. $$$–$$$$.

- The Westin Resort & Spa, 4090 Whistler Way, Whistler, BC V0N 1B4, 604 905-5000, 1-888-634-5577, fax 604 905-5640, www.westinwhistler.com. Condo-style, luxury all-suite hotel, spa, health club, pools, Whistler Kids Club program, Aubergine Grille Restaurant, FireRock Lounge. Deluxe beds, down duvets. Full kitchen, dining room, living room in all suites. $$$–$$$$.

Village North

- The Alpenglow, 4369 Main St., Whistler, BC V0N 1B4, 604 905-3903, 1-866-580-6642, fax 604 905-7053, www.whistler-alpenglow.com. Newer, lodge-style with smaller-size studio, one- and two-bedroom suites. Good value, central location. Fireplaces, full kitchens, air conditioning, fitness facilities with lap pool, hot tub, steam room, sauna. $$$.

- Whistler's Marketplace Lodge, 4360 Lorimer Rd., Whistler, BC V0N 1B4, 604 932-6699, 1-800-663-7711, fax 604 938-6622, www.resortquestwhistler.com. Low-frills lodging, good price, full kitchen, living and dining area with gas fireplace. No pool. Free parking. $$.

Upper Village

- Fairmont Chateau Whistler, 4599 Chateau Blvd., Whistler, BC V0N 1B4, 604 938-8000, 1-800-441-1414, fax 604 938-2291, www.fairmont.com. Rated one of the top ski resort hotels. Canadian Chateau-style luxury with double queen- and king-size beds and goose-down duvets. Wildflower Restaurant, The Mallard Lounge, shopping on-site. Ski-in/ski-out Blackcomb Mountain. Pool, spa, sauna, fitness facilities. $$$$.

- Four Seasons Resort Whistler, 4591 Blackcomb Way, Whistler, BC V0N 1B4, 604 935-3400, fax 604 935-3455, www.fourseasons.com/whistler. Newcomer to Whistler, with 242 spacious "modern rustic" rooms (95 suites) at the base of Blackcomb Mountain. Spa with luxury treatments, full fitness club, pool, steam room, 24-hour concierge, Fifty two 80 Bistro and Bar. $$$$

- Residence Inn by Marriott, 4899 Painted Cliff Rd., Whistler, BC V0N 1B4, 604 905-3400, 1-866-580-6648, fax 604 905-3432, www.whistler-marriott.com. Ski-in/ski-out location on Blackcomb Mountain. Large rooms, fireplaces, full kitchens, pool, hot tubs. Free shuttle bus to and from Whistler Village. Free breakfast buffet, excellent renovated fitness facilities. Pet-friendly. $$$$.

- Summit Lodge & Spa, 4359 Main St., Whistler, BC V0N 1B4, 604 932-2778, 1-888-913-8811, fax 604 932-2716, www.summitlodge.com. Intimate boutique hotel with exceptional service. All suites have full kitchen and gas fireplaces. Free shuttle to Whistler Village and gondolas. Pool, hot tub. $$$.

Creekside

- Lake Placid Lodge, 2050 Lake Placid Rd., Whistler, BC V0N 1B2, 604 932-6699, 1-800-663-7711, fax 604 932-6622, www.resortquestwhistler.com. Good value. Ski in/ski out access to Creekside Gondola. Large pool and patio area. One- and two-bedroom suites, gas fireplaces, fully equipped kitchens. Free underground parking. $$–$$$.
- Legends Whistler Creek, 2036 London Lane, Whistler, BC V0N 1B2, 1-800-332-3152, fax 604 983-9699, www.lodgingovations.com. Ski-in/ski-out access to Creekside Gondola. Opened by Intrawest in 2002, luxury one- to three-bedroom condo-style suites with full kitchens. Family and adult fitness facilities, indoor kids' play area, movie room, two pools, two Jacuzzis. $$$–$$$$.

Other Locations

- Edgewater Lodge and Restaurant, 8020 Alpine Way, north of Whistler (Mailing address: Edgewater Lodge, Box 369, Whistler, BC V0N 1BO), 604 932-0688, 1-888-870-9065, fax 604-932-0686, www.edgewater-lodge.com. Small motel-like lodge in forest setting overlooking Green Lake. Deluxe breakfast, tea and coffee all day, gourmet restaurant. One-bedroom units with bathtub and extra pullout twin bed. Shower-only in six units. Free parking. $$–$$$.
- Hostelling International Whistler, 5678 Alta Lake Rd., Whistler, BC V0N 1B5, 604 932-5492, 1-866-762-4122, fax 604 932-4687, www.hihostels.ca. Located in a former fishing lodge on Alta Lake. Wood-burning stove, common kitchen, dining room, sauna. Dorm rooms, private room sleeps up to four (children must stay with family in private room). Reservations recommended. $.
- Riverside RV Resort and Campground and Cabins, 8018 Mons Rd., Whistler, BC V0N 1B8, 604 905-5533, fax 604 905-5539, www.whistlercamping.com. Tent camping (call to confirm) and RV with amenities in lodge including grocery store and Internet café. Fourteen log cabins with lofts, showers only in units. Free parking. $$.

Bed & Breakfasts

For information on more than 25 B&B members, contact Whistler Visitor Information Centre, 4230 Gateway Dr., Whistler, BC V0N 1B4. 604 935-3357, www.tourismwhistler.com.

- Alpine Lodge Pension, 8135 Alpine Way, Whistler, BC V0N 1B8, 604 932-5966, fax 604 932-1104, www.alpinelodge.com. Casual, European-style pension in a huge cedar lodge. Continental breakfast buffet, down duvets, steam room. Communal kitchen open to guests. Japanese spoken. Free parking, free shuttle bus to mountains. $–$$$.
- Cedar Springs Bed & Breakfast Lodge, 8106 Cedar Springs Rd., Whistler, BC V0N 1B8, 604 938-8007, 1-800-727-7547, www.whistlerbb.com. Pretty cedar and pine lodge. Gourmet breakfast, dining room has wood-burning fireplace, tea and coffee always on. Sauna, hot tub. Showers only in rooms, except family room with soaker tub. Next to Meadow Park and the Valley Trail. Free shuttle in winter. $$.
- Durlacher Hof Pension Inn, 7055 Nesters Rd., Whistler, BC V0N 1B7, 604 932-1924, 1-877-932-1924, fax 604 938-1980, www.durlacherhof.com. Impressive guest rooms, extra-long twin or queen beds, goose-down duvets, private baths with Jacuzzi tubs or showers. Full breakfast, afternoon tea. No telephone or television in rooms. Free hot breakfast with Austrian sweet pancakes. Whirlpool, sauna. No children. $$$.

Whistler Dining

All major credit cards accepted.

Dining: Whistler

Fine Dining on the Mountains

- Christine's on Blackcomb Mountain, 604 938-7437. Elegant, full-service dining. Food rooted in tradition includes BC fish and shellfish, pasta, and steak. L, $$$, V/MC/AX/DC.
- Steeps Grill, Whistler Mountain, 604 905-2379. Alpine bistro at 1,150 metres (3,800 vertical ft.). Seasonal BC fare, includes grilled salmon and chowder. L, $$$, V/MC/AX/DC.

Casual Dining on the Mountains

Whistler Mountain

Ski in to these casual eateries and enjoy the view and people-watching.

- Chic Pea. Top of Garbanzo Express. Pizza, soup, and cinnamon buns. $.
- Dusty's Bar & BBQ. Bottom of Creekside Gondola. Breakfast to BBQ, delicious all day long and into the night. $.
- Raven's Nest. Top of Creekside Gondola. Hearty soups, sandwiches, BBQs. $.
- Roundhouse Lodge. Top of Whistler Express Gondola and PEAK 2 PEAK Gondola terminal. Three open food courts (Pika's, The Mountain Market, and Expressway) serve great food variety, from Asian dishes to artisan sandwiches. $.

Blackcomb Mountain

- Crystal Hut. All-day Belgian waffles, wood-oven baked lunches. Fondue in the evenings. $.
- Glacier Creek Lodge. Base of Jersey Cream Express and Glacier Express. River Rock, upstairs, features 10 market areas, serving up fresh deli sandwiches to fantastic Asian selections. $. Expressway, downstairs, paninis, fresh salads and more. $.
- Horstman Hut. Top of 7th Heaven. Hearty stews, home-style fare, and BBQs. $.
- Merlins Bar & Grill. At base of Blackcomb Mountain. "Whistler's Best Nachos" and spirited après-ski action. L/D, $.
- Rendezvous Lodge. Top of Solar Coaster Express and PEAK 2 PEAK Gondola terminal. Soups, fresh salad bar, pizza, pastas, and fajitas. B/L, $.

Asian

- Amami Restaurant, 4274 Mountain Square, Westbrook Hotel, Whistler Village, 604 932-6431. Japanese and Chinese dishes in a casual setting. L/D, $$, V/MC/AX/DC.
- Mongolie Grill, 201-4295 Blackcomb Way, Whistler Village, 604 938-9416. Notable Chinese stir-fry restaurant, including seafood and noodles, 18 gourmet sauces. No reservations accepted. L/D, $$, V/MC/AX.
- Tandoori Grill, 201–4368 Main St., Village North, 604 905-4900. Mild to hot authentic East Indian dishes. Reservations recommended. Take out and delivery available. L/D, $$$, V/AX/MC.
- Teppan Village Steak House, 301–4293 Mountain Square, Hilton Whistler Resort & Spa, Whistler Village, 604 932-2223. Teppan-yaki–style restaurant features steak, also chicken and seafood. Reservations suggested in peak seasons. D, $$$, V/AX/MC/DC.
- Zen Japanese Restaurant, 2202 Gondola Way, First Tracks Lodge, Creekside, 604 932-3667. Sleek restaurant features traditional Japanese cuisine with West Coast influences. L/D, $$$, V/AX/MC/DC.

Cafés

- Beetroot Café, 129–4340 Lorimer Road, 604 932-1163. Organic café specializing in local ingredients and vegetarian dishes. B/L/D, $$, V/MC.
- Ciao-Thyme Bistro, 1–4573 Chateau Blvd., Whistler Village, 604 932-7051. Tiny café with tasty treats made with fresh local produce. Soups, salads, cinnamon buns. B/L/D, $, AX/MC/V.

- Esquires Coffee House, 127–4338 Main St., Village North, 604 905-3386. Excellent coffee and teas with quiches, wraps, and panini. B/L/D, $, AX/MC/V.
- Splitz Grill, 4369 Main St., Alpenglow Hotel, Village North, 604 938-9300. Burgers galore including all-beef burger and spicy lentil vegetarian. L/D, $$, V/MC.

Alpine

- Bavaria Restaurant, 101–4369 Main St., Village North, 604 932-7518. Traditional fondue, schnitzel, and all dishes Austrian from a superb chef. Desserts include home-made apple strudel and Kaiserchmarn, a caramelized crepe. D, $$$$, AX/MC/V.

Family/Casual

- Black's Original Ristorante, 4270 Mountain Square, Whistler Village, 604 932-6408. Fast-paced service starting with breakfast. Pizzas and pastas. B/L/D, $$, V/AX/MC.
- Caramba! Restaurante, 12–4314 Main St., Town Plaza, 604 938-1879. Pizzas, pastas in a cheery, lively setting. New York steak and calamari à la Plancha on the menu. L/D, $$$, AX/MC/V.
- Old Spaghetti Factory, 4154 Village Green, Crystal Lodge, Whistler Village, 604 938-1081. Adult and children's menu of soups, salads, pastas, sourdough bread, New York steak, chicken, vegetarian lasagna, ice cream. L/D, $$$, AX/MC/V.

Mediterranean

- Kypriaki Norte, 4122 Village Green, Whistler Village, 604 932-0600. •
- Pasta Lupino Gourmet, 121–4368 Main St., Village North, 604 905-0400. Fresh pasta and sauces in a tiny, popular café. L/D, $$$, MC/V.
- Quattro at Whistler, 4319 Main St., Village North, 604 905-4844. Country Italian cooking and extensive wine list. D, $$$$, AX/DC/MC/V.
- Trattoria di Umberto, 4417 Sundial Place, Whistler Village, 604 932-5858. Tuscan cooking features linguine, spaghetti, fettuccine, and more. Seafood cioppino is chef Umberto Menghi's specialty. L/D, $$$$, AX/DC/MC/V.
- Mediterranean restaurant known for its fabulous roast lamb. L (July, August on patio)/D, $$$, AX/MC/V.

Seafood & Steak

- Brewhouse, 4355 Blackcomb Way, Village North, 604 905-2739. Wood-fired pizza and rotisserie-grilled prime ribs and chicken, sandwiches, and burgers. Children's menu. L/D, $$, AX/MC/V.
- Ric's Grill, 4154 Village Green, Crystal Lodge, Whistler Village, 604 932-7427.
  Steak, seafood, and pasta served in a contemporary setting. D, $$$, AX/MC/V.
- Rimrock Café, 2117 Whistler Rd., Creekside, 604 932-5565. Specialize in seafood and game. Very popular, reservations recommended. Free parking. D, $$$$, AX/MC/V.

West Coast Cuisine

- Araxi Restaurant & Bar, 4222 Village Square, Whistler Village, 604 932-4540. Superb menu and 12,000-bottle wine list. West Coast with Italian and French influences. D, $$$$, AX/DC/MC/V.
- The Aubergine Grille, 4090 Whistler Way, Westin Resort & Spa, Whistler Village, 604 935-4344. Breakfast, lunch, dinner with a mountain view. West Coast seafood and salmon plus rustic pizza, certified Angus Beef, pastas. Dazzling desserts. B/L/D, $$$$, AX/MC/V.
- Cinnamon Bear Grille & Lounge, 4050 Whistler Way, Hilton Whistler Resort & Spa, Whistler Village, 604 966-5060. Elegant and casual. Pacific Northwest ingredients with a focus on world fusion. B/L/D, $$$$, AX/MC/V.
- Edgewater Lodge and Restaurant, 8020 Alpine Way, north of Whistler Village, 604 932-0688. Secluded waterfront setting offering gourmet locally grown fare. Venison medallions, chicken, steaks. D, $$$$, AX/MC/V.
- La Rua Restaurante, 4557 Blackcomb

Whistler: Dining

Way, Upper Village, 604 932-5011.
Great food and great wines with six
gourmet pasta selections. D,
$$$–$$$$, AX/DC/MC/V.

- The Wildflower, 4599 Chateau
  Blvd., Fairmont Chateau Whistler,
  Upper Village, 604 938-2033. Daily
  breakfast buffet. Dinner includes
  prime rib, rib-eye steak, free-range
  chicken, cedar-plank wild salmon.
  Over 2,500 bottles of wine. B/D,
  $$$–$$$$, AX/MC/V.

PHOTO CREDITS

Legend: Top – T; Centre – C; Bottom – B; Left – L: Right - R

Photography by Hamid Attie, except those listed below.

adrian8_8 (flickr): 69B; Al Harvey: 167B; aloalosabine (flickr), 51B; Andy Mons: 39; Ayala Moriel: 92B; Ballet British Columbia, Dan Barns: 21T; Berry Leinbach: 113C; Bobak Ha'Eri: 30B; Cait Hurley: 166B; Capilano Suspension Bridge: 75B; Chinese Cultural Centre Museum & Archives: 99T; Chris Cameron: 58T; City of Vancouver Archives, LGN 1045, photographer Harry T. Devine: 16B; Cliff Lemire: 79T; Cord Rodefeld: 83B; Cypress Mountain: cover — skier, 71B; Cyprien Lomas: 116T; Dan Dickinson: 159B; Dan McCormick photographytips.com: 167T; David Burn, 34; David Cooper Photography: 53B, 54T&B, 56B, 57T; David Look: 41B, 46, 95B, 98T, 102T, 103, 104, 106T; dburka (flickr): back cover — skier, 71C; Devlyn (flickr): 19T; Dr. Sun Yat Sen Classical Chinese Garden: 65T; Duncan Rawlinson: 110T; 158B; Ed7 (flickr): 64C; Evan Leeson: 87B; Fish House in Stanley Park: 43B; Furry Creek Golf and Country Club: 70T; Geoff Peters: back cover — Nikkyu sushi, 45; Gerritkb (flickr): 58B; Gill Gunson: 72B; Gio JL (flickr): 44B; Grant Kwok: 64T; Greg Descantes: 69T; Kenny Louie: 19C; Greg Dunham: 160B; Gulf of Georgia Cannery Society: 36; Hans Sipma Photography: 23B; Hisazaku Watanabe: 86T&B; iStock: 9, 10, back cover—sunset, 15R, 97T, 122T; Itzafineday (flickr): 20; Iwona Erskine Kellie: 60C, 73; Jason Rowe: 53T; Jason Vanderhill: 35, 59B; Jenny Lee Silver: 121T; Jhayne Holmes: 105T; Jon Faulknor: 160T, 161T; Kamitakahara: 13B; Kan Chew: 80T; Keith Tyler: 147T; Kent Wang: 37; Keya White: 159T; Kyle Pearce: 60T, 84T; Laura Cox: 128T, 134T, 140B, 148T&B, 150B; Leanna Rathkelly: 75T, 161B; Lili Vieira de Carvalho: 50B; LWY (flickr): 148C; Lynn Baugher: 143, 154, 155T, 156T&B; Maplewood Farm: 77BR; Michael Tedesco: 68B; Mike Martin Wong (flickr): 91T, 96B, 98B; Museum of Anthropology, Vancouver, Canada. Photo, Bill McLennan: 26B; Pacific National Exhibition: 76B; Perry Danforth: 115TR; Po Yang: cover — skytrain, Granville market, back cover: Vancouver Island, 27B; Richard Glasner; 11, 18B, 21B, 28B, 51T, 52T, 81, 87C, 88T, 93T, 95T, 96B, 98C, 99C, 105B, 106B, 108B, 111; Richard Winchell: 48B; Robert Kwong: 70B; Rod Templeton: 116B; Roland Tanglao: 89B, 102C, 114B; roy.susan (flickr): 60B; Royal BC Museum: 136B, 137B; scazon (flickr): 99B; Science World: 24; Sharmini Thiagarajah: 115TL; Sooke Harbour House: 151T, 153T&B; Sooke Harbour House, Andrei Fedorov: 151B; Stephen Ruttan: 164, 166T; Stephen Wu: 118T; Steve Rosset: 78B; Tal Atlas: 90B; TELUS International Ski and Snowboard Festival, Greg Athens: 74; TELUS International Ski and Snowboard Festival, Rob Plato: 159T; Thomas Mascardo: 147B; Thomas Quine: 96T, 166T; Thomas Svab: Vancouver Art Gallery, 59T; Tim Matheson: 54C&B, 55C&B; Tom Stovall: 78T; Tourism Vancouver, Al Harvey: 13C, 14B, 31T, 38T, 47; Tourism Victoria: 150T; Tourism Whistler, Greg Eymundston: 157, 162C; Tourism Whistler, Maureen Provencal: 162B; Tourism Whistler, Scott Hughes: back cover — Whistler forest, 158T; Tourism Whistler, Tim King: 162T; Tourism Vancouver, Tom Ryan: 82T, 85T, 94T, 94B, 101T, 112T, 119B; Tracy Olson: 124T; Translink: 12; Trista B (flickr): 117T; unwritten (flickr): 33; upyernoz (flickr): 61T; Vancouver Maritime Museum: 29T, 29B; Vancouver Opera, Tim Matheson Photography: 55C&B; Vancouver Public Library: 15L, 17T&B, 18T; Vancouver Sun: 72T; Vancouver Symphony Orchestra: 55T; Windzepher (flickr): 67.

Formac Publishing Company Limited acknowledges the financial support of the Government of Canada through the Book Publishing Industry Development Program (BPIDP) for our publishing activities.

Index

Index

Index

Index